ENGLISH POETRY
1400–1580

THE POETRY BOOKSHELF

General Editor: James Reeves

Robert Graves: *English and Scottish Ballads*
Tom Scott: *Late Medieval Scots Poetry*
William Tydeman: *English Poetry 1400–1580*
Martin Seymour-Smith: *Shakespeare's Sonnets*
James Reeves: *John Donne*
Maurice Hussey: *Jonson and the Cavaliers*
Jack Dalglish: *Eight Metaphysical Poets*
James Reeves and Martin Seymour-Smith: *Andrew Marvell*
Dennis Burden: *Shorter Poems of John Milton*
V. de S. Pinto: *Poetry of the Restoration*
Roger Sharrock: *John Dryden*
James Reeves: *Jonathan Swift*
John Heath-Stubbs: *Alexander Pope*
Donald Davie: *The Late Augustans*
F. W. Bateson: *William Blake*
G. S. Fraser: *Robert Burns*
Roger Sharrock: *William Wordsworth*
James Reeves: *S. T. Coleridge*
Robin Skelton: *Lord Byron*
John Holloway: *P. B. Shelley*
James Reeves: *John Clare*
Robert Gittings: *Poems and Letters of John Keats*
Edmund Blunden: *Alfred Lord Tennyson*
James Reeves: *Robert Browning*
James Reeves: *Emily Dickinson*
James Reeves: *G. M. Hopkins*
David Wright: *Seven Victorian Poets*
James Reeves: *The Modern Poets' World*
James Reeves: *D. H. Lawrence*

HENRY HOWARD, EARL OF SURREY

ENGLISH POETRY,
1400-1580

Edited with an Introduction, Notes and Glossary

by

WILLIAM TYDEMAN

HEINEMANN
LONDON

Heinemann Educational Books Ltd
LONDON EDINBURGH MELBOURNE
SINGAPORE JOHANNESBURG
IBADAN HONG KONG
TORONTO AUCKLAND
NAIROBI

SBN 435 15054 5

INTRODUCTION, NOTES AND GLOSSARY

© WILLIAM TYDEMAN 1970

FIRST PUBLISHED 1970

Published by
Heinemann Educational Books Ltd
48 Charles Street, London W1X 8AH
Printed in Great Britain by Morrison and Gibb Ltd
London and Edinburgh

CONTENTS

v

JOHN SKELTON (c. 1460–1529)

ALEXANDER BARCLAY (c. 1476–1552)

? GEORGE BOLEYN, VISCOUNT ROCHFORD (*c.* 1505–1536)

'TOTTEL'S MISCELLANY' (1557)

THOMAS SACKVILLE, EARL OF DORSET (1536–1608)

ARTHUR GOLDING (1536–1606)

BARNABY GOOGE (*c.* 1540–1594)

PREFACE

THIS collection presents a selection of the verse composed in England between the death of Chaucer in 1400 and the publication of Spenser's *The Shepheardes Calender* in 1579. Arguments for suggesting that this period of English poetic history deserves greater attention from critics and readers than it often receives, are put forward in the Introduction. The poets represented include Lydgate at the beginning of the period, Skelton, Wyatt and Surrey towards the middle, and the aspiring Spenser at the close; I have tried to do justice to the wealth of secular and religious lyrics in anonymous fifteenth-century collections, and to the varied contents of *Tottel's Miscellany* and its Elizabethan successors. Briefer selections from writers as various as Hoccleve, Charles D'Orleans, Barclay, Hawes, Sackville, Googe, Turbervile and Gascoigne should indicate something of their poetic abilities, and so persuade the reader to explore further.

For the texts, I am grateful to the many reliable editions cited in the Guide to Further Reading; I have also used their notes and comments where I found them helpful, though there is a sad lack of good, modern, annotated editions of Skelton, Googe, Turbervile and Gascoigne, to name only the most urgent needs. I am also delighted to record my indebtedness to several of my colleagues at the University College of North Wales, and to Professors David Knowles and Kenneth Muir for their ready willingness to elucidate difficulties. I owe a large debt of gratitude to my wife for her support and wise counsel, and, above all, to the General Editor, and his enthusiasm for, and faith in, this project from the outset.

In preparing these works for readers of today, I have tried to bear in mind the ideal poet described by Sidney, whose duty was to make the reader's journey pleasant before making it instructive, and have therefore sought primarily to make these poems as readable as possible; there is no justification, in my view, for abandoning uninitiated readers in a palaeographic desert. Yet to modernize the texts ruthlessly would falsify the impression these poems create in manuscript and early printed books; I have therefore adopted the following principles: FF, I, J, U, V, VV have been changed to the appropriate modern equivalents; long S has been eliminated, and 3 and þ replaced by the least misleading modern symbol. Abbreviations are expanded without comment, and Roman numerals are spelt out. Obvious misprints or scribal errors have been corrected, with comment in the notes where necessary; I have followed modern practice as far as capital letters are concerned, except that where they seem to have been used for emphasis in early printed texts, they are retained. Editorial punctuation has been inserted where its use might clarify the sense for a modern reader.

WILLIAM TYDEMAN

Bangor, North Wales, 1969

INTRODUCTION

I

THE English poetic landscape from 1400 to 1580 is still curiously unfamiliar to many readers, yet anyone willing to explore the century and a half dividing Chaucer from Spenser meets with pleasures as rich and varied as any in our literature. A growing appreciation of the most accomplished fifteenth-century lyrics, the rediscovery of early Tudor poets such as Skelton and Wyatt, attempts to revalue underrated authors such as Lydgate and Gascoigne, have all helped to dispel the antiquated myth that here was a kind of poetic no-man's land, an arid stretch of worthless verbiage separating the glories of *The Canterbury Tales* from the splendours of *The Faerie Queene*. Today it is unnecessary to find excuses for an age that could produce *The Dance of Death* or *London Lickpenny*, 'They fle from me' or Surrey's tribute to Wyatt: the finest verse of the period is now deemed worthy to take its place beside Malory's mighty Arthurian epic, the prose of Tyndale and Cranmer, the sublimity and gaiety of the miracle cycles.

Indeed, the years covered by this collection were vital for the development of English poetry: they saw it assume some of its most distinctive characteristics—its moral seriousness, its ability to argue a case or move a listener, its wit, its colloquial strength—and when the challenge of the classics came, the brasher native traditions fused successfully with the discoveries of the ancients, and so made possible the work of the great Elizabethans. The total pattern is one of consolidation at the beginning of the period, followed by expansion, experiment and innovation; the keynote is search and discovery, which gives to so much verse its air of excitement and enthusiasm. 'The interval between Chaucer and Spenser is long and dreary' claimed William Hazlitt in 1818; I seriously question whether many present-day readers will find themselves agreeing with him.

Collections of medieval verse and collections of Tudor verse abound, but they are rarely found sharing the same volume; it seems to me helpful, however, to regard the period as a whole, without paying much attention to the idea of a 'Renaissance' which split the age into two parts. Historians and philosophers agree that, far from being a breakaway from medieval ideas and ways of thinking, the 'Renaissance' (if any firm definition can now be attached to the term) is in many respects an extension and re-development of them. Among English poets, until the late sixteenth century at least, one detects only a gradual sense of re-birth, and in terms of continuity, I think the reader will find that there is more to be gained from treating poetry written between 1400 and 1580 as a totality, than from trying to suggest that some chronological crash-barrier comes down on English writing in 1485 or 1500.

II

. . . my master Chauceris now is grave,
That noble rethor Poete of Breteine,
That worthy was the laurer to have
Of poetrie, and the palme atteine,
That made firste to distille and reyne
The golde dewe droppis of speche and eloquence
Into oure tounge thourgh his excellence,
And founde the flourys first of rethoryk,
Oure rude speche oonly to enlumyne. . . .

JOHN LYDGATE

2

One way of appreciating the achievement of the poets represented in this selection is to remind ourselves that even by Chaucer's death in 1400, English had hardly established itself securely as a stable and respectable enough language for literary composition. It had certainly thrown off the challenge of Latin and French and produced at least one major poet, but almost the whole of the period under discussion was spent gaining for the vernacular the literary prestige of the classical tongues. The adulation Chaucer received from his successors, including Spenser, was partly an acknowledgement of his genius in evolving a native standard of literary excellence for others to consolidate, even if many were sadly aware that their shots fell short of the target. To such disciples, Chaucer had found the English language crude and clumsy, and left it flexible and sophisticated, bequeathing to his followers a workable literary medium. He was a primary and enduring influence all through the period: his successors worked in the full light of his attainments, and acknowledged him 'the well of English undefyled' (*The Faerie Queene*, IV, ii, 32).

Frequently Chaucer's followers made conscious use of his materials, as Lydgate did in *The Complaint of the Black Knight*, but such affinities should not betray us into naively lamenting that they misunderstood his genius and chose to imitate the wrong poems. We must not allow *The Canterbury Tales*, whose image is untypically modern, to blot out less immediately acceptable areas of Chaucer's work: to us he is apt to wear a very different face from the one his contemporaries saw, and since as Dryden observed, 'Here is God's plenty',[1] we may all find our personal tastes catered for in his work. But when we are tempted to sneer at Lydgate and Hawes for copying what to us seem the least profitable aspects of Chaucer's work, we must remember that our view of it may be equally distorted.

Moreover, one man's accomplishments do not make a poetic renaissance, and it is absurd to suggest that Chaucer's disciples only

[1] Preface to *Fables Ancient and Modern*, 1700.

3

needed to continue tamely imitating the Master to produce great
works, for

> ... one has only learnt to get the better of words
> For the thing one no longer has to say, or the way in which
> One is no longer disposed to say it. And so each venture
> Is a new beginning ...
>
> T. S. ELIOT, East Coker

The modes Chaucer pioneered and polished suited some themes
admirably, but there were still large sectors of human concern
requiring poetic exploitation, many types of verse-form and subject
yet to be attempted, many ingredients in pre-Chaucerian poetry to
be assimilated into the texture of the new; in short, fifteenth-century
writers had to develop what Chaucer had begun, and their work
reflects their pioneering status. Lydgate lacked Chaucer's humour,
intelligence and subtlety, but he attempted to apply the new tech-
niques to epic narration and a comprehensive study of human
history; Charles d'Orleans worked within the tighter bonds of the
ballade and the *roundel*; Hoccleve composed the first truly auto-
biographical pieces in the language; the finest lyrics continued to
develop outside the courtly tradition.

In their choice of style too, writers were free to break new
ground, and often selection was difficult: William Caxton, printer
and author, gives a clear impression of the writer's dilemma in the
preface to his *Aeneid*:

> ... whan I had advysed me in this sayd boke, I delybered and con-
> cluded to translate it into englysshe, and forthwyth toke a penne & ynke,
> and wrote a leef or tweyne, whyche I oversawe agayn to corecte it. And
> whan I sawe the fayr & straunge termes therin I doubted that it sholde
> not please some gentylmen whiche late blamed me, sayeng that in my
> translacyons I had over curyous termes whiche coude not be understande
> of comyn peple, and desired me to use olde and homely termes in my
> translacyons ... And som honeste and grete clerkes have ben wyth me,
> and desired me to wryte the moste curyous termes that I coude fynde.
> And bytwene playn, rude, & curyous, I stande abasshed. But in my

judgemente the comyn termes that be dayli used ben lyghter to be under-
stonde than the olde and auncyent englysshe. . . .

The controversy over literary language continued into the
sixteenth century when the merits and demerits of 'ink-horne terms'
were hotly debated; Caxton's preference for 'the comyn termes
that be dayli used' was shared by Wyatt and William Tyndale, as
Chaucer and John Wycliffe had shared it in the fourteenth century.
But others, feeling the 'plain' style to be bald and mean by com-
parison with Latin, and *too* close to everyday speech, set about
augmenting the language by embellishing their verse with more
elaborate and exotic adornments than ordinary speech could provide.
Labouring under a sense of linguistic inferiority, they endeavoured
to dress up the native tongue by infusing it with sonorous words of
Latin origin and appearance. This love of 'aureate terms' or 'halff
chongyd Latyne' is a feature of verse associated with the nobility
and the court, often ceremonial in character; Lydgate, Hawes, and
even Skelton are among those who take advantage of its stately,
encrusted effects to counteract the presumed rudeness and barbarity
of common speech. Words like *stellify*, *astropotent*, *oreant*, *auricomous*,
equipolent, and *tenebrous* made society verse stiff and ponderous;
Dunbar's *Ane Ballat of Our Lady* is a typical specimen:

> Hale, sterne superne! Hale, in eterne,
> In Godis sicht to schyne!
> Lucerne in derne, for to discerne
> Be glory and grace devyne;
> Hodiern, modern, sempitern,
> Angelicall regyne!
> Our tern inferne for to dispern,
> Helpe rialest rosyne . . .

Imprisoned in its ornate strait-jacket of gold, the theme suffocates
to death.

Both plain and 'curyous' styles are features of a more general
contrast at this time between a discreet, formalized style, restrained

in sentiment and elevated in manner, heard chiefly in pieces maintaining the courtly-love tradition of female coldness and masculine devotion, gracing court functions and extolling a noble patron, and a more uninhibited, colloquial, gay and informal mode used for drinking-songs, poems abusing women, tender lyrics, jocular anecdotes. One is tempted to employ terms such as 'courtly' and 'popular' to suggest the contrast, but actually, the distinction is not based on social differences: the 'popular' idiom found favour with the aristocracy, as the song-books of Henry VIII's court make clear, and the best poets of the period effectively blend the two extremes of diction. Indeed, Skelton is equally at home in the rarified atmosphere of *The Garlande of Laurell* and among the pungent odours of *Elynour Rummynge*, the style of each being fitted to the subject-matter. Similarly, in 'The auncient acquaintance', the poet employs a high-falutin' manner, appropriate to remarks addressed to a court lady, and then, suddenly and rapidly descends to the style of the gutter he considers more suited to the lady's conduct!

The chief faults of the elevated style were excessive regularity and circumlocution, those of the plain were drabness and doggerel. But as the less idiomatic, esoteric manner associated with allegorical narrative and amorous eulogy lost favour, the more colloquial, starker style of *Colin Clout* and Wyatt's satires gained ground, and though it now had to compete with the new challenge from the Petrarchan influence sanctioned by *Tottel's Miscellany*, the sinewy, economical, vernacular style became the medium in which men such as Googe, Turbervile and Gascoigne produced verse which the critic Yvor Winters has praised for its restraint, absence of ornament, and moral concern. Indeed Winters prefers this school of poets to that of Sidney and Spenser, which he views as excessively rhetorical but mentally inactive, an extreme opinion perhaps, but one which provides a necessary antidote to the idea that the only important traditions at work in Tudor poetry are the foreign ones.

On the whole, it is these simpler, more colloquial styles of writing that present-day taste prefers; we find it harder to come to terms with the more elaborate, formal styles, adopted primarily to satisfy fashion-conscious upper-class audiences, and especially when contrivance and artifice seem to obtrude to such a marked degree. It is worthwhile to try and eliminate our prejudices, particularly when considering the use writers made of those literary devices and techniques learnt from the art of Rhetoric, one of the main branches of classical and medieval learning.

Rhetoric was the ancient art of using language to attain some desired end, such as the refutation of an opponent's case in debate, or the acquittal of a man accused of murder, and the same term came to apply to the body of rules laid down for achieving success in the subject. From treatises on rhetoric, orators and writers learnt the best way to present an argument or narrative, to contract or expand it, to give their audience a respite from the main theme, to describe a situation or a series of events in the most effective sequence, to emphasize a point, to vary the presentation of an ove-familiar topic, and so on. In the Middle Ages, treatises on poetic composition (the *artes poeticae*) such as Geoffroi de Vinsauf's *Poetria Nova* (gently satirized by Chaucer in *The Nun's Priest's Tale*) or Mathieu de Vendôme's *Ars Versificatoria* appeared, classroom manuals systematizing the methods of practising poets, and providing examples for imitation. The 'colours' or devices of rhetoric were thus part of any writer's equipment; some of them still linger on as what we call ' figures of speech' today.

The existence of such manuals, along with the notion underlying them that poetry was an art to be learnt and practised according to certain established rules, should not lead us to the belief that most medieval and Renaissance poets were uninspired, pedestrian and convention-ridden: there was nothing mechanical about the way in which the best authors handled rhetorical techniques. The *artes poeticae* provided the tools, but they did not guarantee success with them: individual distinction still lay in treating the 'colours' with skill and imagination.

Rhetorical techniques played an extensive part in poetic composition and evaluation until nearly the end of the eighteenth century, before Romanticism emerged with its emphasis on

7

spontaneity and strong emotion as the distinguishing marks of poetry. Today we are unlikely to respond as enthusiastically as did poets and readers of the past to 'an elegant Epanorthosis' or 'an Ironicall Sarcasmus', but such terms remind us that the age took pleasure in the skilled display of technique for its own sake, and that it was less important for a poet to be a thinker than that he should be a craftsman, a 'maker'.

III

The language used by the poets of this collection should not cause the reader undue difficulty, especially if he is already familiar with Chaucerian English, but the subject of metre forms the most controversial and knotty problem we face in studying poetry between 1400 and 1580. So much of the necessary evidence is missing, that scholars can advance only tentative explanations of what took place. Though Chaucer is clearly central to the discussion, scholars are divided about his habits of scansion: did he write in predominantly regular metres, conforming more or less to rules of classical prosody later accepted as descriptive patterns for English verse, so that we can read

> 'A Knyght ther was, and that a worthy man'

as we read 'The curfew tolls the knell of parting day'?

Or did he retain the native English basis, and organize his rhythms, not by apportioning 'shorts' and 'longs' on a predetermined framework, but by creating patterns of stresses within the line, and only accenting certain syllables? In this case, we would have to assume that

> 'Wel koude she carie a morsel / and wel kepe'

follows the system behind lines like Langland's

> 'In a somere seyson / whan softe was the sonne'

8

though Chaucer did not retain the strong alliterative element in Langland and the *Gawain* poet. Most scholars would now agree that Chaucer's metrical regularity has been exaggerated, though they might not subscribe as readily to the view that his verse is in the same rhythmical pattern as poems such as *Piers Plowman*. The majority opinion is that Chaucer can still be scanned regularly, if on a rather freer basis than the strictly classical one, but at least the prevailing doubts as to his intentions are a warning against being too dogmatic about them.

Whatever the true nature of his prosody, there is little doubt that Chaucer's work displays a more accomplished mastery of verse movement than that of his successors: this has normally been explained by the disappearance of sounded final -e, which, though already archaic in his time, he nonetheless retained to balance his lines syllabically. But his followers were forced to dispense with its aid, and so their metres fell into confusion. However, doubts as to whether Chaucer *did* in fact retain a pronounced final -e, along with other uncertainties, have meant that, metrically, fifteenth-century poetry has assumed the appearance of an impenetrable jungle. There are two possible ways out: assuming that Chaucer stabilized final -e for a time, one can accept that later poets permitted themselves a wide range of variations on standard forms like the decasyllabic line of *The Canterbury Tales*, or one can suggest that many fifteenth-century poets returned to (or followed Chaucer in retaining) the 'stress' principle of works such as *Sir Gawayn and the Grene Knight*. Certainly poets such as Hawes and Barclay seem to have been writing four- or five-stress lines with a strong central pause, rather than fumbling towards some lost iambic pentameter.

Lydgate is something of a special case, in that he seems to follow Chaucer's rhythmic patterns with ruthless fidelity, but without the same flexibility, so that his lines often have a dreary monotony. In addition, Lydgate adopted systematically line-types which Chaucer only employed as variants, and he failed completely in understanding just how subtly and skilfully the older poet had managed to vary the position of the pause within the line.

Further difficulties occur when the iambic pentameter begins to establish (or re-establish) itself early in the sixteenth century; by the time of Surrey and the publication of *Tottel's Miscellany* (1557), the regular iambic had settled itself in as the standard prosodic form, and compared with Wyatt's poems (which were made to conform to regular patterns by Tottel's editor), Surrey's pieces are metrically immaculate and confident. The problem with Wyatt is to decide how far he was aware of the dictates of metrical regularity, or how far he was consciously flouting them to produce those subtle variations of cadence heard in 'They fle from me' and elsewhere in his best work. Certainly he often adheres to a line of five stresses (which may have led the editor of *Tottel's Miscellany* to think that he was striving to write iambic pentameters), but his verse schemes appear to owe more to native stress-patterns than to foreign or classical systems of prosody. There are occasions when Wyatt seems to write like a man floundering out of his metrical depth, but the accomplished and assured rhythms in many of his lyrics must convince most readers that Wyatt at least knew what he was doing well.

When Wyatt turns to decasyllabics, as in his Satires, he is always prepared to relinquish the regularity of the iambic foot, when it conflicts with the rhythms of natural speech. On the other hand, Surrey is not concerned to reproduce such effects, and adheres to the metrical norm close to that found in Tottel, in both his blank-verse and in the popular 'jog-trot' metre known as 'Poulter's Measure', a couplet form consisting of alternate lines of six and seven feet, which Wyatt had unfortunately pioneered, and Surrey helped to establish in literary vogue. Surrey achieved a highly polished metre in his blank-verse, but at the expense of his language, which loses the vitality of living speech and becomes somewhat effete.

For Surrey's successors such as Googe and Turbervile, regularity of metre seems to have become a sufficient ambition in itself, though this is less true of their best work than it is of their imitations of Tottel's poets. But certainly much of the poetry between 1557 and 1579 is marred by metrical monotony, as if poets were anxious to preserve the iambic foot at all costs, even if it meant wresting phrases out of their natural order, and perplexing the reader as a result. This is the worst feature of the work of Golding, Googe and Turbervile, and it was against lines such as

> Now let us go to Temple ours

which manifestly fail to reconcile the habits of normal speech to the metrical pattern, that Gascoigne protested in *Certayne Notes of Instruction* (1575), though he did not quite visualize the implied contradictions of what he asserted. He laid emphasis on poets not deviating from usual word-order and pronunciation, and on taking the iambic foot as the standard measure, insisting that 'all the wordes in your verse be so placed as the first sillable may sound short, or be depressed, the second long or elevate, the third shorte . . .' Gascoigne's 'instruction' that the aspiring poet should subordinate natural stress to metrical demand conflicted with his views on natural word-order, but at least the metrical pattern had been recognized 'as a ruling principle independent of the stresses of the language in a line . . . when the patterns of stress in the language gain a similar status, we have the line in which both patterns can function . . .'[1] Gascoigne's own successes occur either when he permits himself to modify his metres, or when his language coincides most neatly with his verse-scheme. But it was left to Spenser in *The Shepheardes Calender*, with its programme of varied metrical types, and its freedom to depart from the pattern imposed by the metre (however haphazardly the experiment was tried), to indicate the distances that poetic technique might travel in future, under the guidance and example of men such as himself and Sidney.

IV

Many works in this selection will meet with an immediate response from present-day readers: the lively humour of the bawdy lyrics and *London Lickpenny*, the restrained adoration of *The Life of*

---

[1] J. Thompson, *The Founding of English Metre*, 1961, p. 74. The whole of this section is greatly indebted to Thompson's helpful study.

Our Lady, Skelton's grotesque savagery, Wyatt's wry evocation of sexual frustration, cross the dividing centuries without difficulty; no amount of editorial preamble is needed to heighten the pleasure obtained from 'Westron wynde' or *The Lullaby of a Lover*. But to savour some of the verse written between 1400 and 1580 (especially pieces only represented here by extracts), the modern reader must be willing to throw out certain current preconceptions about poetry, and appreciate how poets of the past saw their art.

For us today the poet is essentially independent and individual, using his poem as a confessional, to tell us something about himself, his emotions and opinions, and the way in which he sees the world. A poem to him is a vehicle for communicating something personal, even intimate, self-motivated and self-centred. Indeed, so completely do readers endorse this identification, that they now expect a writer to adopt no other role but the Self, and to speak out on behalf of the rebel, the outsider, and the non-conformist in a world increasingly indifferent to the minority of one. He is required to break down the old orthodoxies, traditions and standards, to challenge authority and convention, by asserting self-made codes and creeds based, not on arbitrary hereditary notions, but on personal experience and empirical exploration. And because we expect poets to tell us something original and arresting, we allow them to create the terms on which they are judged and understood, being prepared to hand ourselves over to the creator's authority, waiting and pondering on his work until its meaning becomes plainer, although believing as we do so that if a poem is complex, then it should not be too long: if we choose depth, we cannot have length.

Few poets in this collection would have sympathized with such ideas: individual experiences were rarely their starting-point, and though a few of them, like Hoccleve, Wyatt and Surrey, do make personal statements in their verse, the poet usually effaces his personality in the interests of his theme, or assimilates his own experiences into the general human pattern. If he does introduce himself, it is normally as a typical member of the family of man, not one of its exceptions or rebels or mystic seers. Such poets are rarely self-absorbed, exalting the events of their lives into illuminating insights or significant symbols: they prefer to take stock parts such as Colin Clout or the dreamer; the wretched, ill-treated lover, condemned to permanent sorrow by his mistress's disdain; the stricken mortal abruptly summoned by Death to account for his sins before the heavenly tribunal; the bemused country bumpkin entangled with the law courts in London; the ingratiating but not very astute pilgrim on the Canterbury road. An audience expected their poet to entertain them with a story, or improve them with a moral lesson, but they hardly urged him to lay bare his soul. For one thing, what authority could be attached to the voice of the individual in an age which believed implicitly in the authority of the Church, or the Word of God, the prestige of the Ancients, or ancestral wisdom? Since these were absolute, the poet was only free to reaffirm the truths that they proclaimed; even at the Reformation when rival truths might clash, most poets prefer to endorse generally accepted attitudes, not create the climate of opinion for the infiltration of novel ones.

Furthermore, since life in the fifteenth and sixteenth centuries was much more of a communal experience than it is today, men and women tended to *feel* in common with one another. The main occurrences in their harsh, grinding lives—the passage of the seasons, the great Church festivals, the older ceremonies of pagan origin, even occasions of a more personal kind, like birth, death and marriage—were experienced communally, and affected everybody. There was less room for private lives and private feelings than in modern suburbia where house-agents guarantee privacy and flats are advertised as 'self-contained'. Even the medieval recluse meditating alone in his cold cell on a winter's night was seeking to align himself with that great unseen community of saints and seraphs enjoying the ultimate sense of union, communion with God. So most writers represented here chose to universalize rather than particularize. They illustrate Dr. Johnson's assertion that 'Great truths are always general'.

The chief method of literary communication for much of this period contributed to the tendency to generalize: even after the introduction of printing to England by Caxton in about 1476, the standard way of digesting poetry was to hear it read: the poet's art was public and oral, especially at court, where nobles considered it bourgeois to publish their literary effusions, and recitation of one's own works was part of the social pattern. Until well into the century, a poet did not abandon his traditional role as bard or *scop*, and fulfilled something of the same function. Many writers, Charles d'Orleans, Surrey, Vaux and Oxford among them, were nobly born; Wyatt, Boleyn, Sackville and Gascoigne served their sovereigns as diplomats and ambassadors; Googe, Golding, Turbervile and Spenser all had dealings with the court; Lydgate, Hawes and Skelton were all professional court poets: it is no wonder that royal and noble tastes governed the literary activities of so many poets found in this anthology. The maker had to satisfy his patron and his audience and would probably perform his work before them in order to do so.

Oral delivery created special problems: the writer was not required to be very original in his initial choice of subject, since a listening audience preferred to know the story in advance, but at the same time, he had to eschew the complexities we permit contemporary authors, since it was vital that his essential meaning was grasped straightaway (no turning back to check on a supposed verbal echo two hundred lines away!). In order to refresh his listeners, he had to provide carefully placed digressions from his main theme; above all, he had to be a sufficient master of his craft to vary and embellish his narrative, so that it retained its interest right to the end. To this goal some of the chief tactics of rhetoric were devoted, and this is often why much medieval literature seems to sprawl and lack coherence today. Perhaps we in our turn have tended to overvalue concise expression and concentrated effects, in an age that specializes in the Digest and the synopsis, where few novels are allowed the luxury of a sub-plot. Variety and compendiousness commended themselves to the Middle Ages, when a book might be required to last a reader the whole winter: the early books of Malory's Arthurian saga or *The Faerie Queene* show how skilfully several single adventures can be interwoven to sustain our interest over a lengthy narration. If too much literature of the period is spoilt for us by its encyclopedic range and its all-inclusive detail, we must remember that classical standards of artistic economy, simplicity and restraint had not yet entered European heads. The Gothic spirit is found in Chartres Cathedral with its relative prodigality of detail, its triumphant diversity of shrine, niche and gargoyle, not in the chaste lucidity of the Parthenon.

V

Despite the activities of the humanists and the consequent re-discovery of the classical spirit, there is no fundamental break in continuity between late medieval and early Tudor verse: the legend of a fully mature poetry suddenly emerging into dazzling light at the wave of Sir Philip Sidney's wand is dispelled by the briefest glance at the work of men such as Surrey, Sackville and Gascoigne. The Elizabethan poetic revolution was pioneered by those who went before and prepared the way, if only by demonstrating that certain of the possible ways ahead were merely cul-de-sacs. Sidney's exasperated denunciation of his contemporaries as 'base men with servile wits' in his *Apologie for Poetrie* is perhaps understandable, but it is a severe epitaph for those poets of the 1560s and 70s who toiled to keep poetry alive, by not only preserving the older types of poem such as the homiletic discourse, the moral satire, the didactic allegory, and the popular lyric, but also by adapting the Petrarchan sonnet, the Latin epigram, and the classical epic to English tastes.

Thus in the latter part of this collection, one may observe how the traditions of medieval English verse, and the fresher moods and subjects borrowed from the classics and from continental literatures, began to run together. There is no need to assume that one is superior to the other, or that the magnificent literary achieve-

15

ments of the Elizabethans did not owe a great deal to both. *The Shepheardes Calender* and *The Faerie Queene* remind us that at least one great Elizabethan poet was steeped in the native traditions of medieval poetry; Marlowe chose to set one of his finest tragedies in the frame of a morality drama; on John Donne there seems to rest the spirit of Thomas Wyatt. Medieval stanza-forms persist everywhere, notably in Gascoigne's fondness for rhyme-royal, a favourite scheme of the fifteenth century. The habit of allegorizing, too, dies hard in the sixteenth century, with Hawes, and Sackville, whose classical Hell is alive with Gothic monsters, while *A Mirrour for Magistrates* as a whole acknowledges itself as a sequel to Lydgate's *Fall of Princes*. In the matter of diction, too, many writers attempt to retain contact with their native predecessors: Sackville in his *Induction* shows a consciousness of linguistic change by giving his language an archaic flavour, and even Wyatt, despite his interest in the contemporary idiom, uses a slightly old-fashioned manner of speech, possibly an indication of his taste for Chaucer. In *The Shepheardes Calender* Spenser exploits antiquated expressions to link his poems to those that have gone before him, and in particular, to pay his tribute to his great predecessor. Wyatt and Spenser are excellent examples of the way in which sixteenth-century pioneers retained contact with the older manner, however much they were concerned to modify and extend it. It is almost as if they needed to base their forays into the unknown territories of continental and classical literatures on solid medieval achievements.

In such ways, continuity between medieval and Tudor poets was maintained: yet Tudor poets were in no sense slaves of their past. What the best authors of the sixteenth century did was to utilize the materials and methods of the past, its conventions and its discoveries, but to meet present requirements, and to serve new artistic ends. This seems notably true of Wyatt, whose best work results from a harmonious fusion between 'tradition and the individual talent', but the same may also be said of the work of Skelton, Surrey, Sackville and Gascoigne. Many writers employed the same rhetorical techniques sanctioned by use in the Middle Ages, but they were now serving slightly different ends. As Douglas Peterson demonstrates in *The English Lyric from Wyatt to Donne*, poets concentrated on those aspects of rhetoric which would best assist them to organize and control their material, for, although hallowed beliefs and traditions about the nature of art retain their importance, a new conception of literary artistry does make itself felt in the sixteenth century, and as one passes from Lydgate to Skelton, from Barclay to Surrey, one detects a developing concern with poetic structure and form, a dawning appreciation of shape and unity, and a growing distaste for sprawl.

This change can be explained in several ways: the impression of streamlining and tightening-up received is very consistent with C. S. Lewis's picture of Renaissance humanism:

> ... it is emphatically not a movement towards freedom and expansion. It is the impulse of men who feel themselves simple, rustic, and immature, towards sophistication, urbanity, and ripeness. In a word, it is the most complete opposite we can find to the Romantic desire for the primitive and the spontaneous. . . .[1]

In addition to their response to this anxious search for elegance and maturity, Tudor poets owed much to that re-discovery of the mood of classical civilizations neatly summarized by Johann Huizinga:

> ... by an inward ripening, the mind, after having been so long conversant with the forms of Antiquity, began to grasp its spirit. The incomparable simpleness and purity of the ancient culture, its exactitude of conception and expression, its easy and natural thought and strong interest in men and in life—all this began to dawn on men's minds. Europe, after having lived in the shadow of antiquity, lived in its sunshine once more. . . .[2]

That spirit began to flow into English poetry perhaps with Wyatt's satires and Surrey's version of the *Aeneid*, and pastorals,

[1] C. S. Lewis, *English Literature in the Sixteenth Century*, 1954, pp. 23–4.
[2] Johann Huizinga, *The Waning of the Middle Ages*, 1924, pp. 307–8.

elegies, epigrams and even epics followed, although Golding's translation of Ovid's *Metamorphoses* may serve to remind us that English writers had a long distance to travel before the classical ethos was securely established and worthily expressed.

Vitally important, too, was the stimulus provided by the continental vernaculars, particularly French and Italian. The Italian influence on English writers has been somewhat over-stressed in the past, and while Petrarch (1304–74), master of the passionate love sonnet, enjoyed a high reputation in England for much of the sixteenth century, by no means all his admirers were content to copy him slavishly. Wyatt, supposedly the importer of the Petrarchan sonnet-form and manner to England, was more attracted by the possibilities of the invention than by its traditional content, and soon learnt to adapt the strict rhyme-scheme of the Italians, to exploit the opportunities latent in the form for developing an argument, and chiefly, to temper the spiritually uplifting, idealized sex relationship enshrined in the Petrarchan sonnet, with some earthy comments of his own. The later Elizabethans in fact copied the Italian more closely than their predecessors, who often resisted the servile assumptions of the original. Typical is Wyatt's sweeping re-handling of Petrarch's sonnet *In Vita* 190, where the poet's love, Laura, is presented as a milk-white hart grazing in the fields early in the morning, wearing about her neck a jewelled collar bearing the legend that her life will be a brief one, since she belongs to God, who will soon claim His own; even as the poet watches, the hart disappears in the midday heat. Wyatt's comment on this piece of symbolism (p. 105) is to give the hart a new meaning but on the cynically ironic level: his beloved is no chaste doe-eyed virgin destined for heaven, but a flighty wanton who enjoys her pursuit by the males at court, secure in the knowledge that she is destined for a prince's bed-chamber. The poet, no longer the awed watcher under the trees, participates in the sex-chase himself, fascinated yet repelled. As in 'You that in love finde lucke' (p. 104) the reality of Wyatt's own personal experience breaks the enchanted spell of *amour courtois*, and all the make-believe comes to an end. Just as

Chaucer had tested the implications of the courtly love code in *Troilus and Criseyde*, so Wyatt analyses the same romantic ethic in terms of human relations, and finds it wanting. Far from 'studiously imitating' the Italian, as Puttenham suggests, Wyatt gives him the lie.

Much of what he introduced into his verse was of native growth: the didactic, disillusioned tone heard not only in the satires but the love-poetry too, is part of a long-established English literary tradition which aims to impart moral instruction and homiletic reflections on the transience and instability of human life. The characteristically rebellious note sounded in many of the love poems represents Wyatt's consolidation of something we discover in Chaucer and anonymous lyrics such as 'O mestres, whye' (p. 64), in which the writer disputes the courtly mistress's traditional right to reduce her man to a servile cipher. Wyatt's use of colloquial speech and proverbial lore is entirely within the plainer style of verse-making, part of a native heritage which he shared with Chaucer, Langland, and Skelton, and handed on to Googe and Gascoigne, who helped to create that very typical mid-century poetry, which is sententious, sober, homely, somewhat melancholy and unemphatic, but which is clearly not adequately defined in C. S. Lewis's misleading epithet 'drab'.[1]

What has been urged of Wyatt's best verse applies to other Renaissance poets represented here: large as their debts to foreign and classical examples may have been, especially in matters of organization, presentation, and style, there was a strong element in their work that remained enduringly English. If readers for too long accepted a picture of poetry between Chaucer and Spenser as lacklustre and effete, it was partly because they over-valued the wrong poets, partly because they assumed that English verse traditions played no part in the new, more polished, more sophisticated work that emerged with Sidney and Spenser. But a rich native element was a vital constituent of the new poetry of the Elizabethans; shaped by centuries of social and cultural change, it stood there to inform

[1] *English Literature in the Sixteenth Century*, 1954; *passim*.

the work of men as various as Marlowe, Drayton, Raleigh, Shakespeare, Jonson, Nashe and Donne. The exotic had to co-exist alongside the traditional. The waves of the continental Renaissance may have made a thunderous impact as they reached the beaches of England, but they certainly did not break on a barren shore.

A GUIDE TO FURTHER READING

The texts in this book have been taken from the following editions, which should be consulted by the reader who wishes to carry his studies further.

Poems by John Lydgate, edited by J. Norton Smith, Oxford, 1966.

The Life of Our Lady, edited by Lauritis, Klinefelter, Gallagher, University of Duquesne, 1960.

The Minor Poems of John Lydgate, II, Early English Text Society, 1934.

English Verse between Chaucer and Surrey, edited by E. P. Hammond, Durham, N. Carolina, 1927.

The English Poems of Charles D'Orleans, edited by R. M. Steele, Early English Text Society, 1941.

Religious Lyrics of the Fifteenth Century, edited by Carleton Brown, Oxford, 1939.

The Early English Carols, edited by R. L. Greene, Oxford, 1935.

English and Scottish Popular Ballads, edited by F. J. Child, 1882–98. Reissued 1965.

Secular Lyrics of the Fourteenth and Fifteenth Centuries, edited by R. H. Robbins, Oxford, 2nd edn. 1955.

'Two minor French lyric forms in English', P. J. Frankis, *Neuphilogische Mitteilungen*, 1959. ('Besse Buntyng').

Songs, Carols and Other Miscellaneous Poems (from Balliol MS 354), edited by R. Dyboski, Early English Text Society, Extra Series, 1907.

The Poetical Works of John Skelton, edited by Alexander Dyce, 2 vols., 1843.

The Eclogues of Alexander Barclay, edited by Beatrice White, Early English Text Society, 1928.

The Pastime of Pleasure, Stephen Hawes, edited by W. E. Mead, Early English Text Society, 1928.

Music and Poetry in the Early Tudor Court, John Stevens, 1961.

Collected Poems of Sir Thomas Wyatt, edited by Kenneth Muir, and Patricia Thomson, Liverpool, 1969.

Poems by Henry Howard, Earl of Surrey, edited by Emrys Jones, Oxford, 1964.

Tottel's Miscellany, edited by H. E. Rollins, 2 vols., Cambridge, Mass., 1928–9.

A Mirror for Magistrates, edited by Lily B. Campbell, Cambridge, 1938.

Eclogs, Epytaphes, and Sonettes, Barnaby Googe, edited by Edward Arber, 1910.

Ovid's Metamorphoses: Arthur Golding's translation of 1567, edited by J. F. Nims, New York, 1965.

The Complete Works of George Gascoigne, edited by J. W. Cunliffe, 2 vols., Cambridge, 1907–10.

A Handfull of Pleasant Delights, edited by H. E. Rollins, Cambridge, Mass., 1924.

The Paradise of Dainty Devises, edited by H. E. Rollins, Cambridge, Mass., 1927.

The Works of Edmund Spenser: The Minor Poems, I, edited by C. G. Osgood and H. G. Lotspeich, Baltimore, 1943.

The poems by George Turbervile have been transcribed from the 1570 edition of *Epitaphs, Epigrams, Songs, and Sonets*, in the British Museum Library.

The following list of suggested further reading is necessarily selective and personal, but most of the works mentioned here contain bibliographies which will lead the reader on to more detailed or specialized studies.

GENERAL BACKGROUND

J. Huizinga, *The Waning of the Middle Ages*, 1924, Pelican Books, 1955.

G. R. Elton, *England Under the Tudors*, 1955.

Perceval Hunt, *Fifteenth Century England*, Pittsburgh, 1962.

Eileen Power, *Medieval People*, 1924, Pelican Books, 1937.

LITERARY BACKGROUND

J. W. H. Atkins, *English Literary Criticism: Medieval*, Cambridge, 1943.

J. W. H. Atkins, *English Literary Criticism: The Renaiscence*, Cambridge, 1947.

H. S. Bennett, *Chaucer and the Fifteenth Century*, Oxford History of English Literature, 1947.

John Buxton, *A Tradition of Poetry*, 1967.

E. K. Chambers, *English Literature at the Close of the Middle Ages*, Oxford History of English Literature, 1945.

Peter Dronke, *The Medieval Lyric*, 1968.

Maurice Evans, *English Poetry in the Sixteenth Century*, 1955, revised 1967.

J. W. Lever, *The Elizabethan Love Sonnet*, 1956.

C. S. Lewis, *The Allegory of Love*, Oxford, 1936.

C. S. Lewis, *English Literature in the Sixteenth Century*, Oxford History of English Literature, 1954.

H. A. Mason, *Humanism and Poetry in the Early Tudor Period*, 1959.

A. K. Moore, *The Secular Lyric in Middle English*, Lexington, 1951.

D. L. Peterson, *The English Lyric from Wyatt to Donne*, Princeton, 1967.

H. Hallett Smith, *Elizabethan Poetry*, Cambridge, Mass., 1952.

A. C. Spearing, *Criticism and Medieval Poetry*, 1964.

John Speirs, *Medieval English Poetry: The Non-Chaucerian Tradition*, 1957, (esp. Sections I, II & VI).

John Stevens, *Music and Poetry in the Early Tudor Court*, 1961.

J. Thompson, *The Founding of English Metre*, 1961.

Yvor Winters, 'The Sixteenth Century Lyric in England', *Poetry*, 53-4, 1939, reprinted in Paul Alpers' anthology, *Elizabethan Poetry, Modern Essays in Criticism*, Galaxy Books, Oxford, 1967.

Individual Authors

LYDGATE

Derek Pearsall, 'The English Chaucerians' in *Chaucer and Chaucerians*, ed. Derek Brewer, 1966.

Alain Renoir, *The Poetry of John Lydgate*, 1967.

Walter Schirmer: *John Lydgate* (Tübingen, 1952), English translation 1961.

SKELTON

H. L. R. Edwards, *Skelton: The Life and Times of an Early Tudor Poet*, 1949.

Stanley E. Fish, *John Skelton's Poetry*, New Haven, 1965.

A. R. Heiserman, *Skelton and Satire*, Chicago, 1961.

John Holloway, *Skelton* (Chatterton Lecture of British Academy, 1958), reprinted in *The Charted Mirror*, 1960.

William Nelson, *John Skelton, Laureate*, New York, 1939.

WYATT

H. A. Mason, *Humanism and Poetry in the Early Tudor Period*, 1959.
Kenneth Muir, *The Life and Letters of Sir Thomas Wyatt*, Liverpool, 1963.
Raymond Southall, *The Courtly Maker*, 1964.
John Stevens, *Music and Poetry in the Early Tudor Court*, 1961.
Patricia Thomson, *Sir Thomas Wyatt and his Background*, 1964.

SACKVILLE

J. Swart, *Thomas Sackville: A Study in Sixteenth Century Poetry*, Groningen, 1948.

THE SHEPHEARDES CALENDER

Paul McLane, *Spenser's Shepheardes Calender*, Notre Dame, 1961.
William Nelson, *The Poetry of Edmund Spenser*, Columbia, 1963.

ANTHOLOGIES

R. T. Davies, *Medieval English Lyrics*, 1963.
R. L. Greene, *A Selection of English Carols*, Oxford, 1962.
J. W. Hebel and H. H. Hudson, *Poetry of the English Renaissance*, 1929.
F. Sidgwick and E. K. Chambers, *Early English Lyrics*, 1907.
Brian Stone, *Medieval English Verse* (translations), Penguin Classics, 1964.

JOHN LYDGATE

From *The Complaint of the Black Knight*

In May, when Flora, the fresshe lusty quene,
The soyle hath clad in grene, rede, and white,
And Phebus gan to shede his stremes shene
Amyd the Bole, wyth al the bemes bryght,
And Lucifer, to chace awey the nyght,
Ayen the morow our orysont hath take,
To bydde lovers out of her slepe awake:

And hertys hevy for to recomforte
From dreryhed of hevy nyghtis sorowe,
Nature bad hem rysen and disporte   10
Ageyn the goodly, glade, greye morowe.
And Hope also, with Seint John to borowe,
Bad, in dispite of Daunger and Dispeyre,
For to take the holsom lusty eyre.

And wyth a sygh I gan for to abreyde
Out of my slombre, and sodenly up-stert
As he, alas, that nygh for sorow deyde;
My sekenes sat ay so nygh myn hert.
But for to fynde socour of my smert,
Or atte lest sum relesse of my peyn,   20
That me so sore halt in every veyn,

I rose anon and thoght I wolde goon
Unto the wode to her the briddes sing,
When that the mysty vapour was agoon,
And clere and feyre was the morwenyng.
The dewe also lyk sylver in shynyng
Upon the leves, as eny baume suete,
Til firy Tytan with hys persaunt hete

Had dried up the lusty lycour nyw
Upon the herbes in the grene mede,   30
And that the floures of mony dyvers hywe
Upon her stalkes gunne for to sprede,
And for to splayen out her leves on brede
Ageyn the sun, golde-borned in hys spere,
That doun to hem cast hys bemes clere.

And by a ryver forth I gan costey,
Of water clere as berel or cristal,
Til at the last I founde a lytil wey
Touarde a parke enclosed with a wal
In compas round; and by a gate smal,   40
Whoso that wolde frely myghte goon
Into this parke, walled with grene stoon.

And in I went to her the briddes songe,
Which on the braunches, both in pleyn and vale,
So loude song that al the wode ronge,
Lyke as hyt shold shever in pesis smale.
And, as me thoghte, that the nyghtyngale
Wyth so grete myght her voys gan out-wrest,
Ryght as her hert for love wolde brest.

The soyle was pleyn, smothe, and wonder softe,   50
Al oversprad wyth tapites that Nature
Had made herselfe, celured eke alofte

26

With bowys grene, the floures for to cure,
That in her beaute they may longe endure
Fro al assaute of Phebus' fervent fere,
Which in his spere so hote shone and clere.

The eyre atempre and the smothe wynde
Of Zepherus, among the blosmes whyte,
So holsom was and norysshing be kynde,
That smale buddes and round blomes lyte   60
In maner gan of her brethe delyte,
To yif us hope that their frute shal take
Ayens autumpne, redy for to shake.

I saw ther Daphene closed under rynde,
Grene laurer, and the holsom pyne,
The myrre also that wepeth ever of kynde,
The cedre high, upryght as a lyne,
The philbert eke, that lowe dothe enclyne
Her bowes grene to the erthe doune
Unto her knyght icalled Demophoune.   70

Ther saw I eke the fresshe hawethorne
In white motele, that so soote doth smelle,
Asshe, firre, and oke, with mony a yonge acorne,
And mony a tre mo than I can telle;
And me beforne I saw a litel welle,
That had his course (as I gan be-holde),
Under an hille, with quyke stremes colde.

The gravel golde, the water pure as glas,
The bankys round the welle environyng,
And softe as velvet the yonge gras   80
That therupon lustely cam spryngyng.
The sute of trees aboute compassyng
Her shadow cast, closyng the welle rounde,
And al the erbes grouyng on the grounde.

From *The Life of Our Lady*

O thoughtfull herte, plunged in distresse
With slombre of slouthe, this long wynter's nyght,
Oute of the slepe of mortall hevynesse
Awake anoon, and loke upon the lyght
Of thelke sterre that with hir bemys bryght
And withe the shynyng of hir stremys merye
Is wonte to gladde all our emysperye,

And to oppresse the derkenesse and the doole
Of hevy hertes that soroen and syghen ofte—
I mene the sterre of the bright poole   10
That with hir bemys whan she is alofte
May al the trowble aswagen and asofte
Of worldely wawes, which in this mortall see
Have us byset, withe grete adversitee,

The rage of whiche is so tempestyuous
That whan the calme is moste blandyshyng,
Then is the streme of dethe most perylous,
If that we wante the light of hir shynyng
And but the syght, allas, of hir lokyng;
From dethes brinke make us to escape,   20
The haven of lif of us may not be take.

This sterre in beautee passethe Pliades,
Both of shynyng and of stremes clere,
Boetes' Arthour, and also Iades,
And Esperus when it dothe appere,
For this is Spica with hir bright spere
That tawarde even, at mydenyght and at morowe,
Downe frome the hevyn adaweth all our sorowe.

28

Whose bright bemys shynyng frome so ferre
That cloudes blake may the light nat fyne;   30
For this of Jacob is the fayrest sterre
That undir wawes nevere doth declyne,
Whose course is not undir the clyptyke lyne
But everyliche of beaute may be sene
Amyddes the arke of our merydyne,

And driethe up the bitter teres wete
Of Aurora, aftir the mourwen gray,
That she in wepyng dothe on floures flete
In listy Aprill and in fresshe May,
And causith Phebus the bright somer's day   40
With his golde wayne, bournede bright and fayre,
T'enchase the miste of our cloudy ayre.

For this is the sterre, that bare the bright sonne
Which holdyth the septre of Juda in his hande,
Whose stremes been oute of Jesse ronne,
To shede hir lyght bothe on see and lande,
Whose gladde beamys without eclypsyng stonde
Estwarde to us in the orient full shene,
With light of grace to voiden all our tene.

Now fayre sterre, O sterre of sterres all,   50
Whose light to see angelles delyte,
So late the golde dewe of thy grace fall
Into my breste, like skales fayre and white,
Me to enspyre of that I wolde endyte
With thilke bame, sent down by myracle
Whan the Hooly Goost the made his habitacle.

This worlde is ful of variaunce
In everything, whoo taketh hede,
That feyth and trust and al constaunce
Exiled ben, this is noo drede;
And, safe oonly in womanhede,
I kan see no sykyrnesse;
But for al that, yet as I rede,
Be-ware alwey of doublenesse.

Also these fresh somer floures,
White and rede, blewe and grene,   10
Ben sodeynly with wynter shoures
Made feynt and fade with-oute wene;
That truste is noon, as ye may sene,
In nothinge, nor noo stedfastnesse,
Except in women, thus I mene;
Yet ay be-ware of doublenesse.

The croked moone—this is no tale—
Som while is shene and bryght of hewe;
And after that ful derke and pale,
And every monyth chaungeth newe;   20
That, who-so the verray sothe knewe,
Alle thynge is bilte on brotilnesse,—
Save that women ay be trewe,
Yet ay be-war of doublenesse.

The lusty fresshe somer's day
And Phebus, with his bemes clere,
Towardes nyght they drawe away
And no lenger lyste appere;
So in this present lyfe now here,

Noo-thinge abytte in hys fairenesse,   30
Save women ay be founde entere
And devoide of doublenesse.

The see eke, with his sterne wawes,
Eche day floweth new ageyn,
And by concourse of his lawes
The ebbe foloweth, in certayn;
After grete drought ther cometh a reyne,
That fare-wel alle her stablenesse,—
Save that women be hool and pleyne;
Yet al be-war of doublenesse.   40

Fortune's whele gooth rounde about
A thousand tymes, day and nyght,
Whos course stondeth ever in doute,
For to transmewe, she ys so lyght;
For which advertyth in your syght
The untrust of worldly fikelnesse,—
Save women which, of kyndely ryght,
Ne have no tachche of doublenesse.

What man may the wynde restreyne,
Or holde a snake by the tayle,   50
Or a slepur eele constreyne
That yt wil voyde, withoute fayle?
Or whoo kan dryve so a nayle
To make sure newfanglenesse,—
Save women that kan guye her sayle
To rowe her boote with doublenesse?

Atte every haven they kan arryve
Whereas they woote ys good passage,
Of innocence they kan not strive
Wyth wawes, nor noo rokkes rage;   60

31

So happe ys her lodmanage
Wyth nelde and stoon her course to dresse,
That Salamon was not so sage
To fynde in hem noo doublenesse.

Wher-fore, who-so hem accuse
Of any double entencion,
To speke roune, outher to muse,
To pynche at hyr condicion—
Alle is but fals collusion,
I dar ryght welle the sothe expresse: 70
They have no bette proteccion
But shrowde hem under doublenesse.

So wel fortuned ys hir chaunce
The dise to turne up so don,
With sis and synke they kan avaunce
And than by revolucion:
They sette a felle conclusion
Of ambes-ase, in sothfastnesse,
Though clerkes make mencion
Ther kynde ys frete with doublenesse!   80

Sampson hadde experience
That women weren ful trewe founde
Whan Dalida of innocence
With sheres gan his hede to rounde;
To speke also of Rosamounde,
And Cleopatris feythfulnesse,
The storyes pleynly wil confounde
Men that apeche her doublenesse.

Sengle thing ne is nat preysed,
Nor oo folde is of noo renoune,   90
In balaunce whan they be peysed

32

For lakke of weght they be bore doune;
And for this cause of juste resoune
These women alle, of ryghtwysnesse,
Of choys and free eleccion,
Muste love eschaunge and doublenesse.

Lenvoy

O ye women whiche ben enclyned,
By influence of youre nature,
To ben as pure as golde y-fyned,
In your trouthe for to endure,   100
Arme your-selfe in strong armure,
Leste men assayle youre sikernesse;
Sitte on your brest, your-self t'assure,
A myghty shelde of doublenesse.

From *The Dance of Death*

DEATH: Ye that amonge lordis and barouns
Han had so longe worship and renoun,
Forgete youre trumpetis and youre clariouns,
This is no dreme ne simulacioun;
Somtime youre custome and entencioun
Was with ladies to daunce in the shade,
But ofte it happith in conclusioun
That o man brekith that anothir made.

33

BAROUN: Ful ofte sithe I have bene auctorised
               To his emprises and thinges of greet fame;   10
               Of hie and lowe my thanke also devised,
               Cherisshed with ladies and wymmen hie of name,
               Ne nevere on me was put no defame
               In lordis court wiche that was notable;
               But deethis strook hath made me so lame,
               Undre hevene in erthe is no thing stable.

DEATH: Come forthe anone, my lady and Princesse,
               Ye muste also goo upon this daunce;
               Not may availle youre grete straungenesse,
               Nouther youre beute ne your greet plesaunce,   20
               Youre riche aray ne youre daliaunce
               That sumtyme cowde so many holde an honde
               In love for al youre double variaunce:
               Ye mote as nowe this footing undirstonde.

LADY: Allas, I see ther is none othir boote—
               Deeth hath in erthe no lady ne maistresse,
               And on his daunce yit muste I nedis foote,
               For there nys qwene, contesse ne duchesse,
               Flouringe in bounte ne in fairnesse,
               That she of deeth mote dethes trace sewe;   30
               For to oure bewte and countirfeet fresshnesse,
               Oure rympled age seith, 'Farewele, adewe.'

DEATH: My lorde, sir Bisshoppe, with youre mytre and croos,
               For al your ricchesse, sothly I ensure,
               For al youre tresour so longe kept in cloos,
               Youre worldly goodes, and goodes of nature,
               And of your sheep the dredly goostly cure
               With charge committid to youre prelacie,
               For to acounte ye shulle be broughte to lure:
               No wight is sure that clymbeth overe hie.   40

BISHOP: My herte truly is nouther glad ne myrie
Of sodein tidinges wiche that ye bring;
My fest is turned into a simple ferye,
That for discomfort me list nothing syng;
The worlde contrarie nowe unto me in workyng,
That alle folkes can so disherite,
He that al withhalt allas at oure parting,
And al shal passe save only oure merite.

DEATH: Come forth, sir Squier, right fresshe of youre aray,
That can of daunces al the newe gise;   50
Though ye bare armes, fressh horsed yisterday,
With spere and shelde at youre unkouthe devise,
And toke on yow so many hy emprise,
Daunceth with us, it wil no bettir be:
Ther is no socour in no manere wise
For no man may fro dethes stroke fle.

SQUIER: Sithen that dethe me holdith in his lace,
Yet shal y speke o worde or y pase:
Adieu al myrthe, adieu nowe al solace,
Adieu my ladies, somtime so fressh of face,   60
Adieu beute, plesaunce and solace!
Of dethes chaunge every day is prime;
Thinketh on youre soules or that deth manace,
For al shal rote and no man wote what tyme.

DEATH: Come forth, sir Abbot, with youre brood hatte,
Beeth not abaisshed, though ye have right;
Greet is your hood, your bely large and fatte,
Ye mote come daunce, though ye be nothing light;
Leve up youre abbey to some othir wight,
Your eir is of age youre state to occupie.   70
Who that is fattest, I have hym behight,
In his grave shal sonnest putrefie.

35

ABBOT: Of thi thretis have I noon envie
That I shal nowe leve al governaunce,
But that I shal as a cloistrer dye,
This doth to me passinge grete grevaunce;
Mi liberte nor my great haboundaunce
What may availe in any manere wise?
Yet axe I mercy with hertly repentaunce,
Though in diynge to late men hem avise.   80

DEATH: And ye, my lady, gentil dame Abbesse,
With youre mantels furred large and wide,
Youre veile, youre wymple passinge of greet richesse,
And beddis softe ye mote nowe leie aside,
For to this daunce I shal be youre guyde;
Though ye be tendre and born of gentil blood,
While that ye lyve, for youresilfe provide,
For aftir deeth no man hath no good.

ABBESSE: Allas, that deeth hath thus for me ordeined
That in no wise I may it not declyne,   90
Though it so be, ful ofte I have constreyned
Brest and throte my notes out to twyne,
My chekes round vernysshed for to shyne,
Ungirt ful ofte to walke at the large:
Thus cruell deth doth all estates fyne;
Who hath no chippe muste rowe in bote or barge.

36

THOMAS HOCCLEVE

From *La Male Regle de T. Hoccleve*

I dar nat telle how that the fressh repeir
Of Venus' femel lusty children deere,
That so goodly, so shaply were and feir,
And so plesant of port and of maneere,
And feede cowden al a world with cheere,
And of atyr passyngly wel byseye,
At Poules heed me maden ofte appeere
To talke of mirthe, and to disporte and pleye.

Ther was sweet wyn ynow thurghout the hous,
And wafres thikke, for this conpaignie   10
That I spak of, been sumwhat likerous
Whereas they mowe a draght of wyn espie,
Sweete, and in wirkinge hoot for the maistrie,
To warme a stomak with, therof they dranke:
To suffre hem paie had been no courtesie,
That charge I took to wynne love and thanke.

Of loves aart yit touchid I no deel—
I cowde nat and eek it was no neede;
Had I a kus, I was content ful weel,
Bettre than I wolde han be with the deede.   20
Theron can I but smal, it is no dreede;

Whan that men speke of it in my presence,
For shame I wexe as reed as is the gleede:
Now wole I torne ageyn to my sentence.

Of him that hauntith taverne of custume,
At shorte wordes, the profyt is this:
In double wyse his bagge it shal consume,
And make his tonge speke of folk amis;
For in the cuppe seelden fownden is
That any wight his neigheburgh commendith: 30
Beholde and see, what avantage is his
That God, his freend, and eek himself offendith?

But oon avantage in this cas I have:
I was so ferd with any man to fighte,
Cloos kepte I me, no man durste I deprave
But rownyngly; I spak nothyng on highte,
And yit my wil was good, if that I mighte,
For lettynge of my manly cowardyse,
That ay of strokes impressid the wighte,
So that I durste medlen in no wyse.   40

Wher was a gretter maister eek than Y,
Or bet aqweyntid at Westmynstre yate
Among the taverneres namely,
And cookes, whan I cam, eerly or late?
I pynchid nat at hem in myn acate,
But paied hem as that they axe wolde;
Wherfore I was the welcomere algate,
And for a verray gentil man y-holde.

38

CHARLES D'ORLEANS

Ballade

Whan fresshe Phebus, day of Seynt Valentyne,
Had whirlid up his golden chare aloft,
The burnyd bemys of it gan to shyne
In at my chambre where Y slepid soft;
Of which the light that he had with him brought,
He wook me of the slepe of hevynes,
Wherin forslepid Y alle the nyght dowtles,
Upon my bed so hard of noyous thought.

Of which this day, to parten there bottyne,
An oost of fowlis semblid in a croft,   10
Myn neye biside, and pletid ther latyne
To have with them as nature had them wrought
Ther makis for to wrappe in wyngis soft,
For which they gan so loude ther cries dresse,
That Y ne koude not slepe in my distres
Upon my bed so hard of noyous thought.

Tho gan Y reyne with teeris of myn eyne
Mi pilowe, and to wayle and cursen oft
My destyny, and gan my look enclyne
These birdis to, and seide, 'Ye birdis ought   20
To thanke Nature, whereas it sittith me nought,

39

That han yowre makis to yowre gret gladnes,
Where Y sorow the deth of my maystres
Upon my bed so hard of noyous thought.'

Als wele is him this day that hath him kaught
A Valentyne that lovyth him as Y gesse,
Whereas discomfort sole Y here me dresse
Upon my bed so hard of noyous thought.

Ballade

O sely ankir, that in thi selle
Iclosid art with stoon and gost not out,
Thou maist ben gladder so for to dwelle
Then Y with wanton wandryng thus abowt
That have me pikid amongis the rowt
An endles woo withouten recomfort,
That of my poore liif Y stonde in dowt:
Go, dul complaynt, my lady this report.

The anker hath no more him for to greve
Then sool alone upon the wallis stare,   10
But welaway! Y stonde in more myscheef,
For he hath helthe and Y of helthe am bare,
And more and more when Y come where ther are
Of fayre folkis, to se a goodly sort,
A thousand fold that doth encrese my care:
Go, dulle complaynt, my lady this report.

It doth me thynke yondir is fayre of face,
But what more fayre yet is my ladi dere;
Yond on is smalle, and yonde streight sidis has,

Her foot is lite, and she hath eyen clere,   20
But alle ther staynyd my lady were she here:
Thus thynke Y, lo! which doth me discomfort,
Not for the sight, but for Y nam hir nere:
Go, dulle complaynt, my lady this report.

Wo worthe them which that raft me hir presence!
Wo worth the tyme to Y to hir resort!
Wo worth is me to be thus in absence!
Go, dulle complaynt, my lady this report.

Roundel

My gostly fadir, Y me confesse,
First to God and then to yow,
That at a wyndow, wot ye how,
I stale a cosse of gret swetnes,
Which don was out avisynes—
But hit is doon not undoon now.
    My gostly fadir, Y me confesse,
    First to God and then to yow.
But Y restore it shalle, dowtles,
Ageyn, if so be that Y mow;   10
And that to God Y make a vow,
And ellis Y axe foryefnes.
    My gostly fadir, Y me confesse,
    First to God and then to yow.

ANONYMOUS

London Lickpenny

In London there I was bent,
I saw myselfe, where trouthe shuld be ateynte,
Fast to Westminstar ward I went
To a man of lawe, to make my complaynt;
I sayd, 'For Mari's love, that holy seynt,
Have pity on the powre that would procede;
I would gyve sylvar, but my purs is faynt:
For lacke of money I may not spede.'

As I thrast thurghe out the thronge
Amonge them all, my hode was gonn;   10
Netheles I let not longe,
To Kyng's Benche tyll I come.
Byfore a juge I kneled anon,
I prayd hym for God's sake he would take hede;
Full rewfully to hym I gan make my mone:
'For lacke of money I may not spede.'

Benethe hym sat clerks, a great rowt;
Fast they writen by one assent;
There stode up one, and cryed round about,
'Richard, Robert, and one of Kent!'   20

42

I wist not wele what he ment,
He cried so thike there in dede;
There were stronge theves shamed and shent,
But they that lacked money mowght not spede.

Unto the Common Place Y yowde thoo,
Where sat one with a sylken houde;
I dyd hym reverence as me ought to do,
I tolde hym my case as well as I coude,
And seyd all my goods by nowrd and by sowde;
I am defrawdyd with great falshed: 30
He would not geve me a momme of his mouthe;
For lake of money I may not spede.

Then I went me unto the Rollis,
Before the clerks of the Chauncerie,
There were many *qui tollis*
But I herd no man speke of me;
Before them I knelyd upon my kne,
Shewyd them myne evidence and they began to reade;
They seyde trewer things might there nevar be—
But for lacke of money I may not spede.   40

In Westminster Hall I found one
Went in a longe gowne of ray;
I crowched, I kneled before them anon,
For Mary's love, of helpe I gan them pray.
As he had be wrothe, he voyded away
Backward, his hand he gan me byd:
'I wot not what thou menest,' gan he say,
'Ley down sylvar, or here thow may not spede.

In all Westminstar Hall I could find nevar a one
That for me would do, thowghe I shulde dye: 50
Without the dores, were Flemings grete woon,

Upon me fast they gan to cry,
And sayd, 'Mastar, what will ye copen or by,
Fine felt hatts, spectacles for to rede
Of this gay gere?'—a great cause why
For lake of money I might not spede.

Then to Westminster gate Y went,
When the sone was at highe prime:
Cokes to me, they toke good entent,
Called me nere for to dyne,   60
And proferyd me good brede, ale and wyne;
A fayre clothe they began to sprede,
Rybbes of befe, bothe fat and fine;
But for lacke of money I might not spede.

Into London I gan me hy,
Of all the lond it bearethe the prise;
'Hot pescods!', one gan cry,
'Strabery rype!', and 'Chery in the ryse!'
One bad me come nere and by some spice,
Pepar and saffron they gan me bede,   70
Clove, grayns, and flowre of rise;
For lacke of money I might not spede.

Then into Chepe I gan me drawne,
Where I sawe stond moche people;
One bad me come ner, and by fine cloth of lawne,
Paris thred, coton, and umple;
I seyde thereupon I could no skyle,
I am not wont thereto indede;
One bad me by a hewre, my hed to hele:
For lake of money I might not spede.   80

Into Cornhill anon I yode,
Where is moche stolne gere amonge;

I saw wher henge myne owne hode
That I had lost in Westminstar amonge the throng!
Then I beheld it with lokes full longe;
I kenned it as well as I dyd my crede:
To by myne owne hode agayne methought it wrong,
But for lacke of money I might not spede.

Then went I forth by London Stone,
Thrwgheout all Canywike Strete;   90
Drapers to me they called anon,
Grete chepe of clothe they gan me hete;
Then come there one, and cried, 'Hot shepes fete!'
'Risshes faire and grene!' anothar began to grete,
Both melwell and makarell I gan mete,
But for lacke of money I myght not spede.

Then I hied me into Estchepe;
One cried 'Ribes of befe, and many a pie!'
Pewtar potts they clatteryd on a heape;
Ther was harpe, pipe, and sawtry;   100
'Ye, by cokke, nay, by cokke' some began to cry;
Some sange of Jenken and Julian, to get themselvs mede:
Full fayne I wold hadd of that mynstralsie,
But for lacke of money I cowld not spede.

Then came the taverner, and toke me by the sleve,
And seyd 'Ser, a pint of wyn would yow assay?'
'Syr,' quod I, 'it may not greve,
For a peny may do no more then it may.'
I dranke a pint, and there fore gan pay;
Sore a-hungred away I yede.   110
Forwell, London, Lykkepeny, for ones and eye!
For lake of money I may not spede.

45

Then I hyed me to Byllingesgate,
And cried, 'Wagge, wagge, gow hens!'
I prayed a bargeman for God's sake,
That they would spare me myn expens.
He sayde 'Ryse up, man, and get the hens!
What, wenist thow I will do on the my almes dede?
Here skapethe no man, bynethe two pens!'
For lacke of money I myght not spede.

Then I conveyed me into Kent,
For of the law would I medle no more;
Bycaws no man to me would take entent,
I dight me to the plowe, even as I ded before.
Jhesus save London, that in Bethelem was bore!
And every trew man of law God graunt hym soul's med,
And they that be other, God theyr state restore,
For he that lackethe money, with them he shall not spede.

Anonymous Lyrics

Adam lay i-bowndyn, bowndyn in a bond,
Fowre thowsand wynter thowt he not to long;
And al was for an appil, an appil that he tok,
As clerkis fyndyn wretyn in here book.

Ne hadde the appil take ben, the appil taken ben,
Ne hadde never Our Lady a ben Hevene Qwen;
Blyssid be the tyme that appil take was,
Ther-fore we mown syngyn, 'Deo gracias!'

I syng of a myden   that is makeles,
Kyng of alle kynges   to here sone che ches.

He cam also stylle   ther his moder was,
As dew in Aprylle,   that fallyt on the gras.

He cam also stylle   to his moderes bowr,
As dew in Aprille,   that fallyt on the flour.

He cam also stylle   ther his moder lay,
As dew in Aprille,   that fallyt on the spray.

Moder and mayden   was never non but che—
Wel may swych a lady   Godes moder be.   10

A god and yet a man?
A mayde and yet a mother?
Witt wonders what witt can
Conceave this or the other.

A god, and can he die?
A dead man, can he live?
What witt can well replie?
What reason reason give?

God, truth itselfe, doth teach it;
Man's witt senckis too farr under,   10
By reason's power to reach it.
Beleeve and leave to wonder!

'Lullay, lullay, my lityl chyld, slepe and be now styll;
If thu be a lytill chyld, yitt may thu have thi wyll.'

'How suld I now, thu fayre may, fall apone a slepe?
Better methynke that I may fall adone and wepe,
Fore he that mad both nyght and day, cold and also hette,
Now layde I ame in a wispe of hay, I cane noder go nore crepe,
Bot wel I wate as well I may—slepe and be now styll—
Suffre the paynes that I may; it is my fader wyll.

'Seys thu noghte, thu fayr may, and heris thu noghte also,
How Kynge Herod, that keyne knyght, and of his peres mo,   10
That be a-bowte nyght and day, my body fore to slo?
Thai seke me both nyght and day that werke me mekyll wo,
Bot well I wate etc.

'How suld I now, thu fayre may, how suld I now myrth make?
My song is mad of walaway, fore dred I begyne to whake,
Fore drede of that ilk day that I my deth sall take,
And suffre the paynes that I may, fore synfull man sake.
Fore well I wate etc.

'Bot yitt methynk it well besett if man have of me mynd,
And al my paynes well besett if man to me be kynd.   20
Thare is no deth that sall me let, and I hym trew fynd,
One the rode fore to sytt, my handis for to bynd.
Bot well I wat etc.'

                    Farewell, this world! I take my leve for evere,
                    I am arested to apere at Goddes face—
                    O myghtyfull God, thu knowest that I had levere
                    Than all this world, to have oone houre space

To make a-sythe for all my grete trespace.
My hert, alas! is brokyne for that sorowe,
Som be this day that shall not be to-morow.

This lyfe, I see, is but a cheyre feyre;
All thyngis passene and so most I algate.
To-day I sat full ryall in a cheyere,   10
Tyll sotell Deth knokyd at my gate,
And on-avysed, he seyd to me, 'Chek-mate!'
Lo! how sotell he maketh a devors—
And wormys to fede, he hath here leyd my cors.

Speke softe, ye folk, for I am leyd aslepe!
I have my dreme, in trust is moche treson.
Fram dethes hold feyne wold I make a lepe,
But my wysdom is turnyd into feble resoun:
I see this worldis joye lastith but a season.
Wold to God, I had remembyrd me be-forne!   20
I sey no more but beware of ane horne!

This febyll world, so fals and so unstable,
Promoteth his lovers for a lytell while,
But at the last he yeveth hem a bable
When his peynted trowth is torned into gile.
Experyence cawsith me the trowth to compile,
Thynkyng this, to late alas! that I began,
For foly and hope disseyveth many a man.

Farewell, my frendis! the tide abidith no man:
I moste departe hens and so shall ye,   30
But in this passage the beste song that I can
Is *Requiem Eternam*—I pray God grant it me!
Whan I have endid all myn adversite,
Graunte me in Paradise to have a mancyon,
That shede his blode for my redempcion.

In a tyme of a somer's day,
The sune shon full meryly that tyde,
I toke my hawke, me for to play,
My spanyellis renyng by my syde.
A fesaunt henne than gan I see;
My howndis put her to flight;
I lett my hawke unto her fle,
To me yt was a deynte syght.

My fawkon flewe fast unto her pray;
My hownd gan renne with glad chere;   10
And sone I spurnyd in my way,
My lege was hent in a breer;
This breer, forsothe, yt dyde me gref:
Ywys yt made me to turn a-ye,
For he bare wrytyng in every leff,
This Latyn word: 'Revertere.'

I hayld and pullid this breer me fro,
And rede this word full meryly;
My hart fell down unto my to,
That was before full lykyngly.   20
I lett my hauke and fesaunt fare;
My spanyell fell down unto my kne;
It toke me with a sighyng sare,
This new lessun: 'Revertere.'

Lykyng ys moder of synnes all,
And norse to every wykyd dede;
To myche myschef she makyth men fall,
And of sorow the dawnce she doth lede.
This hawke of yowth ys high of porte,
And wildnes makyth hym wyde to fle,   30
Anf ofte to fall in wykyd thowght,
And than ys best: 'Revertere.'

A, a, a, a!
Nunc gaudet ecclesia.

Lestenytgh, lordynges, bothe grete and smale,
I shal you telyn a wonder tale,
How Holy Cherche was browt in bale
Cum magna injuria.

The greteste clerk of al this lond,
Of Cauntyrbery, ye understond,
Slawyn he was with wykkyd hond,
Demonis potencia.   10

Knytes kemyn fro Hendry Kyng,
Wykkyd men, withoute lesyng,
Ther they dedyn a wonder thing,
Ferventes insania.

They sowtyn hym al abowtyn,
Withine the paleys and withoutyn;
Of Jhesu Cryst hadde they non dowte
In sua malicia.

They openyd here mowthis wonder wyde,
To Thomeys they spokyn mekyl pryde,   20
'Here, tretour, thou shalt abyde,
Ferens mortis tedia.'

Thomas answerid with mylde chere,
'If ye wil me slon in this manere,
Let hem pasyn, alle tho arn here,
Sine contumilia.'

Beforn his aunter he knelyd adoun,
Ther they gunne to paryn his crown;

51

He sterdyn the braynys up and doun,
Optans celi gaudia.   30

The turmentowres abowtyn sterte,
With dedly wondys thei gunne him hurte,
Thomas deyid in Moder Cherche,
Pergens ad celestia.

Moder, clerk, wedue, and wyf,
Worchepe ye Thomeys in al your lyf,
For fifty-two poyntes he les his lyf,
Contra regis consilia.

Mery hyt ys in May mornyng,
Mery wayys for to gone.

And by a chapell as Y came,
Mett Y wyhte Jhesu to chyrcheward gone,
Petur and Pawle, Thomas and Jhon,
And hys desyplys everychone.

Sente Thomas the bellys gane ryng,
And Sent Collas the Mas gane syng,
Sente Jhon toke that swete offeryng,
And by a chapell as Y came.   10

Owre Lorde offeryd whate he wollde,
A challes alle off ryche rede gollde;
Owre Lady, the crowne off hyr mowlde,
The son owte off hyr bosom schone.

Sent Jorge, that ys Owre Lady knyghte,
He tende the tapyrys fayre and bryte,
To myn yghe a semley syghte,
And by a chapell as Y came.

Lully, lulley; lully, lulley!
The fawcon hath born my mak away.

He bare hym up, he bare hym down;
He bare hym into an orchard brown.

In that orchard ther was an hall,
That was hangid with purpill and pall.

And in that hall ther was a bede;
Hit was hangid with gold so rede.

And yn that bed ther lythe a knyght,
His wowndis bledyng day and nyght.   10

By that bedis side ther kneleth a may,
And she wepeth both nyght and day.

And by that beddis side ther stondith a ston,
'Corpus Christi' wretyn theron.

Seynt Stevene was a clerk in Kyng Herowdes halle,
And servyd him of bred and cloth, as every kyng befalle.

Stevyn out of kechone cam, with boris hed on honde;
He saw a sterre was fayr and bryght over Bedlem stonde.

He kyst adoun the boris hed and went into the halle,
'I forsak the, kyng Herowdes, and thi werkes alle.

'I forsak the, kyng Herowdes, and thi werkes alle;
Ther is a chyld in Bedlem born is beter than we alle.'

'Quat eylyt the, Stevene? quat is the befalle?
Lakkyt the eyther mete or drynk in king Herowdes halle?'   10

'Lakit me neyther mete ne drynk in kyng Herowdes halle;
Ther is a chyld in Bedlem born is beter than we alle.'

'Quat eylyt the, Stevyn? art thu wod, or thu gynnyst to brede?
Lakkyt the eyther gold or fe, or ony ryche wede?'

'Lakyt me neyther gold ne fe, ne non ryche wede;
Ther is a chyld in Bedlem born shal helpyn us at our nede.'

'That is also soth, Stevyn, also soth, i-wys,
As this capoun crowe shal that lyth here in myn dysh.'

That word was not so sone seyd, that word in that halle,
The capoun crew Christus natus est! among the lordes alle.   20

'Rysyt up, myn turmentowres, be to and al be on,
And ledyt Stevyn out of this town, and stonyt hym wyth ston!'

Tokyn he Stevene, and stonyd hym in the way,
And therfore is his evyn on Crystes owyn day.

54

I have a yong suster,
Fer beyondyn the se;
Many be the drowryis
That che sente me.

Che sente me the cherye
With-outyn ony ston,
And so che ded the dowe
With-outyn ony bon.

Sche sente me the brer
With-outyn ony rynde,
Sche bad me love my lemman
With-oute longgyng.

How shuld ony cherye
Be with-oute ston?
And how shuld ony dowe
Ben with-oute bon?

How shuld ony brer
Ben with-oute rynde?
How shuld Y love myn lemman
With-out longyng?

Quan the cherye was a flour,
Than hadde it non ston;
Quan the dowe was an ey,
Than hadde it non bon;

Quan the brer was on-bred,
Than hadde it non rynd;
Quan the maydyn hayt that che lovit,
Che is with-out longing.

I have a gentil cook,
Crowyt me day;
He doth me rysyn erly,
My Matyins for to say.

I have a gentil cook,
Comyn he is of gret;
His comb is of reed corel,
His tayil is of get.

I have a gentyl cook,
Comyn he is of kynde;
His comb is of red corel,
His tayl is of inde.

His legges ben of asor,
So geintil and so smale;
His spores arn of sylver qwyt,
In-to the worte-wale.

His eynyn arn of cristal,
Lokyn al in aumbyr;
And every nyght he perchit hym
In myn ladyis chaumbyr.

In Aprell and in May,
When hartys be all mery,
Besse Buntyng, the myllaris may,
Wythe lyppys so red as chery,
She cast in hyr remembrance
To passe hyr tyme in dalyaunce,
And to leve hyr thowth driery.

Ryght womanly arayd
In a petycote of whytt,
She was nothyng dysmayd—   10
Hyr cowtenance was ful lyghth.

How! Hey! It is non les,
I dar not seygh quan che seyght 'Pes!'

Yyng men, I warne you everychon,
Elde wywys tak ye non;
For I my-self have on at hom—
I dar not seyn quan che seyght 'Pes!'

Quan I cum fro the plow at non,
In a reven dych myn mete is don;
I dar not askyn our dame a spon—
I dar not seyn quan che seyght 'Pes!'   10

If I aske our dame bred,
Che takyt a staf and brekit myn hed,
And doth me rennyn under the bed—
I dar not seyn quan che seyght 'Pes!'

If I aske our dame fleych,
Che brekit myn hed with a dych:
'Boy, thou art not worght a reych!'
I dar not seyn quan che seyght 'Pes!'

If I aske our dame chese,
'Boy,' che seyght, al at ese,   20
'Thou art not worght half a pese.'
I dar not seyn quan che seyght 'Pes!'

I am as lyght as any roe,
To preyse wemen wher that I goo.

To onpreyse wemen yt were a shame,
For a woman was thy dame;
Our Blessyd Lady beryth the name
Of all women wher that they goo.

A woman ys a worthy thyng—
They do the washe and do the wrynge;
'Lullay, lullay,' she doth the synge,
And yet she hath but care and woo.   10

A woman ys a worthy wyght,
She servyth a man both daye and nyght,
Therto she puttyth all her myght,
And yet she hathe bot care and woo.

Whan netilles in wynter bere rosis rede,
And thornys bere figges naturally,
And bromes bere appylles in every mede,
And lorelles bere cheris in the croppis so hie,
And okys bere dates so plentuosly,
And lekes geve hony in ther superfluens—
Than put in a woman your trust and confidens.

Whan whityng walk in forestes, hartes for to chase,
And herynges in parkys hornys boldly blowe,
And flownders more-hennes in fennes enbrace,   10
And gornardes shote rolyons owt of a crosse-bowe,
And gren gese ride in huntyng the wolf to over-throwe,
And sperlynges rone with speris in harnes to defence—
Than put in a woman your trust and confidence.

Whan sparowys bild chirches and stepulles hie,
And wrennes cary sakkes to the mylle,
And curlews cary clothes, horsis for to drye,
And se-mewes bryng butter to the market to sell,
And wod-dowes were wodknyffes, theves to kyll,
And griffons to goslynges don obedyence—   20
Than put in a woman your trust and confidence.

Whan crabbis tak wodcokes in forestes and parkes,
And haris ben taken with swetnes of snaylis,
And camelles with ther here tak swalowes and perchis,
And myse mowe corn with wafeyyng of ther taylis,
Whan dukkes of the dunghill sek the blod of Haylis,
Whan shrewd wyffes to ther husbondes do non offens—
Than put in a woman your trust and confidence.

'Kyrie, so Kyrie,'
Jankyn syngyt merie,
With 'Aleyson.'

As I went on Yol Day in owre prosessyon,
Knew I joly Jankyn be his mery ton.
'Kyrieleyson.'

Jankyn began the Offys on the Yol Day,
And yyt me thynkyt it dos me good, so merie gan he say,
'Kyrieleyson.'

Jankyn red the Pystyl ful fayr and ful wel,   10
And yyt me thinkyt it dos me good, as evere have I sel:
'Kyrieleyson.'

Jankyn at the Sanctus crakit a merie note,
And yyt me thinkyt it dos me good: I payid for his cote:
'Kyrieleyson.'

Jankyn crakit notes, an hunderid on a knot,
And yyt he hakkyt hem smaller than wortes to the pot:
'Kyrieleyson.'

Jankyn at the Angnus beryt the pax-brede,
He twynkelid, but sayd nowt, and on myn fot he trede: 20
'Kyrieleyson.'

Benedicamus Domino, Cryst fro schame me schylde;
Deo gracias therto—alas, I go with chylde!
'Kyrieleyson.'

Were it undo that is y-do,
I wolde be-war.

Y lovede a child of this cuntre,
And so Y wende he had do me;
Now my-self the sothe Y see,
That he is far.

He seyde to me he wolde be trewe,
And change me for non othur newe;
Now Y sykke and am pale of hewe,
For he is far.   10

He seide his sawus he wolde fulfille,
Therfore Y lat him have al his wille;
Now Y sykke and morne stille,
For he is far.

Hogyn cam to bower's dore—
Hogyn cam to bower's dore,
He tryld upon the pyn for love,
Hum, ha, trill go bell—
He tryld upon the pyn for love,
Hum, ha, trill go bell.

Up she rose and lett hym yn—
Up she rose and let hym yn,
She had a-went she had worshipped all her kyn,
Hum, ha, trill go bell—   10
She had a-went she had worshipped all her kyn,
Hum, ha, trill go bell.

When thei were to bed browght—
Whan thei were to bed browght,
The old chorle he cowld do nowght,
Hum, ha, trill go bell—
The old chorle he cowld do nowght,
Hum, ha, trill go bell.

'Go ye furth to yonder wyndow—
Go ye furth to yonder wyndow—   20
And I will cum to you with-in a throw,
Hum, ha, trill go bell—
And I will cum to you with-yn a throw,
Hum, ha, trill go bell.'

Whan she hym at the wyndow wyst—
Whan she hym at the wyndow wyst,
She torned owt her ars and that he kyst,
Hum, ha, trill go bell—
She torned owt her ars and that he kyst,
Hum, ha, trill go bell.   30

61

'Ywys, leman, ye do me wrong—
Ywis, leman, ye do me wrong,
Or elles your breth ys wonder strong,
Hum, ha, trill go bell—
Or elles your breth ys wonder strong,
Hum, ha, trill go bell.'

Drawe me nere, draw me nere,
Drawe me nere, the joly juggelere.

Here beside dwellith a riche baron's daughter;
She wold have no man that for her love had sowght her,
So nyse she was.

She wold have no man that was made of molde,
But yf he had a mowth of gold, to kiss her whan she wold,
So dangerus she was.

Ther-of hard a joly juggeler that layd was on the gren,
And at this ladi's wordis, ywys, he had gret tene: 10
An-angrid he was.

He juggeled to hym a well good stede of an old hors bon,
A sadill and a brydill both, and set hymself ther-on:
A juggler he was.

He priked and pransid both beffore that ladi's gate,
She wend he had ben an angell was com for her sake:
A prikker he was.

He pryked and pransid beffore that lady's bowr,
She went he had ben an angell commen from hevyn towre:
A praunser he was.   20

62

Twenty-four knyghtis lade hym into the hall,
And as many squyres his hors to the stall,
      And gaff hym mete.

They gaff hym ottis and also hay,
He was an old shrew, and held his hed a-way:
      He wold not ete.

The day began to passe; the nyght began to com,
To bede was browght the fayre jentyll woman
      And the juggeler also.

The nyght began to passe, the day began to sprynge,   30
All the brydis of her bowr, they began to synge
      And the cokoo also.

'Wher be ye, my mery maydyns, that ye cum not me to?
The joly wyndows of my bowr lok that you undoo,
      That I may see;

'For I have in myn armes a duk or ellis an erle';
But whan she loked hym upon, he was a blere-eyed chorle;
      'Alas!' she said.

She laid hym to an hill, and hangid shuld he be;
He juggled hymself to a mele pok; the duste fell in her eye;   40
      Begiled she was.

God and Owr Lady and swete Seynt Johan,
Send every giglot of this town such an-other leman,
      Evyn as he was!

We ben chapmen lyght of fote,
The fowle weyis for to fle.

We bern abowtyn non cattes' skynnys,
Pursis, perlis, sylver pynnis,
Smale wympeles for ladyis' chynnys;
Damsele, bey sum ware of me.

I have a poket for the nonys,
Therine ben tweyne precyous stonys;
Damsele, hadde ye asayid hem onys,
Ye shuld the rathere gon with me.   10

I have a jelyf of Godes sonde,
Withoutyn fyt it can stonde;
It can smytyn and hayt non honde;
Ryd yourself quat it may be.

I have a powder for to selle,
Quat it is can I not telle—
It makit maydenys' wombys to swelle:
Therof I have a quantyte.

        O mestres, whye
        Owtecaste am I
        All utterly
        From your pleasaunce?
        Sythe ye and I,
        Or thys, truly,
        Famyliarly
        Have had pastaunce.

64

And lovyngly
Ye wolde aply
Thy company
To my comforte;
But now, truly,
Unlovyngly,
Ye do deny
Me to resorte.

And me to see
As strange ye be,
As thowe that ye
Shuld nowe deny,
Or else possesse
That nobylnes
To be dochess
Of grete Savoy.

But sythe that ye
So strange wylbe
As toward me,
And wyll not medyll,
I truste, percase,
To fynde some grace
To have free chayse,
And spede as welle!

JOHN SKELTON

With, Lullay, lullay, lyke a chylde,
Thou slepyst to long, thou art begylde.

'My darlyng dere, my daysy floure,
  Let me,' quod he, 'ly in your lap.'
'Ly styll,' quod she, 'my paramoure,
  Ly styll hardely, and take a nap.'
  Hys hed was hevy, such was his hap,
All drowsy dremyng, dround in slepe,
That of hys love he toke no kepe.

With ba, ba, ba, and bas, bas, bas,   10
  She cheryshed hym both cheke and chyn,
That he wyst never where he was;
  He had forgoten all dedely syn.
  He wantyd wyt her love to wyn:
He trusted her payment, and lost all hys pray:
She left hym slepyng, and stale away.

The ryvers rowth, the waters wan,
  She sparyd not to wete her fete;
She wadyd over, she found a man
  That halsyd her hartely and kyst her swete: 20
  Thus after her cold she cought a hete.
'My lefe,' she sayd, 'rowtyth in hys bed;
Iwys he hath an hevy hed!'

66

What dremyst thou, drunchard, drousy pate!
  Thy lust and lykyng is from the gone;
Thou blynkerd blowboll, thou wakyst to late,
  Behold, thou lyeste, luggard, alone!
    Well may thou sygh, well may thou grone,
To dele wyth her so cowardly:
Iwys, powle hachet, she bleryd thyne I!   30

The auncient acquaintance, madam, betwen us twayn,
  The famylyaryte, the formar dalyaunce,
Causyth me that I can not myself refrayne
  But that I must wryte for my plesaunt pastaunce:
  Remembryng your passyng goodly countenaunce,
Your goodly port, your bewteous visage,
Ye may be countyd comfort of all corage.

Of all your feturs favorable to make tru discripcion,
  I am insuffycyent to make such enterpryse;
For thus dare I say, without contradiccyon,   10
  That dame Menolope was never half so wyse:
  Yet so it is that a rumer begynnyth for to ryse,
How in good horsmen ye set your hole delyght,
And have forgoten your old trew lovyng knyght.

Wyth bound and rebound, bounsyngly take up
  Hys jentyll curtoyl, and set nowght by small naggys!
Spur up at the hynder gyrth, with, 'Gup, morell, gup!'
  With, 'Jayst ye, jenet of Spayne, for your tayll waggys!'
  Ye cast all your corage uppon such courtly haggys.
Have in, sergeaunt ferrour, myne horse behynde is bare;   20
(He rydeth well the horse, but he rydeth better the mare.)

Ware, ware, the mare wynsyth wyth her wanton hele!
  She kykyth with her kalkyns and keylyth with a clench;
She goyth wyde behynde, and hewyth never a dele:
Ware gallyng in the widders, ware of that wrenche!
  It is perlous for a horseman to dyg in the trenche.
Thys grevyth your husband, that ryght jentyll knyght,
And so with youre servantys he fersly doth fyght.

So fersly he fytyth, hys mynde is so fell,
  That he dryvyth them doune with dyntes on ther day wach;   30
He bresyth theyr braynpannys and makyth them to swell,
  Theyre browys all to-brokyn, such clappys they cach;
  Whose jalawsy malycyous makyth them to lepe the hach;
By theyr conusaunce knowing how they serue a wily py:
Ask all your neybours whether that I ly.

It can be no counsell that is cryed at the cros:
  For your jentyll husband sorowfull am I;
How be it, he is not furst hath had a los:
  Advertysyng you, madame, to warke more secretly,
  Let not all the world make an owtcry;   40
Play fayre play, madame, and loke ye play clenc,
Or ells with gret shame your game wylbe sene.

From *The Boke of Phyllyp Sparowe*

  Pla ce bo,
  Who is there, who?
  Di le xi,
  Dame Margery;
  Fa, re, my, my,
  Wherfore and why, why?
  For the sowle of Philip Sparowe,

68

That was late slayn at Carowe,
Among the Nones Blake,
For that swete soules sake,
And for all sparowes' soules,
Set in our bederolles,
Pater noster qui,
With an *Ave Mari*,
And with the corner of a Crede,
The more shalbe your mede.

Whan I remembre agayn
How mi Philyp was slayn,
Never halfe the payne
Was betwene you twayne,
Pyramus and Thesbe,
As than befell to me:
I wept and I wayled,
The tearys downe hayled;
But nothynge it avayled
To call Phylyp agayne,
Whom Gyb our cat hath slayne.

Gib, I saye, our cat,
Worrowyd her on that
Which I loved best:
It can not be exprest
My sorrowfull hevynesse,
But all without redresse;
For within that stounde,
Halfe slumbrynge, in a sounde
I fell downe to the grounde.

Unneth I kest myne eyes
Towarde the cloudy skyes:
But whan I dyd beholde
My sparow dead and colde,
No creatuer but that wolde
Have rewed upon me,

To behold and se
What hevynesse dyd me pange;
Wherewith my handes I wrange,
That my senaws cracked,
As though I had ben racked,
So payned and so strayned,
That no lyfe wellnye remayned.
 I syghed and I sobbed,   50
For that I was robbed
Of my sparowes lyfe.
O mayden, wydow, and wyfe,
Of what estate ye be,
Of hye or lowe degre,
Great sorowe than ye myght se,
And lerne to wepe at me!
Such paynes dyd me frete,
That myne hert dyd bete,
My vysage pale and dead,   60
Wanne, and blewe as lead;
The panges of hatefull death
Well nye had stopped my breath.
 Heu, heu, me,
That I am wo for the!
Ad Dominum, cum tribularer, clamavi:
Of God nothynge els crave I
But Phyllypes soule to kepe
From the marees deepe
Of Acherontes well,   70
That is a flode of hell;
And from the great Pluto,
The prynce of endles wo;
And from foule Alecto,
With vysage blacke and blo;
And from Medusa, that mare,
That lyke a fende doth stare;

And from Megera's edders,
For rufflynge of Phillip's fethers,
And from her fyry sparklynges,   80
For burnynge of his wynges;
And from the smokes sowre
Of Proserpina's bowre;
And from the dennes darke,
Wher Cerberus doth barke,
Whom Theseus dyd afraye,
Whom Hercules dyd outraye,
As famous poetes say;
From that hell hounde,
That lyeth in cheynes bounde,   90
With gastly hedes thre,
To Jupyter pray we
That Phyllyp preserved may be!
Amen, say ye with me!
   Do mi nus,
Helpe nowe, swete Jesus!
Levavi oculos meos in montes:
Wolde God I had Zenophontes,
Or Socrates the wyse,
To shew me their devyse,   100
Moderatly to take
This sorow that I make
For Phyllip Sparowes sake!
So fervently I shake,
I fele my body quake;
So urgently I am brought
Into carefull thought.
Like Andromach, Hector's wyfe,
Was wery of her lyfe,
Whan she had lost her joye,   110
Noble Hector of Troye;
In lyke maner also

Encreaseth my dedly wo,
For my sparowe is go.
    It was so prety a fole,
It wold syt on a stole,
And lerned after my scole
For to kepe his cut,
With, 'Phyllyp, kepe your cut!'
    It had a velvet cap,   120
And wold syt upon my lap,
And seke after small wormes,
And somtyme white bred crommes;
And many tymes and ofte
Betwene my brestes softe
It wolde lye and rest;
It was propre and prest.
    Somtyme he wolde gaspe
Whan he sawe a waspe;
A fly or a gnat,   130
He wolde flye at that;
And prytely he wold pant
Whan he saw an ant;
Lord, how he wolde pry
After the butterfly!
Lorde, how he wolde hop
After the gressop!
And whan I sayd, 'Phyp, Phyp,'
Than he wold lepe and skyp,
And take me by the lyp.   140
Alas, it wyll me slo,
That Phillyp is gone me fro!
    Si in i qui ta tes,
Alas, I was evyll at ease!
De pro fun dis cla ma vi,
Whan I sawe my sparowe dye!
    Nowe, after my dome,

Dame Sulpicia at Rome,
Whose name regystred was
For ever in tables of bras,   150
Because that she dyd pas
In poesy to endyte,
And eloquently to wryte,
Though she wolde pretende
My sparowe to commende,
I trowe she coude not amende
Reportynge the vertues all
Of my sparowe royall.

    For it wold come and go,
And fly so to and fro;   160
And on me it wolde lepe
Whan I was aslepe,
And his fethers shake,
Wherewith he wolde make
Me often for to wake,
And for to take him in
Upon my naked skyn;
God wot, we thought no syn:
What though he crept so lowe?
It was no hurt, I trowe,   170
He dyd nothynge, perde,
But syt upon my kne:
Phyllyp, though he were nyse,
In him it was no vyse;
Phyllyp had leve to go
To pyke my lytell too;
Phillip myght be bolde
And do what he wolde;
Phillip wolde seke and take
All the flees blake   180
That he coulde there espye
With his wanton eye.

From *The Tunnynge of Elynour Rummynge*

Tell you I chyll,
If that ye wyll
Awhyle be styll,
Of a comely gyll
That dwelt on a hyll:
But she is not gryll,
For she is somwhat sage
And well worne in age;
For her vysage
It would aswage   10
A mannes courage.
   Her lothely lere
Is nothynge clere,
But ugly of chere,
Droupy and drowsy,
Scurvy and lowsy;
Her face all bowsy,
Comely crynklyd,
Woundersly wrynkled,
Lyke a rost pygges eare,   20
Brystled wyth here.
   Her lewde lyppes twayne,
They slaver, men sayne,
Lyke a ropy rayne,
A gummy glayre:
She is ugly fayre;
Her nose somdele hoked,
And camously croked,
Never stoppynge,
But ever droppynge;   30
Her skynne lose and slacke,
Grained lyke a sacke;
With a croked backe.

74

Her eyen gowndy
Are full unsowndy,
For they are blered;
And she gray hered;
Jawed lyke a jetty;
A man would haue pytty
To se how she is gumbed,   40
Fyngered and thumbed,
Gently joynted,
Gresed and annoynted
Up to the knockels;
The bones of her huckels
Lyke as they were with buckels
Togyther made fast:
Her youth is farre past:
Foted lyke a plane,
Legged lyke a crane;   50
And yet she wyll jet,
Lyke a jolly fet,
In her furred flocket,
And gray russet rocket,
With symper the cocket.
Her huke of Lyncole grene,
It had ben hers, I wene,
More then fourty yere;
And so doth it apere,
For the grene bare thredes   60
Loke lyke sere wedes,
Wyddered lyke hay,
The woll worne away;
And yet I dare saye
She thynketh herselfe gaye
Upon the holy daye,
Whan she doth her aray,
And gyrdeth in her gytes

Stytched and pranked with pletes;
Her kyrtel Brystow red,
With clothes upon her hed
That wey a sowe of led,
Wrythen in wonder wyse,
After the Sarasyns' gyse,
With a whym wham,
Knyt with a trym tram,
Upon her braynepan,
Lyke an Egyptian,
Capped about:
Whan she goeth out
Herselfe for to shewe,
She dryveth downe the dewe
Wyth a payre of heles
As brode as two wheles;
She hobles as a gose
With her blanket hose
Over the falowe;
Her shone smered wyth talowe,
Gresed upon dyrt
That baudeth her skyrt.

Primus passus.

And this comely dame,
I understande, her name
Is Elynour Rummynge,
At home in her wonnynge;
And as men say
She dwelt in Sothray,
In a certayne stede
Bysyde Lederhede.
She is a tonnysh gyb;
The devyll and she be syb.
     But to make up my tale,

She breweth noppy ale,
And maketh therof port sale
To travellars, to tynkers,
To sweters, to swynkers,
And all good ale drynkers,
That wyll nothynge spare,
But drynke tyll they stare
And brynge themselfe bare,
With, 'Now away the mare,   110
And let us sley care,'—
As wyse as an hare!

  Come whoso wyll
To Elynour on the hyll,
Wyth, 'Fyll the cup, fyll,'
And syt thereby styll,
Erly and late:
Thyther cometh Kate,
Cysly, and Sare,
With theyr legges bare,   120
And also theyr fete
Hardely full unswete;
Wyth theyr heles dagged,
Theyr kyrtelles all to-jagged,
Theyr smockes all to-ragged,
Wyth tytters and tatters,
Brynge dysshes and platters,
Wyth all theyr myght runnynge
To Elynour Rummynge,
To have of her tunnynge: 130
She leneth them on the same,
And thus begynneth the game.

  Some wenches come unlased,
Some huswyves come unbrased,
Wyth theyr naked pappes,
That flyppes and flappes;

It wygges and it wagges,
Lyke tawny saffron bagges;
A sorte of foule drabbes
All scurvy with scabbes: 140
Some be flybytten,
Some skewed as a kytten;
Some wyth a sho clout
Bynde theyr heddes about;
Some have no herelace,
Theyr lockes about theyr face,
Theyr tresses untrust,
All full of unlust;
Some loke strawry,
Some cawry-mawry;   150
Full untydy tegges,
Lyke rotten egges.
Suche a lewde sorte
To Elynour resorte
From tyde to tyde:
Abyde, abyde,
And to you shall be tolde
Howe hyr ale is solde
To Mawte and to Molde.

Secundus passus.
Some have no mony   160
That thyder commy,
For theyr ale to pay,
That is a shreud aray;
Elynour swered, 'Nay,
Ye shall not beare away
My ale for nought,
By hym that me bought!'
With, 'Hey dogge, hay,

Have these hogges away!'
With, 'Get me a staffe,   170
The swyne eate my draffe!
Stryke the hogges with a clubbe,
They have dronke up my swyllynge tubbe!'
For, be there never so much prese,
These swyne go to the hye dese,
The sowe with her pygges;
The bore his tayle wrygges,
His rumpe also he frygges
Agaynst the hye benche!
With, 'Fo, ther is a stenche!   180
Gather up, thou wenche;
Seest thou not what is fall?
Take up dyrt and all,
And bere out of the hall:
God gyne it yll prevynge
Clenly as yvell chevynge!'
    But let us turne playne,
There we lefte agayne.
For, as yll a patch as that,
The hennes ron in the mashfat;   190
For they go to roust
Streyght over the ale joust,
And donge, whan it commes,
In the ale tunnes.
Than Elynour taketh
The mashe bolle, and shaketh
The hennes' donge away,
And skommeth it into a tray
Whereas the yeest is,
With her maungy fystis: 200
And somtyme she blennes
The donge of her hennes
And the ale together;

79

And sayeth, 'Gossyp, come hyther,
This ale shal be thycker,
And flowre the more quicker;
For I may tell you,
I lerned it of a Jewe,
Whan I began to brewe,
And I have founde it trew;   210
Drinke now whyle it is new;
And ye may it broke,
It shall make you loke
Yonger than ye be
Yeres two or thre,
For ye may prove it by me;
Beholde,' she sayde, 'and se
How bryght I am of ble!
Ich am not cast away,
That can my husband say,   220
Whan we kys and play
In lust and in lykyng;
He calleth me his whytyng,
His mullyng and his mytyng,
His nobbes and his conny,
His swetyng and his honny,
With, "Bas, my prety bonny,
Thou art worth good and monny."
This make I my falyre fonny,
Til that he dreme and dronny;   230
For, after all our sport,
Than wyll he rout and snort;
Than swetely together we ly,
As two pygges in a sty.'

From *Colyn Cloute*

And if ye stande in doute
Who brought this ryme aboute,
My name is Colyn Cloute.
I purpose to shake oute
All my connyng bagge,
Lyke a clerkely hagge;
For though my ryme be ragged,
Tattered and jagged,
Rudely rayne-beaten,
Rusty and moughte-eaten,   10
If ye take well therwith,
It hath in it some pyth.
For, as farre as I can se,
It is wronge with eche degre:
For the temporalte
Accuseth the spiritualte;
The spirituall agayne
Dothe grudge and complayne
Upon the temporall men:
Thus eche of other blother   20
The tone ayenste the tother:
Alas, they make me shoder!
For in hoder moder
The Churche is put in faute;
The prelates ben so haut,
They say, and loke so hy,
As though they wolde fly
Above the sterry skye.
Layemen say indede
How they take no hede   30
Theyr sely shepe to fede,
But plucke away and pull
The fleces of theyr wull,

81

Unethes they leve a locke
Of wull amonges theyr flocke;
And as for theyr connynge,
A glommynge and a mummynge,
And make therof a jape;
They gaspe and they gape
All to have promocyon, 40
There is theyr hole devocyon,
With money, if it wyll hap,
To catche the forked cap:
Forsothe they are to lewd
To say so, all beshrewd!

What trow ye they say more
Of the bysshoppes' lore?
How in matters they be rawe,
They lumber forth the lawe,
To herken Jacke and Gyll, 50
Whan they put up a byll,
And judge it as they wyll,
For other mennes skyll,
Expoundyng out theyr clauses,
And leve theyr owne causes:
In theyr provynciall cure
They make but lytell sure,
And meddels very lyght
In the Churches ryght;
But *ire* and *venire*, 60
And solfa so alamyre,
That the premenyre
Is lyke to be set afyre
In theyr jurisdictions
Through temporall afflictions:
Men say they have prescriptions
Agaynst spirituall contradictions,
Accomptynge them as fyctions.

And whyles the heedes do this,
The remenaunt is amys   70
Of the clergy all,
Bothe great and small.
I wot never how they warke,
But thus the people barke;
And surely thus they say,
Bysshoppes, if they may,
Small houses wolde kepe,
But slumbre forth and slepe,
And assay to crepe
Within the noble walles   80
Of the kynges halles,
To fat theyr bodyes full,
Theyr soules lene and dull,
And have full lytell care
How evyll theyr shepe fare.
    The temporalyte say playne,
Howe bysshoppes dysdayne
Sermons for to make,
Or suche laboure to take;
And for to say trouth,   90
A great parte is for slouth,
But the greattest parte
Is for they have but small arte
And ryght sklender connyng
Within theyr heedes wonnyng.
But this reason they take:
How they are able to make
With theyr golde and treasure
Clerkes out of measure,
And yet that is a pleasure.   100
Howe be it some there be,
Almost two or thre,
Of that dygnyte,

83

Full worshypfull clerkes,
As appereth by theyr werkes,
Lyke Aaron and Ure,
The wolfe from the dore
To werryn and to kepe
From theyr goostly shepe,
And theyr spirituall lammes   110
Sequestred from rammes
And from the berded gotes
With theyr heery cotes;
Set nought by golde ne grotes,
Theyr names if I durst tell.

But they are loth to mell,
And loth to hang the bell
Aboute the cattes necke,
For drede to have a checke;
They ar fayne to play deuz decke,   120
They ar made for the becke.
How be it they are good men,
Moche herted lyke an hen:
Theyr lessons forgotten they have
That Becket them gave:
Thomas *manum mittit ad fortia*,
Spernit damna, spernit opprobria,
Nulla Thomam frangit injuria.
But nowe every spirituall father,
Men say, they had rather   130
Spende moche of theyr share
Than to be combred with care:
Spende! nay, nay, but spare;
For let se who that dare
Sho the mockysshe mare;
They make her wynche and keke,
But it is not worth a leke:
Boldnesse is to seke

84

The Churche for to defend.
Take me as I intende,   140
For lothe I am to offende
In this that I have pende:
I tell you as men say;
Amende whan ye may,
For, *usque ad montem Sare*,
Men say ye can not appare;
For some say ye hunte in parkes,
And hauke on hobby larkes,
And other wanton warkes,
Whan the nyght darkes.   150

   What hath laymen to do
The gray gose for to sho?
Lyke houndes of hell,
They crye and they yell,
Howe that ye sell
The grace of the Holy Gost:
Thus they make theyr bost
Throughowte every cost,
Howe some of you do eate
In Lenton season fleshe mete,   160
Fesauntes, partryche, and cranes;
Men call you therfor prophanes;
Ye pycke no shrympes nor pranes,
Saltfysshe, stocfysshe, nor heryng,
It is not for your werynge;
Nor in holy Lenton season
Ye wyll netheyr benes ne peason,
But ye loke to be let lose
To a pygge or to a gose,
Your gorge not endewed   170
Without a capon stewed,
Or a stewed cocke,
To knowe whate ys a clocke

Under her surfled smocke,
And her wanton wodicocke.
    And howe whan ye gyve orders
In your provinciall borders,
As at *Sitientes*,
Some are *insufficientes*,
Some *parum sapientes*,   180
Some *nihil intelligentes*,
Some *valde negligentes*,
Some *nullum sensum habentes*,
But bestiall and untaught;
But whan thei have ones caught
Dominus vobiscum by the hede,
Than renne they in every stede,
God wot, with dronken nolles;
Yet take they cure of soules,
And woteth never what thei rede,   190
Paternoster, Ave, nor Crede;
Construe not worth a whystle
Nether Gospell nor Pystle;
Theyr Mattyns madly sayde,
Nothynge devoutly prayde;
Theyr lernynge is so small,
Theyr prymes and houres fall
And lepe out of theyr lyppes
Lyke sawdust or drye chyppes.
I speke not nowe of all,   200
But the moost parte in generall.
Of suche vagabundus
Speketh *totus mundus*;
Howe some synge *Laetabundus*
At every ale stake,
With, 'Welcome hake and make!'
By the brede that God brake,
I am sory for your sake.

86

I speke not of the good wyfe,
But of theyr apostles lyfe;
Cum ipsis vel illis
Qui manent in villis
Est uxor vel ancilla,
'Welcome Jacke and Gylla!
My prety Petronylla,
And you wyll be stylla,
You shall have your wylla!'
Of suche Paternoster pekes
All the worlde spekes.

To Maystres Isabell Pennel!

By Saynt Mary, my lady,
Your mammy and your dady
Brought forth a godely babi!
   My mayden Isabell,
Reflaring rosabell,
The flagrant camamell;
   The ruddy rosary,
The soverayne rosemary,
The praty strawbery;
   The columbyne, the nepte,
The jeloffer well set,
The propre vyolet;
   Enuwyd your colowre
Is lyke the dasy flowre
After the Aprill showre;
   Sterre of the morow gray,
The blossom on the spray,
The fresshest flowre of May;

10

87

Maydenly demure,
Of womanhode the lure;
Wherfore I make you sure,
    It were an hevenly helth,
It were an endeles welth,
A lyfe for God hymselfe,
    To here this nightingale,
Amonge the byrdes smale,
Warbelynge in the vale,
Dug, dug,
Jug, jug,
Good yere and good luk,
With chuk, chuk, chuk, chuk!

20

30

ALEXANDER BARCLAY

From *Egloge V*

AMINTAS: The winter snowes, all covered is the grounde,
The north wind blowes sharpe and with ferefull sound,
The longe isesicles at the ewes hang,
The streame is frosen, the night is cold and long;
Where botes rowed, nowe cartes have passage,
From yoke the oxen be losed and bondage,
The ploweman resteth avoyde of businesse,
Save when he tendeth his harnes for to dresse.
Mably, his wife, sitteth before the fyre,
All blacke and smoky, clothed in rude attire,   10
Sething some grewell, and sturring the pulment
Of pease or frument, a noble meat for Lent.
The summer season men counted nowe laudable,
Whose fervour before they thought intollerable;
The frosty winter and wether temperate,
Which men then praysed, they nowe disprayse and
    hate;
Colde they desired, but nowe it is present,
They braule and grutche, their mindes not content.
Thus mutable men them pleased cannot holde,
At great heat grutching, and grutching when it is
    cold.   20

FAUSTUS: All pleasour present of men is counted small;
            Desire obtayned some counteth nought at all;
            What men hope after, that semeth great and deare,
            As light by distaunce appeareth great and cleare.

AMINTAS: Eche time and season hath his delite and joyes,
            Loke in the stretes, beholde the little boyes;
            Howe in fruite season for joy they sing and hop,
            In Lent is eche one full busy with his top,
            And nowe in winter, for all the greevous colde,
            All rent and ragged, a man may them beholde;   30
            They have great pleasour supposing well to dine;
            When men be busied in killing of fat swine,
            They get the bladder and blowe it great and thin,
            With many beanes or peason put within;
            It ratleth, soundeth, and shineth clere and fayre,
            While it is throwen and caste up in the ayre;
            Eche one contendeth and hath a great delite,
            With foote and with hande the bladder for to smite;
            If it fall to grounde, they lifte it up agayne;
            This wise to labour, they count it for no payne;   40
            Renning and leaping, they drive away the colde.
            The sturdie plowmen lustie, strong and bolde,
            Overcommeth the winter with driving the footeball,
            Forgetting labour and many a grevous fall.

FAUSTUS: Men labour sorer in fruiteles vanitie
            Then in fayre workes of great utilitie;
            In suche trifles we labour for domage,
            Worke we despise which bringeth advauntage.

STEPHEN HAWES

From *The Passetyme of Pleasure*

And in meanewhyle the gentyll porteres
Called Countenaunce on my way then me lede,
Into the basse courte of grete wydnes,
Where all of golde there was a conduyte hede
With many dragons enameled with reed,
Whiche dyde spoute oute the dulcet lycoure
Lyke crystall clere with aromatyke odoure.

Alofte the basse toure foure ymages stode,
Whiche blewe the claryons well and wonderly;
Alofte the toures the golden fanes gode   10
Dyde with the wynde make full swete armony;
Them for to here it was grete melody:
The golden toures with crystall clarefyed
Aboute were glased, moost clerely purefyed.

And the gravell whereupon we wente,
Full lyke the golde that is moost pure and fyne,
Withouten spotte of blacke encombremente,
Aboute our fete it dyde ryghte clerely shyne:
It semed more lyke a place celestyne
Than an erthely mansyon whiche shall away   20
By longe tyme and proces another day.

And towarde me I dyde se than comynge
La Belle Pucell, the moost fayre creature
Of ony fayre erthely persone lyvynge,
Whiche with me mette with chere so demure;
Of the shynynge golde was all her vesture:
I dyde me duty, and ones or twyes, ywys,
Her lyppes softe I dyde full swetely kys.

'Aha,' quod she, 'that I am very fayne
That you are come, for I have thought longe   30
Sythen the tyme that we parted in twayne,
And for my sake you have had often wronge,
But your courage so hardy and stronge
Hath caused you for to be vyctoryous
Of your enmyes so moche contraryous.'

With her fayre hande, whyte as ony lyly,
She dyde me lede into a ryall hall
With knottes kerved full ryght craftely;
The wyndowes fayre glased with crystall,
And all aboute upon the golden wall,   40
There was enameled with fygures curyous
The syege of Troye so harde and dolorous.

The flore was paved with precyous stones,
And the rofe of mervaylous geometry
Of the swete sypres wrought for the nones,
Encensynge oute the yll odours mysty;
Amyddes the rofe there shone full wonderly
A poynted dyamonde of mervaylous bygnes,
With many other grete stones of ryches.

So up we wente to a chambre fayre,   50
A place of pleasure and delectacyon,
Strowed with floures flagraunte of ayre,

Without ony spotte of perturbacyon;
I behelde ryght well the operacyon
Of the mervaylous rofe set full of rubyes,
And tynst with saphers and many turkeys.

The walles were hanged with golden aras
Whiche treated well of the syege of Thebes,
And yet all aboute us depured was
The crystallyne wyndowes of grete bryghtnes: 60
I can nothynge extende the goodlynes
Of this palays, for it is impossyble
To shewe all that unto me vysyble.

But La Bell Pucell full ryght gentylly
Dyde syt adowne by a wyndowes syde,
And caused me also full swetely
By her to sytte at that gentyll tyde.
'Welcome,' she sayde, 'ye shall with me abyde,
After your sorowe to lyve in joye and blysse;
You shall have that ye have desrved, ywys.'   70

Up Y arose *in verno tempore*,
And found a maydyn *sub quadam arbore*,
That dyd complayne *in suo pectore*,
Sayng, 'Y fele *puerum movere*;

'Adew, plesers *antiquo tempore*,
Full oft with you *solebam ludere*,
But for my mysse *michi deridere*;
With right goed cause *incipeo flere*.

'Now what shall Y say *meis parentibus*?
Bycause Y lay with *quidam clericus*,   10
They wyll me bete *cum virgis ac fustibus*,
And me sore chast *coram omnibus*.

With the seid child, *quid faciam*?
Shall Y hyt kepe *vel interficiam*?
Yf Y sley hyt, *quo loco fugiam*?
I shall lose God *et vitam eternam*.'

Benedicite! Whate dremyd I this nyght?
Methought the worlde was turnyd up so downe,

The son, the moone, had lost ther force and light;
The see also drownyd both towre and towne:
Yett more mervell how that I hard the sownde
Of onys voice sayyng, 'Bere in thy mynd,
Thi lady hath forgoten to be kynd.'

Westron wynd, when wyll thow blow,
The smalle rayne downe can rayne?
Cryst, yf my love were in my armys,
And I yn my bed agayne!

SIR THOMAS WYATT

Farewell, all my wellfare,
My shue is trode awry;
Now may I karke and care
To syng *lullay by by*.
Alas! what shall I do thereto?
There ys no shyffte to helpe me now.

Who made hytt suche offence
To love for love agayn?
God wott that my pretence
Was but to ease hys payn;   10
For I had ruthe to se hys wo;
Alas, more fole, why dyd I so?

For he frome me ys gone
And makes thereat a game,
And hathe leffte me alone
To suffer sorow and shame.
Alas! he ys unkynd dowtles
To leve me thus all comfortles.

Hytt ys a grevous smarte
To suffer paynes and sorowe;   20
But most it grevyd my hart
He leyde hys feythe to borow:

96

And falshode hathe hys feythe and trowthe,
And he forsworne by many an othe.

All ye lovers, perde,
Hathe cawse to blame hys dede,
Whyche shall example be
To lett yow off yowre spede;
Let never woman agayn
Trust to suche wordes as men can fayn.   30

For I, unto my coste,
Am warnyng to yow all,
That they whom you trust most
Sonest dysceyve yow shall;
But complaynt cannot redresse
Of my gret greff the gret excesse.

What menythe thys when I lye alone?
I tosse, I turne, I syghe, I grone;
My bedd me semys as hard as stone:
 What menys thys?

I syghe, I playne contynually;
The clothes that on my bedd do ly
Always methynks they lye awry:
 What menys thys?

In slumbers oft for fere I quake;
For hete and cold I burne and shake;   10
For lake of slepe my hede dothe ake:
 What menys thys?

97

A mornynges then when I do rysse,
I torne unto my wontyd gysse;
All day after muse and devysse
    What menys thys?

And yff perchanse by me there passe
She unto whome I sue for grace,
The cold blood forsakythe my face:
    What menythe thys?   20

But yff I sytte nere her by,
With lowd voyce my hart dothe cry,
And yet my mowthe ys dome and dry:
    What menys thys?

To aske for helpe no hart I have,
My tong dothe fayle what I shuld crave,
Yet inwardly I rage and rave:
    What menys thys?

Thus have I passyd many a yere,
And many a day, tho nowght apere;   30
But most of that that most I fere:
    What menys thys?

    Ons in your grace I knowe I was,
    Evyn as well as now ys he;
    Tho fortune so hath tornyd my case,
    That I am doune, and he full hye,
        Yet ons I was.

    Ons I was he that dyd you please
    So well that nothyng dyd I dobte;

98

And tho that nowe ye thinke yt ease
To take him in and throw me out,
    Yet ons I was.   10

Ons I was he in tym past
That as your owne ye did retayne;
And tho ye have me nowe out cast,
Shoyng untruthe in you to raygne,
    Yet ons I was.

Ons I was he that knyt the knot,
The whyche ye swore not to unknyt;
And tho ye fayne yt now forgot,
In usynge yowr newfanglyd wyt,
    Yet ons I was.   20

Ons I was he to whome ye sayd:
'Welcomm, my joy, my hole delight!'
And tho ye are nowe well apayd
Of me, your owne, to clame ye quyt,
    Yet ons I was.

Ons I was he to whome he spake:
'Have here my hart, yt ys thy owne!'
And tho thes wordis ye now forsake,
Sayng therof my part ys none,
    Yet ons I was.   30

Ons I was he before reherst,
And nowe am he that nedes must dye;
And tho I dye, yet at the lest,
In your remembrance let yt lye
    That ons I was.

Quondam was I in my lady's gras,
I thynk as well as nou be you;
And when that you have trad the tras,
Then shal you kno my woordes be tru,
      That quondam was I.

Quondam was I. She seyd for ever:
That 'ever' lastyd but a short whyl;
Promis mad not to dyssever.
I thoght she laughte—she dyd but smyl,
      Than quondam was I.   10

Quondam was I: he that full oft lay
In hyr armes wythe kysses many whon.
Yt is enou that thys I may saey:
Tho amonge the moo, nou I be gon,
      Yet quondam was I.

Quondam was I: yet she wyl you tell
That syns the ouer she was furst borne,
She never lovyd non halfe so well
As you. But what altho she had sworne,
      Suer quondam was I.   20

I love lovyd and so doithe she,
And yet in love wee sufer still;
The cause is strange as semeth me,
To lovve so well and want our will.

O deadly yea! O grevous smart!
Worse then refuse, unhappe gaine!
I love: whoever playd this part
To love so well and leve in payn?

Was ever hart soo well agrede,
Sines love was love, as I do trowe,   10
That in ther love soo evell dyd sped,
To love so well and leve in woo?

Thes morne wee bothe and hathe don long,
With wofull plaint and carefull voice:
Alas! it is a grevous wrowng,
To love so well and not rejoice.

And here an end of all our mone!
With sighinge oft my brethe is skant,
Sines of myshappe ours is alone—
To love so well and it to wantt.   20

But they that causer is of thes,
Of all owr cares God send them part!
That they may trowe what greve it is
To love so well and leve in smart.

My lute awake! perfourme the last
Labor that thou and I shall wast,
And end that I have now begon;
For when this song is sung and past,
My lute be still, for I have done.

As to be herd where ere is none,
As lede to grave in marbill stone,
My song may perse her hert as sone;
Should we then sigh, or syng, or mone?
No, no, my lute, for I have done.   10

The rokkes do not so cruelly
Repulse the waves continuelly,
As she my suyte and affection,
So that I ame past remedy:
Whereby my lute and I have done.

Prowd of the spoyll that thou hast gott
Of simple hertes thorough love's shot,
By whome, unkynd, thou hast theim wone,
Thinck not he haith his bow forgot,
Alltho my lute and I have done.   20

Vengeaunce shall fall on thy disdain,
That makest but game on ernest pain;
Thinck not alone under the sonne,
Unquyt to cause thy lovers plain,
Alltho my lute and I have done.

Perchaunce the lye wethered and old,
The wynter nyghtes that are so cold,
Playnyng in vain unto the mone;
Thy wisshes then dare not be told;
Care then who lyst, for I have done.   30

And then may chaunce the to repent
The tyme that thou hast lost and spent
To cause thy lovers sigh and swoune;
Then shalt thou knowe beaultie but lent,
And wisshe and want as I have done.

Now cesse, my lute, this is the last
Labour that thou and I shall wast,
And ended is that we begon;
Now is this song boeth sung and past:
My lute be still, for I have done.   40

They fle from me that sometyme did me seke
With naked fote stalking in my chambre.
I have sene theim gentill, tame and meke,
That nowe are wyld and do not remembre
That sometyme they put theimself in daunger
To take bred at my hand; and nowe they raunge,
Besely seking with a continuell chaunge.

Thancked be fortune, it hath ben othrewise
Twenty tymes better; but ons in speciall,
In thyn arraye after a pleasaunt gyse,   10
When her lose gowne from her shoulders did fall,
And she me caught in her armes long and small;
Therewithall swetely did me kysse,
And softely said, 'Dere hert, howe like you this?'

It was no dreme: I lay brode waking,
But all is torned thorough my gentilnes
Into a straunge fasshion of forsaking;
And I have leve to goo of her goodenes,
And she also to use newfangilnes.
But syns that I so kyndely ame served,   20
I would fain knowe what she hath deserved.

My galy charged with forgetfulnes,
Thorrough sharpe sees in wynter nyghtes doeth pas
Twene rock and rock, and eke myn ennemy, Alas,
That is my lorde, sterith with cruelnes,
And every owre a thought in redines,
As tho that deth were light in suche a case.
An endles wynd doeth tere the sayll apase,
Of forced sighes and trusty ferefulnes.

103

A rayn of teris, a clowde of derk disdain,
Hath done the wered cordes great hinderaunce;
Wrethed with errour and eke with ignoraunce.
The starres be hid that led me to this pain;
Drowned is reason that should me confort,
And I remain dispering of the port.

10

Farewell, Love, and all thy lawes forever:
Thy bayted hookes shall tangill me no more;
Senec and Plato call me from thy lore,
To perfaict welth my wit for to endever.
In blynde error when I did persever,
Thy sherpe repulce, that pricketh ay so sore,
Hath taught me to sett in tryfels no store,
And scape fourth, syns libertie is lever.
Therefore, farewell: goo trouble yonger hertes,
And in me clayme no more authoritie;
With idill yeuth goo use thy propertie,
And theron spend thy many brittil dertes;
For, hetherto though I have lost all my tyme,
Me lusteth no lenger rotten boughes to clyme.

10

You that in love finde lucke and habundance,
And live in lust and joyful jolitie,
Arrise for shame! Do away your sluggardie!
Arise, I say, do May some observance!
Let me in bed lye dreming in mischaunce;
Let me remember the happs most unhappy
That me betide in May most commonly,

As oon whome love list litil to avaunce.
Sephame saide true that my nativitie
Mischaunced was with the ruler of the May: 10
He gest, I prove, of that the veritie.
In May my welth, and eke my liff, I say,
Have stoude so oft in such perplexitie—
Rejoyse! Let me dreme of your felicitie.

Dyvers dothe use, as I have hard and kno,
When that to chaunge ther ladies do beginne,
To mourne and waile, and never for to lynne,
Hoping therbye to pease ther painefull woe.
And some ther be, that whan it chansith soo,
That women change and hate where love hath bene,
Thei call them fals, and think with woordes to wynne
The hartes of them wich otherwhere dothe gro.
But as for me, though that by chaunce indede,
Change hath outworne the favor that I had, 10
I will not wayle, lament, nor yet be sad,
Nor call her fals that falsley ded me fede:
But let it passe and think it is of kinde,
That often chaunge doth plese a woman's minde.

Whoso list to hounte, I knowe where is an hynde,
But, as for me, helas, I may no more:
The vayne travaill hath weried me so sore,
I ame of theim that farthest cometh behinde;
Yet may I by no meanes my weried mynde
Drawe from the diere: but as she fleeth afore,

Faynting I folowe. I leve of therefore,
Sins in a nett I seke to hold the wynde.
Who list her hount, I put him owte of dowbte,
As well as I may spend his tyme in vain: 10
And, graven with diamondes, in letters plain,
There is written, her faier neck rounde abowte:
Noli me tangere, for Cesar's I ame,
And wylde for to hold, though I seme tame.

Tagus, farewell, that westward with thy stremes,
Torns up the grayns of gold alredy tryd:
With spurr and sayle for I go seke the Tems,
Gaynward the sonne that shewth her welthi pryd,
And to the town which Brutus sowght by drems,
Like bendyd mone doth lend her lusty syd.
My Kyng, my Contry, alone for whome I lyve,
Of myghty love the winges for this me gyve.

Syghes ar my foode, drynke are my teares,
Clynkinge of fetters suche musycke wolde crave,
Stynke and close ayer away my lyf wears:
Innocencie is all the hope I have.
Rayne, wynde, or wether I judge by myne eares.
Mallice assaulteth that rightiousnes should have:
Sure I am, Brian, this wounde shall heale agayne,
But yet, alas, the scarre shall styll remayne.

Stond whoso list upon the slipper toppe
Of courtes estates, and lett me heare rejoyce;
And use me quyet without lett or stoppe,
Unknowen in courte, that hath suche brackishe joyes:
In hidden place, so lett my dayes forthe passe,
That, when my yeares be done, withouten noyse,
I may dye aged after the common trace.
For hym death greep'the right hard by the croppe,
That is moche knowen of other, and of himself, alas,
Doth dye unknowen, dazed with dreadfull face.   10

Who lyst his welthe and eas retayne,
Hymselfe let hym unknowne contayne;
Presse not to fast in at that gatte
Wher the retorne standes by desdayne:
For sure, *circa Regna tonat.*

The hye montaynis ar blastyd oft,
When the lowe vaylye ys myld and soft;
Fortune with helthe stondis at debate;
The fall ys grevous frome alofte:
And sure, *circa Regna tonat.*   10

These blodye dayes have brokyn my hart;
My lust, my youth dyd then departe,
And blynd desyre of astate;
Who hastis to clyme sekes to reverte:
Of truthe, *circa Regna tonat.*

The bell towre showed me suche syght
That in my hed stekys day and nyght;
Ther dyd I lerne, out of a grate,

107

For all vavore, glory or myght,
That yet *circa Regna tonat.* 20

By profe, I say, ther dyd I lerne,
Wyt helpythe not defence to yerne,
Of innocence to pled or prate;
Ber low, therfor, geve God the sterne,
For sure, *circa Regna tonat.*

A spending hand that alway powreth owte
Had nede to have a bringer-in as fast,
And on the stone that still doeth tourne abowte
There groweth no mosse: these proverbes yet do last.
Reason hath set theim in so sure a place,
That lenght of yeres their force can never wast.
When I remembre this, and eke the case
Wherein thou stondes, I thowght forthwith to write,
Brian, to the, who knowes how great a grace
In writing is to cownsell man the right. 10
To the, therefore, that trottes still up and downe,
And never restes, but runnyng day and nyght
From reaulme to reaulme, from cite, strete and towne,
Why doest thou were thy body to the bones,
And myghtst at home slepe in thy bed of downe,
And drynck goode ale so noppy for the noyns,
Fede thyself fat and hepe up pownd by pownd?
Lykist thou not this? *No.* Why? *For swyne so groyns*
In stye and chaw the tordes molded on the grownd,
And dryvell on pearles, the hed still in the maunger, 20
Then of the harp the asse to here the sownd.
So sackes of durt be filled up in the cloyster,
That servis for lesse then do thes fatted swyne.

108

Tho I seme lene and dry withoute moyster,
Yet woll I serve my prynce, my lord and thyn,
And let theim lyve to fede the panche that list,
So I may fede to lyve both me and myn.
By God, well sayde! But what and if thou wist
How to bryng in as fast as thou doest spend?
That would I lerne. And it shall not be myst   30
To tell the how. Now, hark what I intend.
Thou knowest well first whoso can seke to plese
Shall pourchase frendes where trowght shall but offend.
Fle therefore trueth: it is boeth welth and ese.
For tho that trouth of every man hath prayse,
Full nere that wynd goeth trouth in great misese.
Use vertu as it goeth nowadayes:
In word alone, to make thy langage swete,
And of the dede yet do not as thou sayse;
Elles be thou sure thou shalt be farre unmyt   40
To get thy bred, eche thing is now so skant.
Seke still thy profett upon thy bare fete;
Lend in no wise, for fere that thou do want,
Onles it be as to a dogge a chese;
By which retorne be sure to wyn a kant
Of half at lest: it is not good to lese.
Lerne at Kittson that in a long white cote,
From under the stall withoute landes or feise,
Hath lept into the shopp; who knoweth by rote
This rule that I have told the here before.   50
Sumtyme also riche age begynneth to dote;
Se thou when there thy gain may be the more:
Stay him by the arme, whereso he walke or goo;
Be nere alway, and if he koggh to sore,
When he hath spit, tred owte, and please him so.
A diligent knave that pikes his maister's purse
May please him so, that he, withouten mo,
Executour is, and what is he the wourse?

But if so chaunce you get nought of the man,
The wedow may for all thy charge deburse:　　　60
A ryveld skyn, a stynking breth, what than?
A tothles mowth shall do thy lips no harme;
The gold is good, and tho she curse or ban,
Yet where the list, thou maist ly good and warme:
Let the old mule byte upon the bridill,
Whilst there do ly a swetter in thyn arme.
In this also, se you be not idell:
Thy nece, thy cosyn, thy sister or thy doghter,
If she be faire, if handsom be her myddell,
Yf thy better hath her love besoght her,　　　70
Avaunce his cause, and he shall help thy nede.
It is but love: turne it to a lawghter.
But ware, I say, so gold the helpe and spede,
That in this case, thow be not so unwise
As Pandare was in suche a like dede,
For he, the fooll, of conscience was so nyse,
That he no gayn would have for all his payne.
Be next thyself, for frendshipp beres no prise.
Laughst thou at me? Why, do I speke in vayne?
No, not at the, but at thy thrifty gest:　　　80
Wouldest thou I should, for any losse or gayne,
Chaunge that for gold that I have tan for best,
Next godly thinges, to have an honest name?
Should I leve that, then take me for a best!
Nay then, farewell! And if thou care for shame,
Content the then with honest povertie,
With fre tong what the myslikes to blame,
And for thy trouth sumtyme adversitie:
And therewithall this thing I shall the gyve—
In this worould now, little prosperite,　　　90
And coyne to kepe as water in a syve.

HENRY HOWARD, EARL OF SURREY

When ragyng love with extreme payne
Most cruelly distrains my hart;
When that my teares, as floudes of rayne,
Beare witnes of my wofull smart;
When sighes have wasted so my breath
That I lye at the poynte of death:

I call to minde the navye greate
That the Grekes brought to Troye towne,
And how the boysteous windes did beate
Their shyps, and rente their sayles adowne,   10
Till Agamemnon's daughter's bloode
Appeasde the goddes that them withstode.

And how that in those ten yeres' warre,
Full manye a bloudye dede was done,
And manye a lord, that came full farre,
There caught his bane, alas, to sone,
And many a good knight overronne,
Before the Grekes had Helene wonne.

Then thinke I thus: sithe suche repayre,
So longe time warre of valiant men,   20
Was all to winne a ladye fayre,
Shall I not learne to suffer then,

And thinke my life well spent to be
Servyng a worthier wight than she?

Therfore I never will repent,
But paynes contented stil endure:
For like as when, rough winter spent,
The pleasant spring straight draweth in ure,
So, after ragyng stormes of care,
Joyful at length may be my fare.   30

Set me wheras the sonne dothe perche the grene,
Or whear his beames may not dissolve the ise;
In temprat heat wheare he is felt and sene;
With prowde people, in presence sad and wyse;
Set me in base, or yet in highe degree,
In the long night, or in the shortyst day,
In clere weather, or whear mysts thikest be,
In loste yowthe, or when my heares be grey;
Set me in earthe, in heaven, or yet in hell,
In hill, in dale, or in the fowming floode;   10
Thrawle, or at large, alive whersoo I dwell,
Sike, or in healthe, in yll fame or in good:
    Yours will I be, and with that onely thought
    Comfort myself when that my hape is nowght.

O happy dames, that may embrace
The frute of your delight,
Help to bewaile the wofull case
And eke the heavy plight

Of me, that wonted to rejoyce
The fortune of my pleasant choyce:
Good Ladies, help to fill my moorning voyce.

In ship, freight with rememberance
Of thoughtes and pleasures past,
He sailes that hath in governance   10
My life, while it wil last;
With scalding sighes, for lack of gale,
Furdering his hope, that is his sail
Toward me, the swete port of his avail.

Alas, how oft in dreames I se
Those eyes, that were my food,
Which somtime so delited me,
That yet they do me good;
Wherwith I wake with his returne
Whose absent flame did make me burne.   20
But when I find the lacke, Lord, how I mourne!

When other lovers in armes acrosse
Rejoyce their chief delight,
Drowned in teares to mourne my losse
I stand the bitter night
In my window, where I may see
Before the windes how the cloudes flee.
Lo, what a mariner love hath made me!

And in grene waves when the salt flood
Doth rise by rage of wind,   30
A thousand fansies in that mood
Assayle my restlesse mind.
Alas, now drencheth my swete fo,
That with the spoyle of my hart did go,
And left me; but, alas, why did he so?

And when the seas waxe calme againe,
To chase fro me annoye,
My doubtfull hope doth cause me plaine:
So dreade cuts of my joye.
Thus is my wealth mingled with wo,   40
And of ech thought a dout doth growe,
Now he comes, will he come? alas, no, no!

When Windesor walles sustained my wearied arme,
My hand my chyn, to ease my restless hedd,
Ech pleasant plot revested green with warm,
The blossomed bowes with lustie Veare yspred,
The flowred meades, the weddyd birds so late
Myne eyes discovered. Than did to mynd resort
The joily woes, the hateles shorte debate,
The rakhell life that longes to love's disporte.
Wherwith, alas, myne hevy charge of care
Heapt in my brest brake forth against my will,   10
And smoky sighes that overcast the ayer.
My vapored eyes such drery teares distill
    The tender spring to quicken wher thei fall,
    And I half bent to throwe me down withall.

So crewell prison howe could betyde, alas,
As prowde Wyndsour, where I in lust and joye
With a kinges soon my childishe yeres did passe,
In greater feast then Priam's sonnes of Troye;

Where eche swete place retournes a tast full sowre.
The large grene courtes, where we wer wont to hove,

114

With eyes cast upp unto the maydens' towre,
And easye syghes, such as folke drawe in love.

The statelye sales; the ladyes bright of hewe;
The daunces short, long tales of great delight,   10
With wordes and lookes that tygers could but rewe,
Where eche of us did plead the other's right.

The palme playe, where, dispoyled for the game,
With dased eyes, oft we, by gleames of love,
Have mist the ball and got sight of our dame
To bayte her eyes which kept the leddes above.

The graveld ground, with sleves tyed on the helme,
On fomynge horse, with swordes and frendlye hertes,
With chere as thoughe the one should overwhelme,
Where we have fought and chased oft with dartes.   20

With sylver dropps the meades yet spredd for rewthe,
In active games of nymbleness and strengthe
Where we dyd strayne, trayled by swarmes of youthe,
Our tender lymes, that yet shott upp in lengthe.

The secret groves, which ofte we made resound
Of pleasaunt playnt and of our ladyes' prayes,
Recording soft what grace eche one had found,
What hope of spede, what dred of long delayes.

The wyld forest, the clothed holtes with grene,
With raynes avald and swift ybrethed horse,   30
With crye of houndes and mery blastes bitwen,
Where we did chase the fearfull hart *à force*.

The voyd walles eke, that harbourd us eche night;
Wherwith, alas, revive within my brest
The swete accord, such slepes as yet delight,
The pleasaunt dreames, the quyet bedd of rest,

The secret thoughtes imparted with such trust,
The wanton talke, the dyvers chaung of playe,
The frendshipp sworne, eche promyse kept so just,
Wherwith we past the winter nightes awaye.   40

And with this thought the blood forsakes my face,
The teares berayne my cheke of dedlye hewe;
The which, as sone as sobbing sighes, alas,
Upsupped have, thus I my playnt renewe:

'O place of blisse, renewer of my woos,
Geve me accompt wher is my noble fere,
Whome in thy walles thou didest eche night enclose,
To other lief, but unto me most dere.'

Eache stone, alas, that dothe my sorowe rewe,
Retournes therto a hollowe sound of playnt.   50
Thus I alone, where all my fredome grew,
In pryson pyne with bondage and restraynt,

And with remembraunce of the greater greif,
To bannishe the lesse I fynde my chief releif.

Wyatt resteth here, that quick could never rest;
Whose heavenly giftes, encreased by disdayn
And vertue, sank the deper in his brest:
Such profit he by envy could obtain.

A hed, where wisdom misteries did frame;
Whose hammers bet styll in that lively brayn
As on a stithe, where that some work of fame
Was dayly wrought to turne to Britaines gayn.

A visage stern and myld; where bothe did grow
Vice to contemne, in vertue to rejoyce;   10
Amid great stormes whom grace assured so
To lyve upright and smile at fortunes choyce.

A hand that taught what might be sayd in ryme;
That reft Chaucer the glory of his wit;
A mark the which, unparfited for time,
Some may approche, but never none shall hit.

A toung that served in forein realmes his king;
Whose courteous talke to vertue did enflame
Eche noble hart; a worthy guide to bring
Our English youth by travail unto fame.   20

An eye, whose judgement none affect could blinde,
Frendes to allure, and foes to reconcile;
Whose persing loke did represent a mynde
With vertue fraught, reposed, voyd of gyle.

A hart, where drede was never so imprest
To hyde the thought that might the trouth avance;
In neyther fortune loft nor yet represt,
To swell in wealth, or yeld unto mischance.

A valiant corps, where force and beawty met;
Happy, alas, to happy, but for foes;   30
Lived and ran the race that nature set;
Of manhodes shape, where she the molde did lose.

But to the heavens that simple soule is fled,
Which left with such as covet Christ to know
Witnesse of faith that never shall be ded;
Sent for our helth, but not received so.

Thus, for our gilte, this jewel have we lost.
The earth his bones, the heavens possesse his gost.

Th'Assyryans' king, in peas with fowle desyre
And filthye luste that staynd his regall harte,
In warr that should sett pryncelye hertes afyre,
Vanquyshd, dyd yeld for want of martyall arte.
The dent of swordes from kysses semed straunge,
And harder then hys ladyes syde his targe;
From glotton feastes to sowldyer's fare a chaunge,
His helmet far above a garlandes charge.
Who scace the name of manhode dyd retayne,
Drenched in slouthe and womanishe delight,
Feble of sprete, unpacyent of payne,
When he hadd lost his honor and hys right,
    Prowde tyme of welthe, in stormes appawld with drede,
    Murdred hymselfe to shew some manfull dede.

Of thy lyfe, Thomas, this compasse well mark:
Not aye with full sayles the hye seas to beat,
Ne by coward dred, in shonning stormes dark,
On shalow shores thy keel in perill freat.
Whoso gladly halseth the golden meane
Voyde of dangers advisdly hath his home:

Not with lothsom muck, as a den uncleane,
Nor palacelyke wherat disdayn may glome.
The lofty pyne the great winde often rives;
With violenter swey falne turrets stepe;   10
Lightninges assault the hye mountains and clives.
A hart well stayd, in overthwartes depe
Hopeth amendes; in swete doth feare the sowre.
God that sendeth withdrawth winter sharp.
Now ill, not aye thus. Once Phebus to lowre
With bow unbent shall cease, and frame to harp
His voyce. In straite estate appere thou stout;
And so wisely, when lucky gale of winde
All thy puft sailes shall fil, loke well about,
Take in a ryft. Hast is wast, profe doth finde.   20

From *Certain Bokes of Virgiles Aenaeis turned into
English metre* . . .

Aurora now from Titan's purple bed
With new daylight hath overspred the earth,
When by her windowes the quene the peping day
Espyed, and navie with splaid sailes depart
The shore, and eke the port of vessels voyde.
Her comly brest thrise or foure times she smote
With her own hand, and tore her golden tresse.
'Oh Jove,' quoth she, 'shall he then thus depart
A straunger thus and scorne our kingdom so?
Shall not my men do on theyr armure prest,   10
And eke pursue them throughout all the town?
Out of the rode some shall the vessells warpe?
Hast on, cast flame, set sayle and welde your owers!
What said I? but where am I? what phrensie

119

Alters thy minde? Unhappy Dido, now
Hath thee beset a froward destenie.
Then it behoved, when thou didst geve to him
The scepter. Lo, his faith and his right hand,
That leades with him (they say) his countrie godes,
That on his back his aged father bore!   20
His body might I not have caught and rent?
And in the seas drenched him and his feers?
And from Ascanius his life with iron reft,
And set him on his father's bord for meate?
Of such debate perchaunce the fortune might
Have bene doubtfull: would God it were assayed!
Whom should I feare, sith I myselfe must die?
Might I have throwen into that navy brandes,
And filled eke their deckes with flaming fire,
The father, sonne, and all their nacion   30
Destroyed, and falln myself ded over al.
Sunne, with thy beames that mortall workes discries,
And thou, Juno, that wel these travailes knowest,
Proserpine thou, upon whom folk do use
To houle and call, in forked wayes by night,
Infernal furies, ye wreakers of wrong,
And Dido's gods, who standes at point of death,
Receive these wordes, and eke your heavy power
Withdraw from me, that wicked folk deserve,
And our request accept, we you besech.   40
If so that yonder wicked head must needes
Recover port, and saile to land of force,
And if Jove's wil have so resolved it
And such ende set as no wight can fordoe,
Yet at the least asailed mought he be
With armes and warres of hardy nacions,
From the boundes of his kingdom farre exiled,
Julus eke rashed out of his armes,
Driven to call for helpe, that he may see

The giltles corpses of his folke lie dead.   50
And after hard condicions of peace,
His realme nor life desired may he brooke,
But fall before his time, ungraved amid the sandes.
This I require, these wordes with blood I shed.
And Tirians, ye his stocke and all his race
Pursue with hate, rewarde our cinders so!
No love nor leage betwixt our peoples be!
And of our bones some wreaker may there spring,
With sword and flame that Troyans may pursue.
And from hencefoorth, when that our powr may stretch,   60
Our costes to them contrary be for aye,
I crave of God, and our streames to their fluddes,
Armes unto armes, and offspring of eche race
With mortal warr eche other may fordoe.'

? GEORGE BOLEYN, VISCOUNT ROCHFORD

O death, O death, rocke mee asleepe,
Bringe mee to quiett rest,
Lett passe my wearie guiltlesse Ghost
Out of my carefull brest.
    Toll on the passing bell,
    Ringe out my dolefull knell,
    Thy sound my death abroad will tell,
    For I must die:
    There is no remedie.

My paines, my paines, who can expresse?   10
Alas, they are so stronge,
My dolowrs will not suffer strength
My life for to prolonge.
    Toll on etc.

Alone, alone in prison stronge,
I waile my destinie;
Woe worth this cruel happ, that I
Must tast this miserie.
    Toll on etc.

Farewell, farewell, my pleasures past,   20
Welcome my present paine:

I feele my torment so increase
That life cannot remaine.
         Cease now then, passing bell,
         Ringe out my dolefull knell,
         For thou my death doth tell;
         Lord, pittie thou my soule,
         Death doth drawe nigh;
         Sound dolefullie,
         For now I dye,   30
         I die, I die.

'TOTTEL'S MISCELLANY'

*The lover disceived by his love repenteth him of the true love
he bare her*

I that Ulysses' yeres have spent,
To finde Penelope,
Finde well that folly I have ment,
To seke that was not so,
Since Troylous' case hath caused me
From Cressed for to go.

And to bewaile Ulysses' truth,
In seas and stormy skies,
Of wanton will and raging youth,
Which have me tossed sore,   10
From Scilla to Caribdis' clives,
Upon the drowning shore.

Where I sought haven, there found I hap,
From daunger unto death:
Much like the Mouse that treades the trap,
In hope to finde her foode,
And bites the bread that stops her breath,
So in like case I stoode.

Till now repentance hasteth him
To further me so fast,   20

That where I sanke, there now I swim,
And have both streame and winde,
And lucke as good, if it may last,
As any man may finde.

That where I perished, safe I passe,
And finde no perill there,
But stedy stone, no ground of glasse,
Now am I sure to save,
And not to flete from feare to feare,
Such anker hold I have.   30

The aged lover renounceth love

I lothe that I did love,
In youth that I thought swete:
As time requires, for my behove
Methinkes they are not mete.

My lustes they do me leave,
My fansies all be fledde:
And tract of time begins to weave
Gray heares upon my hedde.

For Age with stelyng steppes,
Hath clawed me with his clowche,   10
And lusty life away she leapes,
As there had bene none such.

My muse dothe not delight
Me as she did before:
My hand and pen are not in plight,
As they have bene of yore.

125

For reason me denies
This youthly idle rime,
And day by day to me she cryes,
'Leave of these toyes in time!'   20

The wrincles in my brow,
The furrowes in my face,
Say limpyng Age will hedge him now,
Where youth must geve him place.

The harbinger of death,
To me I see him ride;
The cough, the colde, the gaspyng breath,
Dothe bid me to provide.

A pikeax and a spade,
And eke a shrowdyng shete,   30
A house of claye for to be made,
For such a gest most mete.

Me thinkes I heare the clarke
That knols the careful knell,
And bids me leave my wofull warke,
Er nature me compell.

My kepers knit the knot,
That youth did laugh to scorne,
Of me that clene shalbe forgot,
As I had not ben borne.   40

Thus must I youth geve up,
Whose badge I long did weare;
To them I yelde the wanton cup
That better may it beare.

Loe, here the bared scull,
By whose balde signe I know
That stoupyng age away shall pull
Which youthfull yeres did sowe.

For beauty with her bande
These croked cares hath wrought,   50
And shipped me into the lande,
From whence I first was brought.

And ye that bide behinde,
Have ye none other trust:
As ye of claye were cast by kinde,
So shall ye waste to dust.

*The lover accusing hys love for her unfaithfulnesse, purposeth
to live in libertie*

The smoky sighes, the bitter teares,
That I in vaine have wasted;
The broken slepes, the wo and feares,
That long in me have lasted;
The love and all I owe to thee,
Here I renounce and make me free.

Which fredome I have by thy guilt,
And not by my deserving,
Since so unconstantly thou wilt
Not love, but still be swarvyng: 10
To leve me off which was thine owne,
Without cause why as shal be knowen.

127

The frutes were faire, the which did grow
Within thy garden planted,
The leaves were grene of every bough,
And moysture nothing wanted,
Yet, or the blossoms gan to fall,
The caterpiller wasted all.

Thy body was the garden place,
And sugred wordes it beareth,
The blossomes all thy faith it was,
Which as the canker wereth;
The caterpiller is the same,
That hath wonne thee and lost thy name.

I meane thy lover, loved now
By thy pretended folye,
Which will prove lyke, thou shalt fynd how,
Unto a tree of holly,
That barke and bery beares alwayes,
The one byrdes feedes, the other slayes.

And right well mightest thou have thy wish
Of thy love new acquaynted,
For thou art lyke unto the dishe
That Adrianus paynted,
Wherin wer grapes portrayd so fayre
That fowles for foode did there repayre.

But I am lyke the beaten fowle
That from the net escaped,
And thou art lyke the ravening owle
That all the night hath waked,
For none intent but to betray
The sleping fowle before the day.

20

30

40

Thus hath thy love been unto me
As pleasant and commodious
As was the fyre made on the sea
By Naulus' hate so odious,
Therwith to trayn the Grekish host
From Troyes return where they wer lost.

Upon the death of Sir Antony Denny

Death and the Kyng did, as it were, contende,
Which of them two bare Denny greatest love.
The Kyng, to shew his love gan farre extende,
Did him advaunce his betters farre above.
Nere place, much welthe, great honour eke him gave,
To make it knowen what power great princes have.

But when Death came with his triumphant gift,
From worldly cark he quite his weried ghost,
Free from the corps, and straight to heaven it lift;
Now deme that can, who did for Denny most.   10
The king gave welth, but fadyng and unsure,
Death brought him blisse that ever shall endure.

THOMAS SACKVILLE
EARL OF DORSET

From *The Induction* to *A Myrrour for Magistrates*

An hydeous hole al vaste, withouten shape,
Of endles depth, orewhelmde with ragged stone,
Wyth ougly mouth and grisly Jawes doth gape,
And to our sight confounds itselfe in one;
Here entred we, and yeding forth, anone
An horrible lothly lake we might discerne
As blacke as pitche, that cleped is Averne.

A deadly gulfe where nought but rubbishe growes,
With fowle black swelth in thickned lumpes that lyes,
Which up in the ayer such stinking vapors throwes,   10
That over there may flye no fowle but dyes,
Choakt with the pestilent savours that aryse;
Hither we cum, whence forth we still dyd pace,
In dreadful feare amid the dreadfull place.

And first within the portche and jawes of Hell
Sate diepe Remorse of Conscience, al besprent
With teares, and to herselfe oft would she tell
Her wretchedness and cursing, never stent
To sob and sigh, but ever thus lament,

With thoughtful care, as she that all in vayne   20
Would weare and waste continually in payne.

Her iyes unstedfast rolling here and there,
Whurld on eche place, as place that vengeaunce brought,
So was her minde continually in feare,
Tossed and tormented with the tedious thought
Of those detested crymes which she had wrought:
With dreadful cheare and lookes throwen to the skye,
Wyshyng for death, and yet she could not dye.

Next sawe we Dread al tremblyng how he shooke,
With foote uncertayne profered here and there,   30
Benumde of speache, and with a gastly looke
Searcht every place al pale and dead for feare,
His cap borne up with staring of his heare,
Stoynde and amazde at his owne shade for dreed,
And fearing greater daungers than was nede.

And next within the entry of this lake
Sate fell Revenge gnashing her teeth for yre,
Devising meanes howe she may vengeaunce take,
Never in rest tyll she have her desire,
But frets within so farforth with the fyer   40
Of wreaking flames, that nowe determines she,
To dye by death, or vengde by death to be.

When fell Revenge with bloudy foule pretence
Had showed herselfe as next in order set,
With trembling limmes we softly parted thence,
Tyll in our iyes another sight we met:
When fro my hart a sigh forthwith I fet,
Rewing, alas, upon the wofull plight
Of Miserie, that next appered in sight.

His face was leane, and sumdeale pyned away, 50
And eke his handes consumed to the bone,
But what his body was I cannot say,
For on his carkas, rayment had he none
Save cloutes and patches pieced one by one.
With staffe in hand, and skrip on shoulders cast,
His chiefe defence agaynst the winter's blast.

His foode for most, was wylde fruytes of the tree,
Unles sumtime sum crummes fell to his share,
Which in his wallet, long, God wote, kept he,
As on the which full dayntlye would he fare; 60
His drinke the running streame, his cup the bare
Of his palme closed, his bed the hard colde grounde:
To this poore life was Miserie ybound.

Whose wretched state when we had well behelde
With tender ruth on him and on his feres,
In thoughtful cares, furth then our pace we helde,
And by and by, another shape apperes
Of Greedy Care, still brushing up the breres,
His knuckles knobd, his fleshe deepe dented in,
With tawed handes, and hard ytanned skyn. 70

The morrowe graye no sooner hath begunne
To spreade his light even peping in our iyes,
When he is up and to his worke yrunne,
But let the nightes blacke mistye mantels rise,
And with fowle darke never so much disguyse
The fayre bright day, yet ceasseth he no whyle,
But hath his candels to prolonge his toyle.

ARTHUR GOLDING

From *The XV Bookes of P. Ovidius Naso, Entytuled Metamorphosis*

Upon the hilles of Phrygie neere a Teyle there stands a tree
Of Oke enclosed with a wall. Myself the place did see,
For Pithey untoo Pelop's feelds did send mee where his father
Did sumtyme reigne. Not farre fro thence there is a poole which
                                         rather
Had bene dry ground inhabited. But now it is a meare
And Moorecocks, Cootes, and Cormorants doo breede and nestle
                                         there.
The mightie Jove and Mercurie his sonne in shape of men
Resorted thither on a tyme. A thousand houses when
For roome to lodge in they had sought, a thousand houses bard
Theyr doores against them. Nerethelesse one Cotage afterward   10
Receyved them, and that was but a pelting one indeede.
The roofe therof was thatched all with straw and fennish reede.
Howbee't two honest auncient folke, (of whom she Baucis hight
And he Philemon) in that Cote theyr fayth in youth had plight:
And in that Cote had spent theyr age. And for they paciently
Did beare theyr simple povertie, they made it light thereby,
And shewed it nothing to bee repyned at at all.
It skilles not whether there for Hyndes or Maister you doo call,
For all the houshold were but two: and both of them obeyde,
And both commaunded. When the Gods at this same Cotage
                                   staid,   20

And ducking downe their heads, within the low-made Wicket
                                                        came,
Philemon bringing ech a stoole, bade rest upon the same
Their limmes: and busie Baucis brought them cuishons homely
                                                        geere.
Which done, the embers on the harth she gan abrode to steere,
And laid the coales togither that were raakt up overnight,
And with the brands and dried leaves did make them gather might,
And with the blowing of hir mouth did make them kindle bright.
Then from an inner house she fetcht seare sticks and clifted brands,
And put them broken underneath a Skillet with hir hands.
Hir Husband from their Gardenplot fetcht Coleworts. Of the
                                                    which   30
She shreaded small the leaves, and with a Forke tooke downe a
                                                        flitch
Of restie Bacon from the Balke made blacke with smoke, and cut
A peece thereof, and in the pan to boyling did it put.
And while this meate a-seething was, the time in talke they spent,
By meanes whereof away without much tedousnesse it went.
There hung a Boawle of Beeche upon a spirget by a ring.
The same with warmed water filld the two old folke did bring
To bathe their guests' foule feete therein. Amid the house there
                                                        stood
A Couch whose bottom sides and feete were all of Sallow wood,
And on the same a Mat of Sedge. They cast upon this bed   40
A covering which was never wont upon it to be spred
Except it were at solemne feastes: and yet the same was olde
And of the coursest, with a bed of sallow meete to holde.
The Gods sate downe. The aged wife right chare and busie as
A Bee, set out a table, of the which the thirde foote was
A little shorter than the rest. A tylesherd made it even
And tooke away the shoringnesse: and when they had it driven
To stand up levell, with greene Mintes they by and by it wipte.
Then set they on it Pallas' fruite with double colour stripte,
And Cornels kept in pickle moyst, and Endive, and a roote   50

Of Radish, and a jolly lump of Butter fresh and soote,
And Egges reare rosted. All these Cates in earthen dishes came.
Then set they downe a graven cup made also of the same
Selfe kinde of Plate, and Mazers made of Beech whose inner syde
Was rubd with yellow wax. And when they pawsed had a tyde,
Hot meate came pyping from the fyre. And shortly thereupon
A cup of greene hedg wyne was brought. This tane away, anon
Came in the latter course, which was of Nuts, Dates, dryed figges,
Sweete-smelling Apples in a Mawnd made flat of Osier twigges,
And Prunes and Plums and Purple grapes cut newly from the
                                             tree,   60
And in the middes a honnycomb new taken from the Bee.
Besydes all this there did ensew good countnance overmore,
With will not poore nor nigardly. Now all the whyle before,
As ofen as Philemon and Dame Baucis did perceyve
The emptie Cup to fill alone, and wyne to still receyve,
Amazed at the straungenesse of the thing, they gan streyghtway
With fearfull harts and hands hilld up to frame themselves to pray.
Desyring for theyr slender cheere and fare to pardoned bee.
They had but one poore Goose which kept theyr little Tennantree,
And this to offer to the Gods theyr guestes they did intend.   70
The Gander wyght of wing did make the slow old folke to spend
Theyr paynes in vayne, and mokt them long. At length he
                                     seemd to flye
For succor to the Gods themselves, who bade he should not dye.
'For wee bee Gods' (quoth they) 'and all this wicked towneship
                                       shall
Abye their gylt. On you alone this mischeef shall not fall.
No more, but give you up your house, and follow up this hill
Togither, and upon the top therof abyde our will.'
They bothe obeyd. And as the Gods did lead the way before,
They lagged slowly after with theyr staves, and labored sore
Ageinst the rysing of the hill. They were not mickle more   80
Than full a flyghtshot from the top, when looking backe they saw
How all the towne was drowned save their lyttle shed of straw.

And as they wondred at the thing and did bewayle the case
Of those that had theyr neyghbours beene, the old poore Cote
                                                        so base
Whereof they had beene owners erst, became a Church. The
                                                        proppes
Were turned into pillars huge. The straw uppon the toppes
Was yellow, so that all the roof did seeme of burnisht gold:
The floore with Marble paved was. The doores on eyther fold
Were graven. At the sight hereof Philemon and his make
Began to pray in feare. Then Jove thus gently them bespake: 90
'Declare, thou ryghtuowse man, and thou O woman meete to have
A ryghtuowse howsband, what yee would most cheefly wish or
                                                        crave.'
Philemon taking conference a little with his wyfe,
Declared bothe theyr meenings thus: 'We covet during lyfe,
Your Chapleynes for to bee to keepe your Temple. And bycause
Our yeeres in concord wee have spent, I pray when death neere
                                                        drawes,
Let bothe of us togither leave our lives: that neyther I
Behold my wyve's deceace, nor shee see myne when I doo dye.'
Theyr wish had sequele to theyr will. As long as lyfe did last,
They kept the Church. And beeing spent with age of yeares
                                                        forepast,   100
By chaunce as standing on a tyme without the Temple doore,
They told the fortune of the place, Philemon, old and poore,
Saw Baucis floorish greene with leaves, and Baucis saw likewyse
Philemon braunching out in boughes and twigs before hir eyes.
And as the Bark did overgrow the heades of both, eche spake
To other whyle they myght. At last they eche of them did take
Theyr leave of other bothe at once, and therewithall the bark
Did hyde theyr faces both at once. The Phrygians in that park
Doo at this present day still shew the trees that shaped were
Of theyr two bodies, growing yit togither joyntly there.   110

BARNABY GOOGE

To M. Henrye Cobham, of the most blessed state of lyfe

The happyest lyfe that here we have,
My *Cobham*, yf I shall defyne,
The goodlyest state twyxte byrth and grave,
Most gracious dayes and swetest tyme,
The fayrest face of fadynge Lyfe,
Race ryghtlyest ronne in ruthfull wayes,
The safest meanes to shun all stryfe,
The surest Staffe in fyckle Dayes:
I take not, I, as some do take,
To gape and gawne for Honours hye,   10
But Court and *Cayser* to forsake,
And lyve at home full quyetlye.
Remembrest thou what he once sayde,
Who bad, 'Courte not in any case,
For Vertue is in Courtes decayed,
And Vyce with States hath chyefest place'?
Not Courte but Countreye, I do judge,
Is it wheare lyes the happyest lyfe,
In Countreye growes no gratynge grudge,
In Countreye standes not sturdye stryfe,   20
In Countreye *Bacchus* hath no place,
In Countreye *Venus* hath defecte,
In Countreye *Thraso* hath no grace,

137

In Countreye fewe of *Gnatoes* secte.
But these same foure and many more
In Courte, thou shalt be sure to fynde,
For they have vowed, not thence to goe,
Bycause in Courte dwels ydle mynde.
In Countrye mayste thou safelye rest,
And flye all these, yf that thou lyste;   30
The Countrey therfore judge I best,
Where godly lyfe doth vyce resyste;
Where vertuous exercyse with joye,
Doth spende the yeares that are to run,
Where Vyces fewe maye the annoye:
This lyfe is best whan all is done.

Goyng towardes Spayne

Farewell, thou fertyll soyle, that *Brutus* fyrst out founde,
When he, poore soule, was driven clean from out his Countrey
    ground;
That Northward layst thy lusty sides amyd the ragyng Seas;
Whose welthy Land doth foster upp thy people all in ease,
While others scrape and carke abroad, theyr symple foode to gett,
And selye Soules toke all for good, that commeth to the Net,
Which they with painfull paynes do pynch in barrain, burning
    Realmes,
While we have all without restreint among thy welthy streames.
O blest of God, thou Pleasaunt Ile, where welth herself doth dwell,
Wherin my tender yeares I past, I byd thee now farewell.   10
For Fancy dryves me forth abroad, and byds me take delyght
In levyng thee and raungyng far, to see some straunger syght,
And sayth I was not framed heare to lyve at home with eas,
But passynge forth for knowledge sake, to cut the fomyng seas.

O Ragyng Seas, and myghty Neptune's rayne,
In monstrous Hylles, that throwest thyselfe so hye;
That, wyth thy fludes, doest beate the shores of Spayne,
And breake the Clyves, that dare thy force envie;
Cease now thy rage, and laye thyne Ire asyde,
And thou that hast the governaunce of all,
O myghty God, grant Wether, Wynd and Tyde,
Tyll on my Countreye Coast, our Anker fall.

GEORGE TURBERVILE

An Epitaph of Maister Win drowned in the Sea

Whoso thou art that passest by this place,
And runst at random on the slipper way,
Recline thy listning eare to mee a space,
Doe stay thy ship and hearken what I say:
Cast Ankor here untill my tale be donne,
So maist thou chaunce the like mishaps to shonne.

Learne this of me, that men doe live to die
And Death decaies the worthiest Wightes of all;
No worldly wealth or kingdomes can supplie
Or garde their Princes from the fatall fall: 10
One way to come unto this lyfe we see,
But to be rid thereof a thousand bee.

Mv gallant youth and frolick yeares behight
Mee longer age, and silver haires to have;
I thought my day would never come to night,
My prime provokte me to forget my grave:
I thought by water to have scapte the death
That now amid the Seas doe lose my breath.

Now, now, the churlish chanell me doe chock,
Now surging Seas conspire to breede my carke,   20

Now fighting flouds enforce me to the rock,
Charybdis' Whelps and *Scylla's* Dogs doe barke,
Now hope of life is past, now, now, I see
That W. can no more a livesman bee.

Yet I doe well affie for my desart,
(When cruell death hath done the worst it may),
Of well-renowmed Fame to have a part
To save my name from ruine and decay:
And that is all that thou or I may gaine,
And so adue, I thank thee for thy paine.   30

To His Love that sent him a Ring wherein was gravde,
            Let Reason rule

Shall *Reason* rule where *Reason* hath no right?
Nor never had? shall *Cupid* loose his landes?
His claim? his crown? his kingdome? name of might?
And yeeld himselfe to be in *Reason's* bandes?
No, (Friend), thy Ring doth will me thus in vaine,
Reason and *Love* have ever yet beene twaine.

They are by kinde of such contrarie mould,
As one mislikes the other's lewde devise;
What *Reason* willes, *Cupido* never would,
Love never yet thought *Reason* to be wise.   10
To *Cupid* I my homage earst have donne;
Let *Reason* rule the hearts that she hath wonne.

To an olde Gentlewoman, That painted hir face

   Leave off, good *Beroe*, now
   To sleeke thy shrivled skin,

141

For *Hecube's* face will never be
As *Helen's* hue hath bin.

Let Beautie go with youth,
Renownce the glosing Glasse,
Take Booke in hand: that seemely Rose
Is woxen withred Grasse.

Remoove thy Pecock's plumes,
Thou cranck and curious Dame;   10
To other Trulles of tender yeares
Resigne the flagge of Fame.

GEORGE GASCOIGNE

A Sonet written in prayse of the browne beautie, compiled
for the love of Mistresse E.P.

The thriftles thred which pampred beauty spinnes,
In thraldom binds the foolish gazing eyes,
As cruell Spiders with their crafty ginnes,
In worthlesse webbes doe snare the simple Flies.
The garments gay, the glittring golden gite,
The tysing talk which flowes from *Pallas'* pooles,
The painted pale, the (too much) red made white,
Are smiling baytes to fishe for loving fooles.
But lo, when eld in toothlesse mouth appeares,
And hoary heares in steede of beauties blaze,   10
Then 'had I wist' doth teach repenting yeares
The tickle track of craftie *Cupides* maze.
Twixt faire and foule therfore, twixt great and small,
A lovely nutbrowne face is best of all.

The Lullabie of a Lover

Sing lullaby, as women doe,
Wherewith they bring their babes to rest,
And lullaby can I sing to,
As womanly as can the best.

With lullaby they still the childe,
And if I be not much beguild,
Full many wanton babes have I,
Which must be stild with lullabie.

First, lullaby my youthfull yeares,
It is nowe time to go to bed, 10
For croocked age and hoary heares,
Have wone the haven within my head:
With Lullaby then, youth, be still,
With Lullaby, content thy will,
Since courage quayles, and commes behind,
Go sleepe, and so beguile thy minde.

Next, Lullaby my gazing eyes,
Which wonted were to glaunce apace.
For every Glasse maye nowe suffise,
To shewe the furrowes in my face: 20
With Lullabye then, winke awhile,
With Lullabye, your lookes beguile:
Lette no fayre face nor beautie brighte,
Entice you efte with vayne delighte.

And Lullaby, my wanton will,
Lette reason's rule nowe reigne thy thought,
Since all to late I finde by skyll
Howe deare I have thy fansies bought:
With Lullaby, nowe tak thyne ease,
With Lullaby, thy doubtes appease: 30
For trust to this, if thou be styll,
My body shall obey thy will.

Eke Lullaby my loving boye,
My little Robyn, take thy rest,
Since age is colde, and nothing coye,
Keepe close thy coyne, for so is best:

With Lullaby, be thou content,
With Lullaby, thy lustes relente,
Lette others pay which hath mo pence,
Thou art to pore for such expence.   40

   Thus Lullabye, my youth, myne eyes,
My will, my ware, and all that was,
I can no mo delayes devise,
But welcome payne, let pleasure passe:
With Lullaby, now take your leave,
With Lullaby, your dreames deceive,
And when you rise with waking eye,
Remember then this Lullabye.

Magnum vectigal parcimonia

The common speech is, spend and God will send,
But what sendes he? a bottell and a bagge,
A staffe, a wallet and a wofull ende,
For such as list in bravery so to bragge.
Then if thou covet coyne enough to spend,
Learne first to spare thy budget at the brinke,
So shall the bottome be the faster bound:
But he that list with lavish hand to linke
(In like expence) a pennye with a pound,
May chaunce at last to sitte aside and shrinke   10
His harbraind head without Dame Dainties' dore.
Hick, Hobbe, and Dick, with clouts upon their knee,
Have many times more goonhole grotes in store
And change of crownes more quicke at cal then he,
Which let their lease and take their rent before.
For he that rappes a royall on his cappe,
Before he put one penny in his pursse,

Had neede turne quicke and broch a better tappe,
Or els his drinke may chance go downe the wursse.
I not denie but some men have good hap,   20
To climbe alofte by scales of courtly grace,
And winne the world with liberalitye:
Yet he that yerks old angells out apace,
And hath no newe to purchase dignitye,
When orders fall, may chaunce to lacke his grace.
For haggard hawkes mislike an emptie hand:
So stiffely some sticke to the mercer's stall,
Till sutes of silke have swet out all their land.
So ofte thy neighbours banquet in thy hall,
Till Davie *Debet* in thy parler stand,   30
And bids the welcome to thine owne decay.
I like a Lion's lookes not worth a leeke
When every Foxe beguiles him of his praye:
What sauce but sorrow serveth him a weeke,
Which all his cates consumeth in one daye?
First use thy stomacke to a stand of ale,
Before thy Malmesey come in Marchantes' bookes,
And rather were (for shifte) thy shirte of male,
Than teare thy silken sleves with teynter hokes,
Put feathers in thy pillowes great and small,   40
Let them be princkt with plumes, that gape for plummes,
Heape up bothe golde and silver safe in hooches,
Catche, snatche, and scratche for scrapings and for crommes
Before thou decke thy hatte (on high) with brooches.
Lette first thyne one hand hold faste all that commes,
Before that other learne his letting flie:
Remember still that soft fire makes sweet malte,
No haste but good (who meanes to multiplye:)
Bought witte is deare, and drest with sower salte,
Repentaunce commes to late, and then saye I,   50
Who spares the first and keepes the last unspent,
Shall finde that sparing yeeldes a goodly rent.

A HANDEFULL OF PLEASANT DELITES

A proper Song, Intituled: Fain wold I have a pretie thing to
give unto my Ladie
To the tune of Lustie Gallant

Fain would I have a pretie thing,
  To give unto my Ladie:
I name no thing, nor I meane no thing,
  But as pretie a thing as may bee.

Twentie jorneyes would I make,
  And twentie waies would hie me,
To make adventure for her sake,
  To set some matter by me: But faine, etc.

Some do long for pretie knackes,
  And some for straunge devices: 10
God send me that my Ladie lackes,
  I care not what the price is, Thus faine, etc.

Some goe here, and some go there,
  Wheare gases be not geason:
And I goe gaping everywhere,
  But still come out of season. Yet faine, etc.

147

I walke the towne, and tread the streete,
  In every corner seeking:
The pretie thinge I cannot meete,
  That's for my Ladies liking. Faine, etc.   20

The Mercers pull me going by,
  The Silkie wives say, 'What lacke ye?'
'The thing you have not,' then say I,
  'Ye foolish fooles, go packe ye.' But fain, etc.

It is not all the Silke in Cheape,
  Nor all the golden treasure:
Nor twentie Bushels on a heape,
  Can do my Ladie pleasure. But faine, etc.

The Gravers of the golden showes,
  With Juelles do beset me,   30
The Shemsters in the shoppes that sowes,
  They do nothing but let me: But faine, etc.

But were it in the wit of man,
  By any meanes to make it,
I could for Money buy it than,
  And say, 'Faire Lady, take it.' Thus, fain, etc.

O Lady, what a lucke is this,
  That my good willing misseth:
To finde what pretie thing it is,
  That my good Lady wisheth.   40

Thus fain wold I have had this preti thing
  To give unto my Ladie:
I said no harme, nor I ment no harme,
  But as pretie a thing as may be.

The Lover compareth himself to the painful Falconer
To the tune, I loved her over wel

The soaring hawk from fist that flies,
    Her Falconer doth constraine
Sometime to range the ground unknown,
    To find her out againe:
And if by sight or sound of bell,
    His falcon he may see:
'Wo, ho!' he cries, with cheerful voice,
    The gladdest man is he.

By Lure then, in finest sort,
    He seekes to bring her in: 10
But if that she ful gorged be,
    He cannot so her win:
Although her becks and bending eies,
    She manie proffers makes:
'Wo ho ho!' he cries, awaie she flies,
    And so her leave she takes.

This wofull man with wearie limmes,
    Runnes wandring round about:
At length by noise of chattering Pies,
    His hawke againe found out,   20
His heart was glad his eies had seen
    His falcon swift of flight:
'Wo ho ho!' he cries, she emptie gorgde,
    Upon his Lure doth light.

How glad was then the falconer there,
    No pen nor tongue can tel:
He swam in blisse that lately felt
    Like paines of cruel hel.
His hand somtime upon her train,

Somtime upon her brest: 30
'Wo ho ho!' he cries with chearfull voice,
 His heart was now at rest.

My deer, likewise, beholde thy love,
 What paines he doth indure:
And now at length let pitie move,
 To stoup unto his Lure.
A hood of silk, and silver belles,
 New gifts I promise thee:
'Wo ho ho!' I crie; 'I come,' then saie,
 Make me as glad as hee! 40

THE PARADYSE OF DAYNTY
DEVISES

Donec eris Felix multos numerabis amicos,
Nullus ad amissas ibit amicus opes

Even as the Raven, the Crowe, and greedie Kite
Doe swarming flocke, where carren corpes doth fall:
And tiring teare with beake and talentes might,
Both skin and fleshe to gorge their guttes withall,
And never cease, but gather moe to moe,
Doe all to pull the carkase too and froe,
Till bared bones at last they leave behinde,
And seeke elsewhere, some fatter foode to finde.

Even so I see, where wealth doth waxe at will,
And Golde doth growe to heapes of great encrease: 10
There frendes resort, and profering frendship still,
Full thicke they throng, with never-ceasing prease,
And slilie make a shew of true intent,
When nought but guile, and inwarde hate is ment:
For when mischaunce shall chaunge such wealth to want,
They packe them thence, to place of ritcher haunt.

151

What watche, what wo, what want, what wracke
Is due to those that toyle the Seas?
Life ledd with losse, of paines no lacke,
In stormes to winne muche restlesse ease.
A bedlesse borde, in seas unrest,
Maie happ to hym that chaunseth best.

How sundrie sounds with lead and line,
Unto the depe, the shipman throwes:
'No foote to spare,' he cries oft tyme,
'No nere,' when 'How'? the master blowes.   10
If Neptune frown, all be undoen,
Straitwaie the shipp the wrack hath won.

These daungers greate doe oft befall
On those that shere upon the sande:
Judge of their lives, the best who shall,
How vile it is, fewe understande.
Alacke! who then maie judge their game?
Not thei, whiche have not felt the same.

But thei that fall in stormes and winde,
And daies and yeres have spent therein: 20
Suche well may judge, since profe thei find
In rage, no rest, till calme begin.
No more then those, that love doe faine,
Give judgement of true lovers' paine.

The Judgement of Desire

The lively Larke did stretche her wyng,
The messenger of mornyng bright:

And with her cherefull voyce did syng,
The daies approche, dischargyng night.
When that Aurora, blushyng redd,
Discride the gilt of Thetis' bedd:
Laradon tan tan, Tedriton teight.

I went abroad to take the aire,
And in the meadds I mett a knight,
Clad in carnation colour faire,   10
I did salute the youthfull wight.
Of hym I did his name enquire,
He sight and saied, 'I am Desire,
Laradon tan tan, Tedriton teight.'

Desire I did desire to staie,
Awhile with hym I craved talke:
The courteous wight saied me no naie,
But hande in hande with me did walke.
Then in desire I askte againe,
What thing did please, and what did pain,   20
Laradon, tan, tan, Tedriton teight.

He smild and thus he answered than,
'Desire can have no greater paine:
Then for to see another man,
The thyng desired to obtaine;
No joye no greater to then this,
Then to injoye what others misse,
Laridon, tan, tan, Tedriton teight.'

Bethinking hymself of his ende

When I beholde the baier, my laste and postyng horsse,
That bare shall to the grave, my vile and carren corsse,

Then saie I, 'Seely wretche, why doest thou put thy truste
In thyngs erthe made of claye, that sone will tourne to duste?

'Doest thou not see the young, the hardie and the faire,
That now are paste and gone, as though thei never were?
Doest thou not see thyself drawe hourly to thy laste,
As shaft whiche that is shotte at birds that flieth faste?

'Doest thou not see how death through smiteth with his launce,
Some by warre, some by plague, and some with worldlie
                                chaunce?   10
What thyng is there on yearth, for pleasure that was made,
But goeth more swifte awaie then doeth the Sommer shade?

'Loe here the Sommer floure, that sprong this other daie,
But Winter weareth as faste, and bloweth cleane awaie:
Even so shalt thou consume, from youth to lothsome age,
For death he doeth not spare the prince more then the page.

'Thy house shall be of claie, a clotte under thy hedde,
Untill the latter daie, the grave shall be thy bedde:
Untill the blowyng trumpe doeth saie to all and some,
"Rise up out of your grave, for now the Judge is come."'   20

EDMUND SPENSER

The Shepheardes Calender. Aegloga decima: October

PIERCE: *Cuddie*, for shame, hold up thy heavye head,
        And let us cast with what delight to chace
        And weary thys long, lingring *Phoebus'* race.
        Whilome thou wont the shepheards' laddes to leade,
        In rymes, in ridles, and in bydding base:
        Now they in thee, and thou in sleepe art dead.

CUDDYE: *Piers*, I have pyped erst so long with payne,
        That all mine oten reedes bene rent and wore:
        And my poore Muse hath spent her spared store,
        Yet little good hath got, and much lesse gayne.   10
        Such pleasaunce makes the Grashopper so poore,
        And ligge so layd, when Winter doth her straine.

        The dapper ditties that I wont devise,
        To feede youthes fancie, and the flocking fry,
        Delighten much: what I the bett forthy?
        They han the pleasure, I a sclender prise.
        I beate the bush, the byrds to them doe flye:
        What good thereof to Cuddie can arise?

PIRES: *Cuddie*, the prayse is better then the price,
        The glory eke much greater then the gayne: 20

O what an honor is it, to restraine
The lust of lawlesse youth with good advice,
Or pricke them forth with pleasaunce of thy vaine,
Whereto thou list their trayned willes entice.

Soone as thou gynst to sette thy notes in frame,
O how the rurall routes to thee doe cleave!
Seemeth thou dost their soule of sence bereave,
All as the shepheard that did fetch his dame
From *Plutoes* balefull bowre withouten leave:
His musick's might the hellish hound did tame. 30

CUDDIE: So praysen babes the Peacock's spotted traine,
And wondren at bright *Argus'* blazing eye:
But who rewards him ere the more forthy,
Or feedes him once the fuller by a graine?
Sike prayse is smoke that sheddeth in the skye;
Sike words bene wynd, and wasten soone in vayne.

PIERS: Abandon then the base and viler clowne;
Lyft up thyselfe out of the lowly dust,
And sing of bloody Mars, of wars, of giusts,
Turne thee to those that weld the awful crowne, 40
To doubted Knights, whose woundlesse armour rusts,
And helmes unbruzed wexen dayly browne.

There may thy Muse display her fluttryng wing,
And stretch herselfe at large from East to West:
Whither thou list in fayre *Elisa* rest,
Or if thee please in bigger notes to sing,
Advaunce the worthy whome shee loveth best,
That first the white beare to the stake did bring.

And when the stubborne stroke of stronger stounds
Has somewhat slackt the tenor of thy string, 50

Of love and lustihead tho mayst thou sing,
And carrol lowde, and leade the Myller's rownde;
All were *Elisa* one of thilke same ring,
So mought our *Cuddie's* name to Heaven sownde.

CUDDYE: Indeede, the Romish *Tityrus*, I heare,
Through his *Mecoenas*, left his oaten reede,
Whereon he earst had taught his flocks to feede,
And laboured lands to yield the timely eare,
And eft did sing of warres and deadly drede,
So as the Heavens did quake his verse to here.   60

But, ah, *Mecoenas* is yclad in claye,
And great *Augustus* long ygoe is dead,
And all the worthies liggen wrapt in leade,
That matter made for Poets on to play:
For ever who in derring doe were dreade,
The loftie verse of hem was loved aye.

But after vertue gan for age to stoupe,
And mighty manhode brought a bedde of ease,
The vaunting Poets found nought worth a pease,
To put in preace emong the learned troupe;   70
Tho gan the streames of flowing wittes to cease,
And sonnebright honour pend in shamefull coupe.

And if that any buddes of Poesie
Yet of the old stocke gan to shoote agayne,
Or it men's follies mote be forst to fayne,
And rolle with rest in rymes of rybaudrye,
Or as it sprong, it wither must agayne:
Tom Piper makes us better melodie.

PIERS: O pierlesse Poesye, where is then thy place?
If nor in Prince's pallace thou doe sitt,   80

(And yet is Prince's pallace the most fitt),
Ne brest of baser birth doth thee embrace,
Then make thee winges of thine aspyring wit,
And, whence thou camst, flye backe to heaven apace.

CUDDIE: Ah, *Percy*, it is all to weake and wanne,
So high to sore, and make so large a flight,
Her peeced pyneons bene not so in plight,
For *Colin* fittes such famous flight to scanne:
He, were he not with love so ill bedight,
Would mount as high, and sing as soote as Swanne.   90

PIRES: Ah, fon! for love does teach him climbe so hie,
And lyftes him up out of the loathsome myre;
Such immortall mirrhor as he doth admire,
Would rayse one's mynd above the starry skie,
And cause a caytive corage to aspire,
For lofty love doth loath a lowly eye.

CUDDIE: All otherwise the state of Poet stands,
For lordly love is such a Tyranne fell,
That where he rules, all power he doth expell;
The vaunted verse a vacant head demaundes,   100
Ne wont with crabbed care the Muses dwell:
Unwisely weaves that takes two webbes in hand.

Whoever casts to compasse weightye prise,
And thinks to throwe out thondring words of threate,
Let powre in lavish cups and thriftie bitts of meate,
For *Bacchus'* fruite is frend to *Phoebus* wise;
And when with Wine the braine begins to sweate,
The nombers flowe as fast as spring doth ryse.

Thou kenst not, *Percie*, howe the ryme should rage:
O if my temples were distaind with wine,   110

And girt in girlonds of wild Yvie twine,
How I could reare the Muse on stately stage,
And teache her tread aloft in buskin fine,
With queint *Bellona* in her equipage.

But, ah, my corage cooles ere it be warme,
Forthy, content us in thys humble shade,
Where no such troublous tydes han us assayde;
Here we our slender pipes may safely charme.

PIRES: And when my Gotes shall han their bellies layd,
Cuddie shall have a Kidde to store his farme.   120

Cuddies Embleme
Agitante calescimus illo etc.

ABBREVIATIONS USED IN THE NOTES

A.V.   The Bible (Authorised Version).

B.C.P.   *The Book of Common Prayer.*

Brown   *English Lyrics of the 13th Century*, ed. Carleton Brown, 1932.

C.T.   *The Canterbury Tales* (refs. to F. N. Robinson, *The Complete Works of Geoffrey Chaucer*, 1933; revised 1957).

E.L.   Everyman's Library.

Muir   *Collected Poems of Sir Thomas Wyatt*, ed. Kenneth Muir and Patricia Thomson, 1969.

O.D.E.P.   *The Oxford Dictionary of English Proverbs*, 2nd edn., 1948.

O.E.D.   *The Oxford English Dictionary.*

Stevens   John Stevens, *Music and Poetry in the Early Tudor Court*, 1961.

T. & C.   *Troilus and Criseyde* (refs. to Robinson edn.).

Tilley   *A Dictionary of Proverbs in England in the 16th and 17th Centuries*, ed. M. P. Tilley, Michigan, 1950.

COMMENTARY

JOHN LYDGATE

(c. 1370–c. 1450)

LIFE

Born of humble parents near Newmarket, Lydgate showed enough intellectual promise to attract the notice of the authorities at the Benedictine Abbey at near-by Bury St Edmunds, for in about 1385, he entered the monastery as a novice. With the Abbey 'the Monk of Bury' was to be associated all his life, though like others, he spent much time 'out of his cloystre'. It was probably through his connection with this important ecclesiastical and cultural centre that Lydgate came to the attention of influential patrons, though he may have met others at the home of Thomas Chaucer, the poet's son, whose circle included aristocratic humanists such as Humphrey, Duke of Gloucester. (Possibly Lydgate, like Hoccleve, knew Chaucer himself, whose poetic superiority he often acknowledges: '. . . in our tunge was nevere noon hym like.')

Lydgate spent part of his novitiate as an Oxford student; ordained priest in 1397, he subsequently turned verse composition into a minor industry, continuing throughout life to produce poems to suit various occasions and honour various commissions, including two from the Prince of Wales, later Henry V: *The Life of Our Lady* (1409–11) and *The Troy Book* (1412–20). From 1423–34 Lydgate was Prior of Hatfield Broad Oak, Essex, though for much of the period he was with the court of the young Henry VI, in Paris, London and Windsor. During these years he wrote much official 'formal' verse, like his lines on the approaching marriage of Duke Humphrey in 1422, a *roundel* and a *ballade* for Henry's coronation in 1429, stanzas for his entry into Paris in 1431, as well as composing didactic, satiric and religious pieces, and devising 'mummings' and tableaux for public and private ceremonials. In about 1431 Humphrey commissioned Lydgate's monumental re-working of Boccaccio's *De Casibus Virorum Illustrium*, which the poet entitled *The Fall of Princes*; in 1439 he received a life-grant of ten marks a year.

The poet's latter years coincided with a decline in the tone of English political life, and saw her military fortunes at a low ebb; his writings often labour the horrors of civil unrest and the perils of ambition. Many former patrons died or suffered eclipse, though Lydgate won the favour of William de la Pole, Earl of Suffolk, despite being attached to Duke Humphrey's circle. He died in 1449–50, and was buried in the Abbey of Bury St Edmunds.

POETRY

Although his complete writings totalling over 140,000 lines, will always daunt all but the dedicated specialist, there is much accomplished and satisfying verse in a Lydgate rescued from forbidding-looking footnotes by formidably scholarly philologists. Lydgate's time may never come again, but at least we can pay him the compliment of re-appraisal.

Much of his work is prolix by today's standards. Even *The Troy Book*, his most finished and possibly greatest production, is admittedly long-winded, much of the narrative appearing excessively rambling and off-the-point; but we have to remember that Lydgate is not only telling the history of Troy, he is pointing a moral, that worldly fame is transient and warfare ugly; he is demonstrating his own ability to handle rhetoric, and command a wide range of facts. These varied aims are maintained in *The Siege of Thebes* into which he injected topical significance, particularly in his discussions of the nature of kingship and the ethics of war. *The Fall of Princes*, an immense *tour de force* of 36,365 lines, is a roll-call of the great names of history and their tragic fates, recited at 'the measured pace of a funeral march'; it has a somewhat cumbersome dignity and inexorable earnestness of intention, and is not to be hurried along or diverted.

Yet there are many less compendious works which deserve rescuing from library vaults: Lydgate's cheerful colloquial fable, *The Churl and the Bird*, remains extremely lively; many of the satires, if mild, are pointed and accurate: *Bycorne and Chichevache*, *The Order of Fools*, *A Ballade of Jak Hare* are among the best. A handful of poems on the stock theme of earthly transience, *That Now is Hay Some-tyme was Grase*, *Timor Mortis Conturbat Me*, and particularly *As a Mydsomer Rose*, are worthy to rank with the most memorable medieval expressions of this attitude.

It may be as well to repeat that Lydgate was neither deliberately perverse nor regrettably incompetent in matters of diction and metre. His decasyllabics usually conform to patterns which Chaucer's usage appears to sanction, and his 'aureate' terms can be seen as analogous to Milton's Latinisms in *Paradise Lost*, as devices adopted to extend and dignify the range of ordinary speech. Lydgate's floribund expressions and elaborate periphrases seem pretentious adornments today, but to men who felt their native language to be crudely inadequate for the tasks required of it, to deck it out in a borrowed costume was not affectation, but a step towards concealing its naked shame.

Originally entitled *A Complaynt of a Loveres Lyfe*, this courtly love-lament was probably composed early in Lydgate's poetic career, and is a piece of close Chaucerian imitation, depending on reminiscences of poems such as *The Boke of the Duchesse*, *The Parlement of Foules*, *The Compleynt unto Pity* and *Troilus and Criseyde*. The figure of the narrator, the spring weather suggestive of love's rejuvenating effect, the idealized artificial landscape of the park representing nature in its orderly harmonious aspect, all belong to the conventional legacy of *Le Roman de la Rose*, but Lydgate succeeds in uniting these commonplaces, and giving the final amalgam an unpretentious charm by taking unaffected pleasure in describing it.

*ll.*1–4. Compare *T. & C.* II. 50–55:

> In May, that moder is of monthes glade,
> That fresshe floures, blew and white and rede,
> Ben quike agayn, that wynter dede make,
> And ful of bawme is fletyng every mede;
> Whan Phebus doth his bryghte bemes sprede,
> Right in the white Bole. . . .

*l.*3. *Phebus:* Apollo, the sun-god.

*l.*4. *the Bole:* Taurus, or the Bull, one of the twelve signs of the Zodiac, through which the sun 'moved' in May.

*l.*5. *Lucifer:* the morning-star, which appears on the horizon towards dawn.

*l.*12. *to borowe:* 'as a pledge' or 'surety'.

*l.*13. *Daunger:* in the context of *amour courtois*, arbitrary disfavour, indifference or high-handedness towards the lover on the part of the lady (see C. S. Lewis *The Allegory of Love*, Appendix II).

*l.*18. *My sekenes:* Lydgate may have cast himself in the role of love-sick narrator through recollection of Chaucer's self-portrait in *The Boke of the Duchesse*. The pains and sufferings of unrequited love are a frequent and wearisome convention of the period.

*l.*28. *firy Tytan:* In Greek mythology, the Titans reigned as gods before the Olympians; the name was often used in later classical poetry to signify Hyperion or the sun.

*l.*34. *golde-borned:* 'burning golden', a typical Chaucerian epithet.

*l.*37. *berel:* beryl is a pale-green precious stone.

*l.*42. *grene stoon:* probably decorated with jewels like jasper, emerald, or beryl (cf. *The Parlement of Foules*, *l.*122: 'a park walled with grene stone').

*l.*52. *celured:* apparently coined by Lydgate from 'celure' a canopy. The image of a roof of boughs protecting flowers from the sun's rays is found in the classics and *Le Roman de la Rose*.

*l.*58. *Zepherus:* the West wind.

l.63. redy for to shake: 'ready for shaking down'.

ll.64–74. Lydgate's catalogue of trees, like Chaucer's in *The Parlement of Foules*, 176–182, and *The Knight's Tale* (*C.T.* I. 2920–3), follows a traditional rhetorical formula deriving from Latin literature.

l.64. Daphene: Daphne was changed into a laurel to save her from being raped by Apollo. (See Ovid's *Metamorphoses* I.)

l.66. The myrre also: myrrh, a gum resin from several trees of the *Commiphora* family, was used from ancient times for perfumes and incense.

l.70. Demophoune: In *The Legend of Good Women* VIII, Chaucer tells the story of the deception of Phyllis by Demophoön, son of Theseus, basing his account partly on Ovid's *Heroides* II, but not mentioning the tradition that she was changed into an almond-tree after her suicide. The filbert, or nut-tree, may have been introduced by Gower in his *Confessio Amantis*.

l.72. motele: parti-coloured garments, white and green here. A similar image (probably adopted from Lydgate) is used by Sackville, *Induction*, *l.*15.

ll.75–7. a litel welle: one of the stock ingredients of Love's garden (cf. *The Romaunt of the Rose*, *ll.*110–25).

l.82. The sute of trees: 'sute' means a set or series of similar objects.

28. THE LIFE OF OUR LADY

The fullest 'history' of the Virgin in English, Lydgate's offering at the extensive shrine of Marian literature covers only certain episodes in her life, and *The Life of Our Lady* is certainly not one of his best works. He chooses to lay stress on Mary's sublime, rather than human, qualities, his aim being to exalt her deity above mortal comprehension, but excessive adulation, with its literary accompaniment, aureation, stifles any interest. However, the dignity, awe and tenderness with which he approached his theme are clearly demonstrated in these pellucid stanzas from the Prologue, which are strong and majestic, without the ornate decoration which renders later parts of the work difficult to penetrate.

l.1. thoughtfull: in the sense of sorrowful meditation, troubled thought.

l.8. oppresse: used here in the literal sense of 'press down, crush'.

l.10. the sterre of the bright poole: this phrase would seem to indicate that Lydgate is referring to the North Star, but from what follows it must refer to Spica (see note on l.26).

l.19. 'If she ceases to look down and watch over us.'

l.21. 'So that the refuge of life may not be taken from us.'

ll.22–6. Pliades: the Pleiades or 'Seven Sisters', a group of stars found in the Northern hemisphere. *Boetes Arthour* (MS reads 'Botetes'): Arcturus, the brightest star known in England apart from Sirius, is the most prominent star in the constellation Boötes or 'the Wagoner'. *Iades:* the Hyades, a group of stars near the Pleiades, the chief member of which is Aldebaran. *Esperus:*

164

Hesper, the evening star (in fact, the planet Venus). *Spica:* the most prominent star of the constellation Virgo, the Virgin. The name means 'ear of wheat', and in classical times, seen as being held in the Virgin's hand, symbolized fertility and harvest. Christian star-cataloguers identified the constellation with the Virgin Mary holding the Christ Child.

l.31. this of Jacob: one of the many titles of the Virgin Mary was 'the star out of Jacob' (cf. Numbers, xxiv. 17: 'there shall come a Star out of Jacob, and a Sceptre shall rise out of Israel').

l.33. the clyptyke lyne: the apparent path of the sun round the sky during the course of a year; Spica lies just below the Southern ecliptic.

l.35. the arke of our merydyne: the arc described by the line of the celestial meridian as it spans a place; so, here, 'in the area of sky above us'.

l.37. Aurora: the goddess of the dawn.

l.40. the bright somer's day: on a bright summer day.

l.45. oute of Jesse: Jesse was father of King David (1 Samuel xvi); St Joseph was 'of the house and lineage of David'. (Cf. Isaiah xi. 1: 'And there shall come forth a rod out of the stem of Jesse, and a branch shall grow out of his roots'.) Medieval art abounds in representations of the 'tree of Jesse', illustrating Christ's genealogy.

l.53. skales: was Lydgate thinking of the protection afforded by the overlapping plates of military scale-armour?

30. BEWARE OF DOUBLENESS
This poem also follows a medieval literary tradition, that of anti-feminist satire (for a full discussion, see Louis Solomon, *The Devil Take Her*, and F. E. Utley, *The Crooked Rib*); medieval authors alternated between abject veneration and absolute vilification of the female sex, and these twin attitudes form fixed poles for the arguments of many debate-poems. As a satirist, Lydgate rarely employs the 'spice of malignity' that makes satire great; he is sarcastic rather than ironic, and his essentially chivalrous temper and affability outweigh the gentle mockery. But the poem is a skilful handling of a standard theme, and the touches of wit go beyond anything mere convention demanded.

l.26. Phebus: the sun.

ll.49–54. Many of the aphorisms in this stanza have a proverbial sound, but none of them appears in exactly Lydgate's form in the standard collections. The closest seems to be 'He holds a wet eel by the tail', which is found in Erasmus's *Adagia*, Heywood's *Proverbs* (1546) etc.

l.49. the wynde restreyne: cf. Wyatt 'Whoso list to hounte', (p. 105, *l.*8): 'Sins in a nett I seke to hold the wynde'.

l.61. 'Their navigation is so fortunate, to direct their course with the aid of a compass-needle and magnet ("loadstone") . . .'

*l.*63. *Salamon:* Solomon was celebrated for his references to feminine guile; (see Proverbs, ii. 16–19, v. 3–10, vi. 24–6, vii. 6–27). Lydgate says ironically that even Solomon was not wise enough to detect woman's deceit!

*ll.*73–80. *So wel fortuned:* Alludes to a dice game called Hazard, an older form of 'Craps', played with two dice. A player calls a 'main', a number between five and nine which, if thrown, wins him the game; if he throws double-one or deuce-ace ('ambes-ase'), he loses. There are also other winning and losing combinations. If he neither wins nor loses outright, the number he throws becomes his 'chance' (*l.*73), and he continues to play until he throws his 'chance', which means a win, or his original 'main' which loses. The best main to call is seven, which can be thrown in six different ways; eleven ('sis and synke') was an approved throw to win a 'main' of seven. (Cf. *Man of Lawe's Prologue, C.T.* II. *l.*124; *The Pardoner's Tale, C.T.* VI. *l.*653). Lydgate's meaning seems to be: 'Women's luck in throwing the dice is so good that they always make a winning score, giving short shrift to double-one, though learned men are always saying that "doubleness" is the ruling principle of their lives!'

*l.*81. *Sampson:* Samson's betrayal to the Philistines by his wife Delilah (Judges xiv–xvi) was a stock example of female treachery for medieval authors (cf. *Sir Gawain and the Grene Knight, ll.*2417–8).

*l.*85. *Rosamounde:* 'Fair Rosamond', Rosamond Clifford (*d.* 1176?) was the celebrated mistress to Henry II; she hardly seems an *exemplum* of female deceit, since her status was publicly acknowledged; perhaps Lydgate is thinking of her implied treachery to Queen Eleanor (who, according to legend, poisoned Rosamond in her bower at Woodstock!).

*l.*86. *Cleopatris:* Again, not an obvious choice; Chaucer praises Cleopatra's constancy in *The Legend of Good Women*, and Lydgate himself in *Of Her that Hath All Virtues* refers to 'Cleopatres abyding stabulnesse' (*l.*19). He may be alluding here to her conduct at the battle of Actium.

*l.*89. *Sengle thing:* cf. the proverb 'One is no number' (Tilley O 54).

*l.*90. *oo folde:* again, this has a proverbial tone, but I have been unable to trace it further. (But cf. 'One swallow does not make a summer'.) In this stanza Lydgate faintly foreshadows Donne's method of proof by logical paradox.

*l.*97. Lydgate's gently ironic yet diffident attitude here resembles that of Chaucer's clerk in *C.T.*

*l.*103. *sitte:* set.

33. THE DANCE OF DEATH

The Dance of Death, or *The Dance Macabre*, is Lydgate's version (as he himself said, 'not word by word, but following the substance') of an anonymous French original, probably written to accompany a set of frescoes painted on the walls of the cemetery of the Église des Innocents at Paris in 1424–5, and doubtless seen by the poet when he was in the city between 1426 and 1429. The earliest of these pictorial renderings of Death leading the various classes of medieval society in dance, appears to date from early fourteenth-century Switzerland and Germany; the cult became widespread in the fifteenth century, and St Paul's Churchyard boasted a celebrated set of paintings by about 1430. (Was Lydgate's translation intended for St Paul's?) Lydgate expands his original slightly, but his main contribution is to retain the powerful tensions, dramatic variety and lively characterization of the French version. The chilling impact of the theme on Lydgate's audience has been considerably weakened for modern readers, but Ingmar Bergmann made use of the same visual image to great effect in his film, *The Seventh Seal*. (On the whole 'death-cult' of the fifteenth century, see Huizinga, *The Waning of the Middle Ages*.)

l.3. clariouns: shrill narrow trumpets, much used for signalling in war.

ll.9–10. 'On very many occasions I have been appointed to carry out important undertakings . . .' (Note the self-congratulatory tone of the Baron's lines.)

l.11. my thanke also devised: 'acknowledgement was rendered me'.

ll.17–32. These two stanzas are not in the French, and appear to be Lydgate's own.

l.22. holde an honde: command, control (cf. 'keep on a string').

l.31. countirfeet fresshnesse: a reference to make-up? Or perhaps 'counterfeit' because of the illusion that beauty will endure for ever.

l.36. worldly goodes, and goodes of nature: the medieval Christian believed that man was endowed with gifts of nature: strength and beauty; of fortune: goods and friends; of grace: knowledge and good deeds (cf. A. C. Cawley's edition of *Everyman*, Manchester, 1961: Everyman first loses his gifts of fortune, then those of nature, and is left with only his knowledge (of God) and his good deeds (cf. line 48 of the present poem).

l.39. brought to lure: a hawk was trained to fly to the lure after it had killed; the lure was a dummy made from leather and feathers to resemble a bird. This image is often used in Middle English verse to suggest enticement or capture.

l.40. No wight is sure: many proverbs of the period allude to this theme, a stock commonplace of the *De Contemptu Mundi* type.

l.43. a simple ferye: a '*feria*', a holiday not associated with a feast day of the Church.

l.52. unkouthe devise: Hammond suggests 'to your special desire'; the word might convey that the Squire fought in tournaments under an unknown heraldic blazon ('device'), so that he went unrecognized, a common occurrence in the pages of Malory and elsewhere in romance.

*l.*57. *in his lace:* in his snare or net.

*l.*62. *every day is prime:* 'every day is a new start'. Prime was the first hour of the day, usually 6 a.m., when worshippers celebrated 'Prime'.

*l.*70. *Your eir:* it would be a nice touch if Lydgate were alluding here to the Abbot's having a son, and indeed the words 'of age' might support this interpretation, but 'eir' can mean simply 'successor'.

*l.*73. *envie:* Lydgate uses this word here in its more modern sense; in Old French it means 'desire'.

*l.*80. *hem avise:* 'reflect' (cf. French *s'aviser*).

*ll.*81–96. These stanzas also appear to be Lydgate's own addition.

*l.*82. *mantels furred:* fur was commonly worn in medieval England; the rich wore ermines, the poor sheepskin. Chaucer's Monk in the Prologue wears a gown trimmed with grey fur; excessive opulence of dress among ecclesiastics was frequently censured by the authorities, and it formed part of John Wycliffe's 'platform' against the clergy.

*l.*83. *wymple:* a woman's head-covering of linen or silk, which enveloped the head, sides of the face, chin and cheeks.

*l.*83. *passinge of greet:* of passing great.

*ll.*91–2. *my notes out to twyne:* 'turn a song'. Cf. Chaucer's Prioress (*C.T.* I. *ll.*122–3):

> Ful weel she soong the service dyvyne,
> Entuned in hir nose full semely.

F. N. Robinson's note is applicable here, too: 'This mode of nasal intonation is traditional with the recitative portions of the Church service'; however, the fact that Lydgate mentions this along with other habits of which he clearly disapproves, suggests that his nun draws undue attention to herself by her vocal feats. The comparison with Chaucer's Prioress is worth careful study; Lydgate may have had his predecessor's portrayal in mind.

*l.*93. *chekes round vernysshed:* the Abbess's 'embellished' complexion suggests that she uses cosmetics, a habit condemned frequently, even in the laity.

*l.*94. *Ungirt:* Hammond suggests this refers to the Abbess's unchastity; nuns were sometimes admonished for not wearing the 'cingula' or girdle; 'at the large' implies 'freely, where I pleased', but the whole phrase may simply imply that the Abbess has never submitted herself truly to the disciplines of her order.

*l.*96. *Who hath no chippe:* this has a definite proverbial tone, but it appears in none of the major collections.

THOMAS HOCCLEVE

(1368–c. 1450)

LIFE

Hoccleve (or Occleve), was destined originally for Holy Orders, and thus probably educated at a monastery school, but ultimately he served for nearly thirty-five years as a Clerk in the Privy Seal Office in the Palace of Westminster. He obtained the post as a stop-gap till a suitable benefice was found, but he remained a civil servant for life, frequently lamenting in his verse the strain of his clerical duties and the irregularity with which his annuity of ten marks a year (granted in 1399 by Henry IV) was paid to him. Possibly a friend and admirer of Chaucer, he may well have been at the death-bed of his poetic mentor in 1400; his poems are full of grateful remembrances of 'the honour of englyssh tonge':

> Mi dere maistir–god his soule quyte!–
> And fadir, Chaucer, fayn wolde han me taght;
> But I was dul, and lerned lite or naght

Despite his onerous profession, Hoccleve's life as a young bachelor clerk in London seems to have been enjoyable enough, but extravagance (and possibly conviviality) took their traditional revenge; debts, ill-health and marriage in about 1410 seem to have persuaded Hoccleve to renounce his spendthrift habits; in 1412 comes his longest and most didactic work, *De Regimine Principium*, or *The Regement of Princes*, addressed to Henry, Prince of Wales, later Henry V.

In 1416 the poet suffered some kind of nervous breakdown, possibly the result of anxiety and over-work, and a long illness was followed by a period of temporary insanity and amnesia; Hoccleve discusses his symptoms and recovery in his moving *Complaint* of 1421–2. During this time he must have been absent from his official duties, and in 1424 he retired from the Privy Seal Office, being well provided for with the grant of sustenance for life in the Priory of Southwick in Hampshire, where it must be presumed he died, at some time before 1450.

POETRY

Hoccleve is possibly the most seriously underrated poet in this book, and it is good to feel that he, like Lydgate, is currently receiving a well-justified re-appraisal. Temperamentally, he is perhaps closer to Chaucer than any other disciple, reproducing that blend of colloquial and educated (though not elaborated) diction which follows the best traditions of his 'maistir'. His finest poetry is personal: his *Complaint* describing the effects of his spell of insanity; the *Dialogue with a Friend; La Male Regle*, an assured piece of tragi-comic self-deprecation; his Dialogue with the Beggar which introduces *The Regement of Princes*, a vigorous performance of nearly 2,000 lines, which maintain the reader's interest by counterpointing the beggar's cheerful resignation and penitence with Hoccleve's depression, and impatience at the frustrations and anxieties of life. The piety and garrulity of the old man are balanced by the poet's gratitude and affection, and the whole is characterized by the mellow, urbane, 'social' tone of much of Chaucer's work. Above all, Hoccleve matches an individual and intriguing personality with a simple, unemphatic style which follows the cadences and idioms of genuine speech, leaving the impression of a relaxed and accomplished creator working unobtrusively within his accepted limits.

37. LA MALE REGLE DE T. HOCCLEVE

This *apologia* is one of the earliest self-portraits in our literature, and a pleasing example of fifteenth-century 'polite' writing at its most colloquial and unembellished. Certainly the picture of the poet himself as a would-be sower of wild oats, self-deprecating, hopefully trying to cut a figure in Bohemian society, is delicately yet humorously drawn, and the usual request for money that lies behind the poem is never allowed to disturb the rueful, well-mannered, intensely personal tone of the verse.

l.1. *fressh repeir:* the lively visits.
l.2. *Venus' femel lusty children dere:* children: subjects or followers (cf. *The Squire's Tale, C.T.,* V. *l*.272: 'lusty Venus children dere').
l.7. *Poules heed:* the Paul's head, an inn. Stow (*The Survey of London,* E.L. edn., p. 324) mentions one of this name in Sermon Lane, near Blackfriars.
l.10. *wafres:* light crisp cakes or biscuits baked between wafer-irons, often served with wine. 'Wafereres' wait on the three rioters in *The Pardoner's Tale.*
l.11. *likerous:* usually 'lecherous', but here 'fond of delicious food, greedy for delicacies'.
l.13. *for the maistrie:* 'extremely, surpassing all others'.
l.21. 'I wasn't very good at that sort of thing, no doubt of that.'
l.27. *bagge:* money-bag or purse. Kurath and Kuhn in their *Middle English Dictionary* (1952–) cite Hoccleve, but offer no explanation of 'double wyse'; I would identify it here with the dialect meaning of 'bag' given in *The English Dialect Dictionary* (1898) and in Webster's *3rd New International*

Dictionary Vol. I (1961), which is 'belly'. Kurath and Kuhn do not admit this meaning, but it makes sense of Hoccleve's phrase.

*l.*37. 'and yet my will was good, to be rid of my cowardly nature, if I could, for it was always imagining the weight of the blows I'd receive in exchange for my abuse, so that I never dared to stick my nose in.'

*l.*42. *Westmynstre yate:* traditional haunt of cooks and caterers. (Cf. *London Lickpenny, ll.*57–64 and notes.)

*l.*43. *taverneres:* cf. *London Lickpenny, l.*105 and note.

*l.*45. 'I never found fault with them in the course of buying', i.e. 'I never queried the bill'.

CHARLES, DUKE OF ORLEANS

(1394–1465)

LIFE

Charles d'Orleans was born in 1394, son of Louis, Duke of Orleans, whose assassination in 1407 left Charles the successor to one of the most important dukedoms in France. Nephew to the 'mad king' Charles VI of France, he first married Isabella, widow of Richard II of England, who died in 1409 at the age of twenty; in the following year Charles married Blanche, daughter of Bernard d'Armagnac, leader of the Orleans party against the Burgundians. At the Battle of Agincourt in October 1415, Charles, joint commander-in-chief of the French army, was captured on the field. (Shakespeare includes him as a character in *Henry V*.) There followed twenty-five years as a prisoner of the English, first at the court and then in various castles throughout the country; Charles learnt English in captivity, and at the time of his release in 1440 is said to have spoken it better than he did his native tongue; indeed, he had lived longer in England than in France. He also made a number of friendships with members of the English nobility, including the ill-fated William de la Pole, Earl of Suffolk, who was his guardian for some years.

On his return to France, Charles married a third time, Mary of Cleves's dowry helping to pay his ransom money, and maintained a cultivated court at Blois, to which François Villon appears to have attached himself briefly, and where an heir was born to Charles and Mary in 1462. He died on 4th January 1465.

POETRY

Charles's poems have sometimes been over-valued, standing out as they do from the ruck of bad fifteenth-century courtly love-verses for their relatively taut construction, and the occasional beauty or vitality of phrases like

> Be nyse, myn hert, as purse is of an ay (egg) or:
> Sett tyme or that the wynd apalle
> And clowdid be the mone aloft

which remind one of Wyatt's sudden departures from the conventional terminology of courtly love. Often in Charles's work there is the same sense of actuality and intensity, the same elliptical ironic note detected in Wyatt, and the use of French forms gives his pieces a shape notably lacking in his

English contemporaries. But we must not exaggerate Charles's good qualities: his verse still abounds in stylized clichés and attitudes, the relationship between lover and lady is rarely developed, and there is too much abstraction, and too little illustration in his compliments and complaints. Perhaps the most vivid and sprightly passages occur in the narrative links between his lyrics, where Charles is plainly under a debt to Chaucer's dream-vision poems and even *The Canterbury Tales*.

39. WHAN FRESSHE PHEBUS

One of the typical *ballades* found among Charles's English poems, this is a version of his French original, 'Le beau soleil le jour saint Valentin'. The tradition of the birds choosing their mates on 14th February, Saint Valentine's Day, is found all over medieval Europe, and occurs notably in Chaucer's *The Parlement of Foules*; cf. too, Elizabeth Brews' letter to John Paston, February 1477: 'And, Cosyn, uppon Fryday is Sent Volentynes Day, and every brydde chesyth hym a make.' Charles develops the pathos of his situation by contrasting the happiness of the mated birds with his own fate, deprived by death of a human lover. Such an antithesis is part of a deep-rooted literary tradition (see 'Foweles in the frith', Brown, No. 8), which Charles somewhat stiffly re-animates.

l.1. the day of Seynt Valentyne: 'on Saint Valentine's Day'.

l.2. whirlid up his golden chare: cf. the opening of the pseudo-Chaucerian *The Flower and the Leaf*:

> When that Phebus his chare of gold so hy
> Had whirled up the starry sky aloft

(Also cf. *The Squire's Tale, C.T.*, V. *ll.*435–6.) Phoebus Apollo drove the chariot of the sun.

l.4. slepid soft: 'slept quietly', a standard phrase.

l.8. noyous thought: 'wearisome, troubled thoughts'.

l.9. parten there bottyne: 'share out their booty'.

l.10. an oost of fowlis: cf. *The Parlement of Foules, ll.*309–11.

l.11. pletid ther latyne: 'pleaded in their own language'. 'Latin' (Old English 'laeden') basically means 'speech'.

l.21. 'It doesn't suit me at all.'

l.25. Als: as. (A Northern form; Charles probably began to learn English in the North.)

l.27. discomfort sole: this reading eliminates some difficulties. The French reads 'Seul me tendray de confort desgarny'; the MS has 'this comfort sole'. Hammond tried to make 'sole' mean 'without', Steele's amendment to 'discomfort' seems to me preferable. The sense is then: 'Whereas I prepare only discomfort for myself' or 'Whereas I prepare discomfort for my solitary self'.

173

Another *ballade*, built on the contrast between the lover's melancholy state of mind and that of the religious recluse, whose devotion to God costs him less anguish than the lover's devotion to his lady. The theme of painful absence is well explored in the literature of courtly love, and it is only Charles' animation and relative objectivity that render his version of this well-worn subject in any way unusual.

*l.*1. *sely:* a host of meanings are attached to this word, which has its roots in Old English 'sel' meaning 'luck, happiness'. In this context its connotations include holiness, innocence, blessedness, with 'fortunate' as the dominant sense.

*l.*11. *stonde in more myscheef:* 'I am in worse discomfort'.

*l.*12. *Y of helthe am bare:* sickness and languor were inevitable accompaniments of the onset of romantic love in the later Middle Ages, and the effects of unrequited passion were often described in terms of illness and disease.

*ll.*17-20. The women described here in general terms conform very much to the medieval ideals of feminine beauty (see D. S. Brewer, *Modern Language Review* 50 (1955), pp. 257-69).

*l.*21. 'My lady would put all these in the shade if she were here.'

*l.*23. *nam:* I have adopted Steele's suggested emendation of the MS 'nare'; 'nam' is a common contraction for 'I am not'.

*ll.*25-7. These lines show the sparing use of anaphora, the repetition of a certain word or phrase.

*l.*25. *them which that raft me hir presence!:* often in Provençal troubadour lyric, figures who cause discord between lovers are tale-bearers or slanderers whose sharp eyes and gossiping tongues prevent lovers from meeting or acknowledging each other. Such *'losengiers'* occur in the love poetry of Wyatt and even in Spenser's *Amoretti*.

*l.*26. *Wo worth the tyme to Y to hir resort!:* 'curse on the time till I return to her!'

41. MY GOSTLY FADIR

This sprightly (and thus rather untypical) poem is in *roundel* form, whose octosyllabic lines and repetitions give it a youthful character not found in the more stately *ballade*. Setting a love poem in the context of a religious confession is not original, but the wit and charm of this parody are neatly sustained, and offer a foretaste of pieces like 'Kyrie so Kyrie' and *Phyllyp Sparowe*. The best part of the joke is that the chief requirement of the Church before absolving the sinner was that the sin should be atoned for; in the case of a theft, by the restitution of the stolen object.

*l.*5. *out avisynes:* 'without pre-meditation'. (In Catholic theology, this would reduce the gravity of the crime.)

l.11. *that to God:* I have adopted Steele's suggestion that the word 'to' be inserted into the MS reading 'that God'.

l.12. 'And otherwise if I can't I shall ask forgiveness' – (but of the girl, not God!).

42. LONDON LICKPENNY

This lively, anonymous poem, whose title might be rendered 'London lap-up-the-pennies', is an early handling of a comic theme dear to later dramatists, that of the unwary countryman at the mercy of wily townsfolk. This bustling and graphic impression of fifteenth-century London life was attributed to Lydgate by John Stow in his *Survey of London* (E.L. edn. p. 195; see also pp. 178–9); satires against the legal profession are found widely distributed through medieval literature. I have ventured to alter the order of stanzas as printed by Miss Hammond; see note to *l*.65.

l.3. *to Westminstar ward:* ('towards Westminster'), then as now, a separate city from London. The countryman makes his way to Westminster Hall, where three courts of law were to be found: the King's Bench, where trespasses against the King's peace were tried; the Court of Common Pleas ('Common Place') where civil disputes and private matters were heard; the Court of Chancery which concerned itself with matters of revenue, and was presided over by the Lord Chancellor and the Master of the Rolls. (See Stow, E.L. edn., p. 416.)

l.7. *faynt:* 'weak', i.e. unable to support him.

l.20. '*Richard*' etc.: presumably the names of the participants in the next action to come before the court.

l.23. *stronge:* 'gross, flagrantly guilty'.

l.26. *one with a sylken houde:* only Sergeants-at-Law (who wore silken hoods) could plead in the Court of Common Pleas.

l.29. *seyd:* 'told, recited'.

l.31. *a momme of his mouthe:* there is an interestingly close parallel to this passage in *Piers Plowman* 'A' text (ed. Kane) *ll*.84–9:

> There hovide an hundrit in howis of silk,
> Seriauntis it semide that servide at the barre;
> Pleten for penis and poundide the lawe,
> Ac nought for love of oure lord unlose here lippes ones.
> Thou mightest betere mete myst on Malverne hilles
> Thanne gete a mom of here mouth til mony be shewid.

l.35. *many qui tollis:* I am grateful to Mr G. A. Usher for the suggestion that the speaker, remembering his 'Agnus Dei', here refers to the assembled attorneys as those 'who take away' their clients' legal problems.

l.42. *longe gowne of ray:* ray was a striped cloth, apparently much worn by the legal profession.

l.51. Flemings grete woon: 'a great crowd of Flemings'. Flemish traders were a familiar part of the London scene at this period; their presence contributed to the outbreak of the Peasants' Revolt in 1381. They were especially skilled at weaving cloth and grinding lenses.

ll.54–5. spectacles for to rede/of this gay gere?: not for reading, but to help the wearer to examine the 'gear' for sale. Spectacles had not been long in use; we know Lydgate wore them; Hoccleve tells us he was too vain to do so!

ll.57–9. Westminster gate: the traditional haunt of cooks (cf. *La Male Regle*, p. 37, *l.*57 and note). Their calls to passers-by are also mentioned in the Prologue of *Piers Plowman*.

l.58. highe prime: The end of the three-hour period starting at Prime (6 a.m.), hence 9 a.m., the time when the medieval worker took his first substantial meal of the day.

ll.65–121. Into London: the narrator's progress can now be traced in detail, though it presents certain problems. He leaves Westminster by the city gate, passes into London, presumably via the Strand and Fleet Street, entering the city through Ludgate, and so past St Paul's into Cheapside (*l.*73). It seems to me more plausible if he next strays into Cornhill, and I have therefore inserted after *l.*80 a stanza which the manuscripts introduce two stanzas later. (This not only seems to me to make a more credible itinerary, but also creates a better narrative sequence, whereby the taverner of *l.*105 is associated with the 'Pewtar potts' and 'mynstralsie of *ll.*99 and 103.) After his visit to Cornhill (*l.*81), the narrator passes down Candlewick (now Cannon) Street, into Eastcheap (*l.*97), wanders into Billingsgate (*l.*113) where he attempts to cross the river by ferry-boat, and then finally takes the road home to Kent by crossing London Bridge into Southwark.

ll.67–8. 'Hot pescods!': London Lickpenny is one of the earliest sources which records London street-cries. 'Pescods' are pea-pods. *'Chery in the ryse':* cherries sold still on the branch.

l.70. Pepper was very highly prized in the Middle Ages; saffron, a rare and expensive spice made from the stigmas of the mauve crocus, was used for medicinal and culinary purposes, and as a dye. It was grown extensively at Saffron Walden in Essex, and the name is also preserved in Saffron Hill, London, E.C.1.

l.71. grayns: Grains of Paradise or Guinea grains, the seeds of a West African plant, used as a drug and a spice, especially to flavour wine. *flowre of rise:* rice-flour, or ground-rice.

l.75. lawne: a fine linen cloth like cambric.

l.76. umple: a fine gauze cloth (cf. lawn).

ll.77–8. I could no skyle: 'I had no knowledge of such things, and indeed, wasn't used to dealing with them'.

l.79. a hewre, my hed to hele: 'a cap to cover my head'. (Since his own hat has been stolen.)

l.82. Stow refers to 'Fripperiers or Upholders, that sold old apparel and household stuff', living in the Cornhill region in the reign of Henry VI (1422–61) (E.L. edn., p. 178).

l.89. London Stone: a celebrated landmark, possibly the oldest relic in London, this stone may have been the point from which the Romans measured distances out of the city. Formerly on the South side of Cannon Street, it was moved in 1798 to the wall of St Swithin's Church, where it survived the London blitz, though the church was destroyed. The stone is now set in the wall of the Bank of China, which occupies the site.

l.91. Stow mentions the rich drapers of Candlewick Street, and the Eastcheap meat market (*l.98*).

l.92. 'They started to offer me fabulous bargains in cloth.'

l.94. '*Risshes faire and grene*': rushes were used as floor coverings.

l.100. sawtry: an ancient and medieval instrument, consisting of a shallow box with ten to twelve strings stretched across it, played by plucking with the fingers or a plectrum.

l.101. '*Ye, by cokke*': a common oath, a corruption of 'By God!'

l.102. Jenken and Julian: obscure. St Julian was the patron saint of hospitality, but I have been unable to trace the allusion any further.

ll.107–8. 'I wouldn't mind, but a penny will only go so far.'

l.114. '*Wagge, wagge, gow hens!*': possibly a traditional call for a ferry-boat, like the Elizabethan 'Eastward Ho!' 'Wagge' means to stir or move, and in this context, it may have the force of the modern military command, 'Move!'

l.118. 'Do you think I'll make you my good deed for the day?' i.e. by ferrying you free as an act of religious devotion. 'almsdede' is an act of Christian charity.

ANONYMOUS LYRICS

One of the great unqualified glories of fifteenth-century English poetry is its wealth of anonymous lyrics, religious and secular: at one extreme are painstakingly transcribed, formal, 'adorned style' pieces; at the other, ribald or convivial scraps jotted down on margins and fly-leaves. Between, lies a wide variety of poems. In the religious area, devotional lyrics still predominate, but pride of place must be given to the rise of the carol, a lyric form probably derived from the Old French *carole* or round dance, where a choric burden alternates regularly with uniform stanzas suitable for a soloist. Carols did not necessarily have a connection with Christmas (cf. *The Corpus Christi Carol*, p. 53) though they were principally associated with times of celebration. At a time when too many of the standard types of religious lyric were becoming over-formalized, many carols marked the resurgence of a freer vernacular impulse, though the simpler, more tender kinds of religious effusion had points of contact with the mood and style of popular ballads (see pp. 52–3).

Inevitably many secular lyrics from the period have perished, but enough survive to indicate that the form was healthy, where it managed to escape the ossifying hand of aureation. Embellished love-complaints and eulogies there are in plenty, but their frigid idealism is off-set by the utterance of more earthy (though no less 'unrealistic') sexual aspirations. Lyrics embodying *sententiae* and gnomic wisdom abound, alongside drinking-songs, hymns to the Virgin, satires on women, mock-Valentines, erotic riddles, political ballads, all testifying to the strength and variety of late medieval lyric.

46. ADAM LAY I-BOWNDYN

The immediate simplicity, freshness and joy of this beautiful lyric should not blind us to the fact that it discusses a profound theological paradox, sometimes referred to as 'the Fortunate Fall', which teaches that the original sin for which Adam and Eve were punished nonetheless gave God an opportunity to reveal his infinite love for mankind by sending Christ to die on the cross, and so release man from Satan's bondage. The 'divine destiny of love' (Speirs) absolves the crime and remits the punishment, and the poet exults that Adam's 'felix culpa' made it necessary for Mary to conceive Christ and so become Queen of Heaven. (For a further discussion, see Herbert Weisinger, *Tragedy and the Paradox of the Fortunate Fall.*)

This poem is taken from the most important single manuscript collection of fifteenth-century lyrics: Sloane MS 2593, which contains English and Latin songs, carols, and ballads and is almost certainly from Lydgate's Abbey of Bury Saint Edmunds. Many of the poems, like this lyric, owe a debt to popular traditions of verse-making.

l.1. Adam: standing here for mankind subject to Satan's bondage through sin, and as a result to death and damnation.

l.2. Fowre thowsand wynter: there is an old tradition that creation took place in the year 4004 B.C. The stress on 'wynter' accentuates the desolation of Adam's situation until Christ released him from his bonds.

l.3. And al was for an appil: the note of incredulity at the seeming disproportion between crime and punishment is neatly caught.

l.4. clerkis: learned men. *here book:* possibly the Vulgate, but probably unspecific.

47. I SYNG OF A MYDEN

This most delicate and tender evocation of Christ's conception by Mary has been so frequently discussed that to dismiss it here in a few words seems superficial. Attention must be focussed on the spring-time setting, the season of birth and fertility (associated here with the renewal of man's life by Christ's redemption); the connection of the life-giving dew with the word of God descending upon Mary, naturally yet miraculously; the whole aura of stillness and wonder surrounding the 'mystery of the Incarnation', heightened by the semi-liturgical repetitions, which carry with them echoes of an older folk-ritual. The whole is a wonderful synthesis of literary simplicity and theological sophistication. Like the previous poem, it appears in Sloane MS 2593.

l.1. makeles: several meanings are present here; Mary is without a 'mate'—her child's father is not human—yet she is also 'matchless', being flawless in her perfect virginity, and so unique (cf. *Pearl, l.780:* 'A makeles may and a maskelles'). The probable source of the phrase is in a thirteenth-century poem:

> Of on I wille singen that is makeles,
>
> The king of alle kinges to moder he hire ches

(see Brown, No. 31).

l.2. to here sone: as her son.

l.4. As dew in Aprylle: the Medieval Church celebrated the Feast of the Annunciation on 25th March, the medieval New Year's Day. The notion of dew falling recalls that one of Mary's titles was 'Fleece of Gideon' (see Judges

179

vi, 36–40, for the story of Gideon spreading a fleece to catch dew sent from God); cf. Brown, No. 60, *l.*26: 'On thee light the Hevene dews').

*ll.*4–8. John Speirs, whose discussion of this lyric is excellent (*Medieval English Poetry: the Non-Chaucerian Tradition*, pp. 67–9), draws attention to the upward movement of the imagery, from grass, to flower, to branch.

*l.*9. *Moder and mayden*: cf. *l.*2 of the next poem: 'A mayde and yet a mother?'

47. A GOD AND YET A MAN?

Like the two previous poems, this lyric exploits tensions inherent in the fabric of the Christian faith: unlike them, however, it is very much a 'wit' poem, depending on verbal economy, ellipsis, and play on words. It is based on an original by Bishop Reginald Pecock (1395?–1460?), Bishop of St Asaph, and Chichester, an ardent opponent of the Lollards and an equally fervent advocate of English as a literary medium. His quatrain on this theme runs:

> Witte hath wondir that resoun ne telle kan,
> How maidene is modir, and God is man.
> Leve thy resoun and bileve in the wondir,
> For feith is aboven and reson is undir.

*ll.*3–4. 'Common sense (or intelligence) marvels what calibre of mind can apprehend and devise either of these problems.' *Conceave:* both meanings given above seem to be present.

*l.*12. *leave to wonder!*: 'stop puzzling yourself about it'.

48. LULLAY, LULLAY, MY LITYL CHYLD

This lyric is one of a large group in which the newly born Christ Child is imagined speaking with his mother, of the world into which He has been born, and of the sorrows and suffering He must bear for the sake of sinful mankind.

*l.*4. *adone*: the MS reads 'apone', probably transferred from *l.*3.

*l.*6. *go nore crepe*: 'walk nor crawl'.

*l.*9. '*Seys*': 'seest'.

*l.*12. *that*: I have regularized the MS reading, which is 'at', the colloquial form (also at *ll.*16 and 21).

*l.*16. *take*: 'receive, get'.

*l.*19. 'I consider it well bestowed if man ponders on my example.'

*l.*21. 'No death shall obstruct my purposes, if I find man faithful to me.'

*l.*22. *sytt*: 'rest', though there is a rare sense meaning 'endure'.

48. FAREWELL, THIS WORLD!

A straightforward, dignified treatment of a hackneyed medieval subject, remarkable for its economy and dramatic force, enhanced by its blend of graphic, homely imagery (esp. in proverbs of everyday usage) and pious, orthodox morality. The lyric provides a moving illustration of the *Vanitas vanitatum* theme beloved of the Middle Ages, and the opening recalls the sudden 'arrest' of Everyman in the morality play.

l.7. Som be this day: very close to the proverb 'Today a man, tomorrow none'.

l.8. cheyre feyre: a fair held in the cherry orchard while the fruit was being sold, frequently the scene of gaiety and licence. Often used in medieval writing to symbolize the shortness of life (cf. *T. & C.* V. 1840–1).

l.12. 'Chek-mate!': there is a close association between Death and the game of chess in sermons at this time. (See G. R. Owst, *Preaching in Medieval England,* 1926, p. 326.) Ingmar Bergmann made use of the same image in the film *The Seventh Seal.*

l.16. in trust is moche treson: proverbial. (Tilley T 549.)

l.19. worldis joye: cf. the early lyric, 'Worldes blis ne last a throwe' (Brown, No. 46).

l.21. ane horne: i.e. Gabriel's horn summoning man to the Last Judgement.

l.25. 'Experience forces me to make a true assessment of the situation'. *compile:* lit. 'heap together'.

l.29. the tide abidith: proverbial. (Tilley T 323.) Cf. Lydgate *The Fall of Princes* III. 2081: 'The tide abit nat for no maner man'.

l.32. Requiem Eternam: eternal rest. The opening phrase of the Introit to the Mass for the Dead in Roman Catholic liturgy.

ll.34–5. 'May he that shed his blood . . . grant me . . .' Cf. A.V., John xiv. 2: 'In my Father's house are many mansions'.

50. IN A TYME OF A SOMER'S DAY

This lyric preserves the traditional opening of the *chanson d'aventure,* which dates back to Provençe and the *trouvères* of Northern France: 'as I rode out this morning, I chanced to see (or hear). . . .' Both secular and religious lyrics making use of this introductory formula are found in Middle English poetry; it often enables the narrator to become a participant in the action.

There are longer versions of this lyric in other manuscripts; I have chosen a terser variant from Balliol MS 354, another important collection dating from the sixteenth century, though the contents are mostly fifteenth century in date. The manuscript formed the commonplace book of Richard Hill, a London grocer, and contains family records, a historical chronicle, puzzles and riddles, as well as some unique copies of English religious and secular lyrics.

l.3. me for to play: 'to enjoy myself, for my pastime'.

l.4. My spanyellis: some breeds of spaniel were employed specifically for starting and retrieving game.

l.14. a-ye: 'again'.

l.16. 'Revertere!': Lambeth MS 853 glosses 'In Englisch tunge, Turne agen!'

l.20. before full lykyngly: 'formerly full of pleasure, self-will'.

l.25. Lykyng: 'pleasure', 'having one's own way'.

51. THE MARTYRDOM OF BECKET

This account of the martyrdom of St Thomas À Becket in Canterbury Cathedral on 29th December 1170 is cast in carol form, a separable burden being repeated between the quatrains. (For a further discussion of carols see p. 178.) This excellent, ballad-like narrative is found in four different manuscripts; I have used Greene's text, which takes Sloane MS 2593 as its basis. (*The Early English Carols*, No. 114.) The poem follows in vivid detail the actual sequence of events that led up to the Archbishop's murder: the flight from palace to cathedral (*l.16*); the charge of traitor levelled at Becket by his murderers (*l.21*); his concern for his followers' safety (*l.25*); authentic details of Thomas's injuries and his death at the altar in the North-West transept of the Cathedral (*ll.27–9*).

l.2. 'Now the Church rejoices.'

l.5. browt in bale: 'was made to suffer'.

l.6. 'With great harm.'

l.10. 'Through the devil's might.'

l.11. kemyn: 'came'. *Hendry Kyng:* Henry II.

l.14. 'Raving in their madness.'

l.18. 'In their wickedness.'

l.20. spokyn mekyl pryde: 'spoke most arrogantly'.

l.22. 'Enduring the pains of death.'

l.25. Let hem pasyn: all but three of Becket's followers took the opportunity to leave him.

l.26. 'Without ill-treatment.'

l.28. paryn his crown: 'slice off (cf. 'pare') the top of his skull' (eye-witnesses testified that this was what actually occurred). Carleton Brown objects to the sequence given here, in that these events precede the attack mentioned in *ll.31–2*, but popular narrative does not always follow strict logic.

l.30. 'Hoping for the joys of Heaven.' Obviously, this refers back to Thomas in *l.27*.

l.34. 'Making his way to the heavens.'

l.37. fifty-two poyntes: this total has puzzled many commentators, since it is found in other poems on Becket, and the tradition persisted into the sixteenth century. The Constitutions of Clarendon which Becket provisionally accepted in 1164 are usually considered as having 16 clauses. But as Mr G. A. Usher has pointed out to me, medieval and modern principles of enumeration are very different, and it may be quite feasible to divide the Constitutions of Clarendon (or other medieval charters or documents) into 52 shorter clauses if one chooses to break down the modern divisions further.

*l.*38. 'Contrary to the king's intentions.'

52. MERY HYT YS IN MAY MORNYNG

This charming, unusual carol employs the spring-time convention and the *chanson d'aventure* opening to create the setting for a piece of religious allegory unparalleled elsewhere in Christian liturgy or iconography. Perhaps the burden is taken from a popular 'Maying' song, and this lyric was sung to the original tune: certainly it reads unlike 'official' religious verse, and one must doubtless seek a source in some surviving tradition, perhaps originally associated with pagan ritual. 'Folk-elements' like the presence of St George, the 'ryche rede gollde', and the unconventional assembly suggest the co-existence of two alien mythologies brought into temporary harmony by the strength of the popular imagination.

The poem occurs in Porkington MS 10, which dates from 1450–75 and contains about fifty-five items of English poetry and prose, secular and religious.

*l.*4. *whyte Jhesu:* some editors favour 'wight' meaning 'strong, mighty'. I prefer the simpler senses of 'white', i.e. 'pale, fair, pure' or even 'dressed in white'.

*l.*8. *Sent Collas:* probably St Nicholas.

*l.*9. *toke that swete offeryng:* 'received that sweet gift'.

*l.*12. *challes:* 'chalice'.

*l.*15. *Owre Lady knyghte:* a traditional epithet for St George. Cf. the burden of a carol in Egerton MS 3307 (Greene, *A Selection of English Carols*, No. 62):

> Enfors we us with all our myght,
> To love Seynt Georg, Our Lady knyght.

St George was still a very popular figure in fifteenth-century England; his figure was said to have been seen above the battlefield at Agincourt in 1415.

53. THE CORPUS CHRISTI CAROL

This piece (from Balliol MS 354), is possibly the best-known of all anonymous lyrics of the period; it is certainly one of the most beautiful and intriguing, and much space has been devoted to its elucidation. It is clearly related to popular tradition, like the preceding poem, and it may also be an adaptation for religious purposes of an existing secular song or carol, of which the refrain is still retained. (There are, of course, several more modern parallels to this poem including a Scots version, 'The heron flew east', and one from North Staffordshire, 'Over yonder's a park'.)

If we leave aside R. L. Greene's theory that the poem describes in symbolic terms the displacement of Catherine of Aragon in Henry VIII's affections by Anne Boleyn (see *Medium Aevum* 29 (1960), pp. 10–21), we are left with two main interpretations: presentation in chivalric terms of Christ's death and burial, followed by a recognition of his bodily presence in the Eucharist, or an allegorical treatment of the legend of the Maimed (or 'Fisher') King of the Waste Land, whose wounds cannot be healed without the Mass wafer being served him on the Holy Grail, the dish used at the Last Supper and said to have been brought to England by Joseph of Arimathea. (See *The Works of Thomas Malory* Book VI, and Jessie L. Weston, *From Ritual to Romance*). It may be that both elements are present; some of the appeal of this lyric undoubtedly lies in its 'enigmatic' quality.

l.4. brown: suggesting that the leaves of the trees are also dead?

l.6. purpill and pall: a Middle English poetic formula. 'pall' comes from 'paell', the Old English word for 'purple', though it can also mean 'canopy'.

l.11. may: 'maiden'. This may suggest the Virgin or Mary Magdalene watching over Christ's body, but a maiden also attends on the Maimed King in the Waste Land Legend.

l.13. ston: the paten or shallow dish used at the Mass service, symbolizing the stone at the door of Christ's tomb.

l.14. 'Corpus Christi': the feast of Corpus Christi was ordained by Pope Urban IV in 1264, in honour of the Real Presence of Christ; a new office was written for its celebration by St Thomas Aquinas, but the order was not confirmed till the Council of Vienne in 1311 when it was ratified by Clement V. It was first celebrated in England in about 1320, and took place on the Thursday before Trinity Sunday, when a procession of the Host through the streets formed the most prominent feature of the festivities. The feast became associated (in certain cities) with the performance of the miracle cycles by the guilds of the town. The phrase is used here either to suggest the Real Presence at the Mass, or the rôle of the Mass wafer in curing the wounds of the bleeding Knight.

53. SEYNT STEVENE WAS A CLERK

The story of Stephen and King Herod is found in many European literatures, and the legend of the resurrected capon is associated with it in several of the Scandinavian versions. (It was also a theme in religious art of the Middle Ages, deriving ultimately from a Greek source.) The tradition that Stephen was a servant in Herod's household (or a groom in his stables) is a long-standing one. The lyric printed here from Sloane MS 2593 has all the best qualities of ballad narration: vividness of idiom, economical narration, a matter-of-factness and lack of falsely sentimental colouring, telling use of repetitions, and a skill in characterizing the protagonists which transcends the medium. Herod's bullying tone corresponds very closely to that of the familiar tyrant of the miracle cycles, his blustering caustic wit in *l.*13, for instance, contrasts well with Stephen's quiet persistent conviction. In fact, the whole poem resembles a brief scene from one of the cycle plays.

*l.*2. 'And served him his food, and attended him as he dressed, as happens to every king.'

*l.*9. *eylyt:* 'ails'.

*l.*13. 'Are you mad, or are you starting a baby?'

*l.*20. *Christus natus est!:* the cock was supposed to have made the birth of Christ known to the other animals by crowing these words, which reproduce the rhythm of a cock's crow.

*l.*21. *be to and al be on:* i.e. 'as one man'.

*l.*23. *Tokyn he:* 'they took'.

*l.*24. *evyn:* 'Eve', the day before a church festival, a saint's day etc. St Stephen's Day is 26th December.

55. I HAVE A YONG SUSTER

This is a poem with many analogues, familiar to most readers from folk-song and nursery-rhyme. F. J. Child prints a ballad called 'Captain Wedder-burn's Courtship' (No. 46), where a man wins a wife by guessing riddles of the same type. From *ll.*11–12 and 27–8, the speaker of the present lyric appears to be female; it is taken from Sloane 2593.

*l.*3. *drowryis:* 'tokens of affection, keep-sakes'.

*l.*23. *ey:* 'egg'. Caxton tells in the preface to his paraphrase of the Aeneid (1490) of an amusing confusion resulting from 'eggs' and 'eyren' both being used to mean 'eggs' in different regions of Britain in the fifteenth century. (See A. C. Baugh, *A History of the English Language*, pp. 236–7.)

*l.*25. *on-bred:* 'in the seed'.

56. I HAVE A GENTIL COOK

One attraction of this poem, apart from its gaiety and emblematic precision, lies in its close relationship with the description of Chauntecleer in *The Nun's Priest's Tale* (*C.T.*, VII. 2859–2865); the resemblance may be conscious, or perhaps both poems draw on common popular tradition. Chaucer's lines are printed here for comparison:

> His coomb was redder than the fyn coral, (cf. *l.*7)
> And batailled as it were a castel wal;
> His byle was blak, and as the jeet it shoon; (cf. *l.*8)
> Lyk asure were his legges and his toon; (cf. *l.*13)
> His nayles whitter than the lylye flour, (cf. *ll.*15–16)

And lyk the burned gold was his colour.
This gentil cok. . . . (cf. *l.*1)

The final ambiguity, of course, recalls the exploits of 'Goosey goosey gander':
Sloane MS 2593 also contains several other poems of this type.

*l.*1. *gentil:* 'well-bred, of noble birth'. *cook:* 'cock'.
*l.*2. 'tells me when it's day by crowing'.
*l.*3. *doth me rysyn:* 'gets me up'.
*l.*4. *Matyins:* early morning devotions.
*l.*6. 'He comes of a distinguished line', i.e. the cock is well-born as well as well-bred.
*l.*10. *of kynde:* 'of a good family'.
*l.*11. *corel:* the MS reads 'scorel'.
*l.*12. *inde:* 'indigo'. (Originally a blue dye coming from India.)

56. BESSE BUNTYNG

This sparkling portrait, discovered by Mr P. J. Frankis as a scribble on a manuscript in the Bodleian Library, Oxford, has affinities with some early French lyrics which describe how 'Bele Aliz' or another married woman decks herself out to meet her lover early in the morning. Bess is in a lower class of society from these amorous dames, and the poem depicting her, like most of the 'Harley lyrics' (from Harley MS 2253), is less sophisticated and courtly than its continental counterparts. Bess's name is well chosen: a 'bunting' was a pet bird, and often used as a term of endearment (cf. 'Baby Bunting'), but to 'bunt' means to 'sift meal', an appropriate occupation for a miller's daughter!

*l.*8. 'Dressed in a really feminine manner.'
*l.*9. *petycote:* a petticoat at this period was any kind of skirted garment, worn beneath the gown by the better-off, but often by itself among the poorer classes.

57. HOW! HEY! IT IS NON LES

Many poems of the period treat of the theme of marriage and its attendant tribulations; in these pieces, anti-feminist satirists often become most biting and admonitory. Sloane MS 2593 and a similar manuscript, Bodleian MS Eng. poet. e.l. have a number of carols on themes like

> Man, bewar of thin wowyng,
> For weddyng is the longe wo

or:

> In soro and car he led hys lyfe
> That have a schrow ontyll his wyfe

The theme survives in folk-song; one collected by Cecil Sharp at Hambridge in 1903, has a verse closely resembling stanza 3 of the present poem:

> When dinner time come to home I repair
> And a hundred to one if I find my wife there
> She's gossipin' about with the child upon her knee
> And the turk of a sign of a dinner for me.
>
> (James Reeves (ed.), *The Idiom of the People* (1958), No. 95.)

l.2. seygh: 'speak'.
l.4. R. L. Greene points out that the marriage of young men to older women was bound to be more common in the Middle Ages, when early widowhood was frequent, and the importance of married status was recognized in property transactions.
l.8. mete: not 'meat' here but 'food'.
l.13. bed: an alternative reading 'led', meaning 'a large cauldron', has been put forward. *doth me rennyn:* 'makes me run'.
l.15. fleych: 'meat' (cf. German 'Fleisch').
l.17. reych: 'rush', i.e. 'not worth the floor covering'.
l.20. al at ese: 'quite unmoved, blandly'.

58. I AM AS LYGHT AS ANY ROE

This cheerful defence of women represents the other side of the anti-feminist debate; as is usual in this kind of retort, the virtues of the Virgin Mary are advanced to strengthen woman's claim to respect from her husband and men in general.

l.9. i.e. 'She looks after the children for you'.

58. WHAN NETILLES IN WYNTER

This catalogue of paradoxes reminds one, in its fantastic variety and grotesque humour, of the profusely decorated margins on medieval manuscripts; we are confronted with a series of almost surrealistic images that conjure up a kind of comic Hieronymus Bosch. The jaunty blatancy and sheer inventiveness of the satire dissipate any sense of monotony, though I have rejected the longer version (in Bodl. MS Eng. poet. e.l.) for this rendering from Balliol MS 354, on the grounds that one can have too much, even of a good thing.

l.3. bromes: 'brooms' (shrubs).
l.4. croppis: 'tops of trees'.
l.11. gornardes: 'gurnards', warm-water fishes with large spiny heads, and three very distinctive lower rays, thick enough to finger the ocean bottom.

rolyons: Old French *rouillons*, identified with the modern *trigle* or red gurnard or gurnet. (I am grateful to Mr J. H. Watkins for help with this identification.)

l.12. gren gese: 'goslings'.

l.13. sperlynges: 'smelts', member of the salmon family. *harnes:* armour.

l.17. 'And curlews carry cloths to rub down horses.'

l.18. se-mewes: 'sea-mews', common gulls.

l.19. wod-dowes: 'wood-doves'.

l.20. griffons: 'vultures'.

l.24. perchis: 'perches' (fish).

l.25. 'And mice mow corn by waving their tails.'

l.26. the blod of Haylis: Hailes Abbey in Gloucestershire was a place of pilgrimage for those seeking to view the alleged blood of Christ preserved in a phial there (cf. *The Pardoner's Tale, C.T.,* VI. 652: 'And "By the blood of Crist that is in Hayles".')

l.27. shrewd: used in its earlier sense of 'ill-natured, malignant', derived from 'shrew', an abusive person of either sex.

59. 'KYRIE, SO KYRIE'

This rollicking seduction poem forms part of a whole class of lyrics on similar themes, in which clerics invariably play notorious rôles; these earthy poems form an excellent corrective to the more stylized and artificial verse of the courtly love tradition. Probably the work of a cleric, this lyric represents an extensive literature that grew up in the Middle Ages, parodying the Mass and other parts of the Church liturgy, of which the best-known examples are found in the work of the wandering scholars, the *vagantes* or 'goliards'; the *Carmina Burana* include several examples. The 'Kyrie Eleison' ('Christ have mercy upon us') forms part of the Ordinary of the Mass, but it also puns on the girl's name, which is presumably Alison. (It is curious to note that Chaucer's Wife of Bath's name was Alison, and her clerkly husband's Jankin.)

In 'A Lutel Soth Sermun', a piece of verse moralizing of roughly the same period, occur the following lines, describing various members of society who will not be spared from the pains of hell on the Day of Judgement:

> 'Ne theos prude yunge men, (proud)
> That luvieth Malekin,
> And theos prude maidenes
> That luvieth Janekin.
> At chirche and at cheping, (market)
> Hwanne heo to-gadre come, (when they come together)
> Heo runeth to-gaderes (whisper)
> And speketh of derne luve.' (secret)

l.4. Yol Day: Christmas Day.

l.7. the Offys: the introit sung at the beginning of the Mass.

l.10. the Pystyl: a portion of one of the apostolic Epistles was read by the sub-deacon as part of the Mass service.

l.13. the Sanctus: 'Holy, holy, holy'–a section of the Mass, concluding the Preface, sung by the choir.

l.13. crakit a merie note: Greene glosses this as a description of the rapidly sung notes of polyphonic church music, as opposed to the longer notes of plainsong. But the habit appears to have been condemned by Wycliffe and his followers: 'thanne strumpetis and thevys preisen Sire Jacke or Hobbe and Williem the proude clerk, hou smale thei knacken here notis . . .' ('Of feyned contemplatif lif')

l.16. an hunderid on a knot: 'a hundred at a time'.

l.19. Angnus: the *Agnus Dei* ('O Lamb of God . . .'), part of the liturgy of the Mass sung by the Choir, prior to the Communion of the celebrant.

l.19. the pax-brede: originally the exchange of a 'kiss of peace' formed part of the Mass. In the thirteenth century, a substitute was introduced, in the shape of a small wooden, metal or silver disc with a handle, bearing the image of the Virgin or a saint, or more often the Crucifixion. The 'pax' was kissed by the celebrant with the words 'Pax tecum' and was then carried by an acolyte to the members of the congregation to be kissed.

l.22. Benedicamus Domino: 'We give thanks to the Lord', a general liturgical phrase.

l.23. Deo gracias: 'praise to the Lord'. *chylde:* the MS reads 'schylde'.

60. WERE IT UNDO THAT IS Y-DO

The *chanson de jeune fille*, or the lament of the seduced maiden, occurs as a stock type in medieval French lyric, and English literature has several examples of the genre, including Wyatt's 'Farewell, all my wellfare' (p. 96). Most are marked by a mocking, ribald tone, and this lyric and Wyatt's are notable for their tenderness and sympathy for the girl's situation, while the speaker's rueful words never slide into exaggerated self-pity.

The manuscript from which this poem is taken, (Gonville and Caius MS 383), seems to be the exercise book of an Oxford student of the mid-fifteenth century, who has scribbled down the words of carols and songs in the blank spaces between his notes.

l.1. y-do: 'done'.

l.3. child: a 'childe', a young squire of noble birth seeking to attain the rank of knight (cf. Byron's *Childe Harold's Pilgrimage*, and Browning's 'Childe Roland to the Dark Tower Came').

l.8. non othur newe: a cliché of the courtly love tradition.

l.12. al his wille: 'all he wanted' (another stock phrase).

This poem has certain affinities with medieval *fabliaux*, racy, predominantly comic tales of *bourgeois* and low domestic life, of which *The Miller's Tale* and *The Reeve's Tale* are the best-known examples in English. 'Hogyn cam to bower's dore' (from Balliol MS 354) bears a close relationship to the former, especially in the use of the folk-tale motif of 'the Unfortunate Kiss', of which many examples exist. Old Hogyn, the lecherous but senile lover, is himself a traditional figure in medieval art and literature; one is reminded of the comic portrayal of Joseph in the miracle plays as an aged cuckold, and of old January married to young May in *The Merchant's Tale*. His presence is frequently felt in the *chanson de mal mariée*, the lament of the young girl tied in marriage to a husband too old to satisfy her.

l.1. bower's dore: the word 'bower' has many senses, but they are usually associated with sexual encounters of this kind (cf. 'The Joly Juggelere' (p. 62) *ll.*18, 31, 34). Perhaps 'boudoir' is the most satisfactory modern rendering.

l.3. He tryld upon the pyn: 'he rattled the latch up and down'.

l.9. 'She thought she was conferring honour on the whole family' (presumably Hogyn is a person of some worldly substance, like old January).

l.19. '*Go ye furth to yonder wyndow*': the motivation is not quite clear. Is the girl offering a farewell kiss through the window?

l.25. 'When she realized he was at the window.'

62. THE JOLY JUGGELERE

A vivid piece of story-telling, from Balliol MS 354, quite self-contained and explicit: the tale of the proud lady humiliated has many analogues in folk-literature and elsewhere.

l.1. Drawe me nere: this couplet is part of the singer's 'patter' to attract a crowd and announce his title.

l.2. juggelere: not in its modern sense, but a jester, more particularly one who does tricks and magic, and hence one who deceives. All three senses seem required here.

l.3. beside: 'hard by, near'.

l.5. nyse: 'absurdly choosey'.

l.6. molde: 'earth', i.e. 'normal substance'.

l.8. dangerus: 'difficult to please', but also guilty of 'danger'. (See note to *The Complaint of the Black Knight, l.*13.)

l.17. a prikker: 'a rider' (to 'prick' a horse was to urge it on by spur, then simply to ride it). But in this context, the word obviously carries sexual connotations, as does 'praunser' (*l.*20).

l.18. bowr: the word creates problems; one of its meanings, 'boudoir' or 'bedroom', suits the sense here and at *l*.34, but it can also mean 'a shady recess or arbour out of doors', which fits better at *l*.31 – or are 'the brydis of her bowr' cage-birds? (but the 'cokoo'?).

l.25. *held his hed a-way:* being a magic horse, and not requiring food?

l.25. *shrew:* rascal.

l.32. *cokoo:* frequently introduced to underline a piece of trickery or deception, especially when a husband has been cuckolded, a stale joke that Shakespeare always seems to have found irresistible.

l.34. *joly wyndows:* 'pretty' (from French *joli*).

l.38. *'Alas!' she said:* a delicious piece of comic understatement.

l.39. *mele pok:* 'a sack of meal'.

l.43. *giglot:* 'sexy piece', 'flapper'.

64. WE BEN CHAPMEN

This cheeky medley of *double-entendres* in carol form is found in Sloane MS 2593, and succeeds in catching the jocular, buoyant, confident tones (and traditional habits!) of the eternal salesman.

l.1. *chapmen:* 'pedlars, traders'.

l.1. *lyght of fote:* suggests the careless ease with which the speakers evade their responsibilities.

l.2. *fowle weyis:* 'muddy roads'; medieval roads were notoriously bad, especially in winter.

l.3. *cattes' skynnes:* the speaker disparages his rivals' goods: 'we carry round no mangy furs'.

l.6. *ware:* a play on the meanings (1) 'merchandise', (2) 'the male sexual organ'.

l.7. *poket:* a small pouch worn on the person (especially inserted into a garment, hence the modern usage) for carrying a purse. Used here with obvious double meaning.

l.11. *jelyf:* 'jelly'. (In modern slang the scrotum is sometimes referred to as the 'jelly-bag.')

64. O MESTRES, WHYE

A lyric which, though utilizing the sentiments and vocabulary of *amour courtois*, nevertheless anticipates Wyatt in its more down-to-earth attitudes and diction, and its complete rejection of the traditional rôle of the down-trodden and apologetic suitor for the lady's favour. 'The rebel lover' who refuses to prostrate himself before the mistress is not a new phenomenon in European love poetry, but in the sixteenth century, he becomes a more established figure, and part of a more naturalistic presentation of sexual passion in verse. The lady's 'strangeness' is very closely akin to 'Danger' of the *Roman de la Rose.*

l.4. pleasaunce: probably 'pleasantness', though a pleasaunce was a pleasure-ground or garden, attached to a great house, where knights and ladies would resort to spend their leisure.

l.11. Note the brief change of pronoun from 'ye' to 'thou', the intimate form.

l.20. shuld nowe deny: 'ought to deny me'.

ll.23–4. dochess Of grete Savoy: This reference means that the poem cannot be dated before 1416, when the dukedom of Savoy was created. If the writer had a particular duchess in mind, he may have been thinking of Anne of Lusignan, daughter of the King of Cyprus, who dominated her spineless husband, Louis, Duke of Savoy from 1449–65, or, more probably, of Yolande, sister of Louis XI of France, who controlled the duchy from 1465–72, due to the ill-health of her husband, Amadeus IX.

l.29. percase: 'by chance'.

l.31. To have free chayse: 'to hunt freely'.

JOHN SKELTON

(c. 1460–1529)

LIFE

Skelton, born in 1460, probably of Northern stock, made his reputation first as a scholar; for his learned achievements, he was given the academic title of Poet Laureate by the universities of Oxford, Cambridge, and Louvain. He had just been awarded his Oxford 'laurels' when Caxton mentioned in the preface to his *Boke of the Eneydos* (1490) that Skelton had translated certain classics 'not in rude and olde langage, but in polysshed and ornate termes craftely, as he that hath redde Vyrgyle, Ovyde, Tullye, and all other noble poetes and oratours to me unknowen . . .'

Skelton seems to have branched out into a literary career at court in 1494, becoming tutor in the household of Henry VII, with special responsibility for the education of the young Duke of York (afterwards Henry VIII), at Eltham Palace; he wrote several books for the use of his illustrious pupil, and Erasmus lavished praise on him during his English visit of 1499. The death of Prince Arthur in 1502 led to a reorganization of the heir apparent's household, and Skelton departed probably from mixed motives, to accept the living of Diss in Norfolk, having taken Holy Orders in 1498. Here he made a controversial and highly irregular rector, probably residing in his parish as little as possible. Despite his strictures on court life, set forth in the allegorical morality-poem *The Bouge of Court* (c. 1499), Skelton lost no time in seeking court preferment when his former pupil succeeded to the throne in 1509; in 1512 he was created *Orator Regius*, a post roughly akin to the modern laureateship, in which capacity he wrote a number of political pieces, including a jeering attack on the Scots after their defeat at Flodden Field in 1513.

Skelton viewed with misgivings the rapid rise to power of Wolsey, created Archbishop of York and Cardinal in 1514, and Lord Chancellor in 1515. Skelton warned Henry against Wolsey's influence in his political morality play *Magnyfycence* (1516), and in three dynamic though diffuse satires, *Speke Parrot*, *Colin Cloute*, and *Why Come Ye Not to Court?* all excellent specimens of vigorous polemic. Wolsey apparently took offence, and for a time Skelton was glad to remain in the sanctuary of his house in Westminster; he also attempted to placate the Cardinal in works such as *A Replycacion*, in which he exalts Catholic doctrines and launches a blistering attack on heretics. His last allegorical poem, *The Garlande of Laurell*, depicting its author as a companion of the great English poets of the past, was written in 1523 at the home of the Countess of Surrey, the poet's mother: it contains a long list of works, many now lost, but is chiefly remembered today for the brief lyrics in honour of various ladies of the household:

> Mirry Margarete,
> As mydsomer flowre,
> Ientyll as fawcoun
> Or hawke of the towre. . . .

Skelton died in Westminster on 21st June 1529, and was buried before the high altar of St Margaret's Church.

POETRY

Even if Pope's epithet 'beastly' is not taken seriously today, Skelton still enjoys the reputation of a literary maverick, and it is necessary to remember that not only is he at home with the stylistic intricacies and lofty sentiments of the aureate manner, but that in matters of form, theme, content and belief, he is an arch-conservative, whose skill (like that of Pope and Swift), in irony and invective, serves a traditionalist philosophy. His satires are in a very highly developed medieval convention, however much he may extend the form; *Phyllyp Sparowe* and *Elynour Rummynge* depend on established rhetorical patterns; his outrage is not so much more revolutionary as more thorough-going than that of his contemporaries.

At the same time, Skelton does deserve commendation for bringing back into the main stream of English poetry the spirit and vigour of demotic verse, after the reign of the 'Chaucerians' had tended to exalt technique as an end in itself; his very idiosyncratic temper is essentially down-to-earth, opposed as much to faded literary stereotypes as it is to all forms of hypocrisy and cant in life. Though his first major poem, *The Bowge of Court*, is cast as an allegorical vision, it takes place, not in a lush garden landscape, but on the deck of a ship, and the dreamer or 'Drede', instead of falling asleep over a book, drops off in an ale-house in Harwich. Always in Skelton actuality and tradition work hand-in-hand, and he attained more subtleties in his narrator-figures (the 'I' of many pieces) than any since Chaucer. The dynamic portraits of Drede's fellow-passengers, Favell (flattery), Riot, Suspect and others, reveal the poet at his happiest, working on morality-type personifications of the decaying, sordid and evil; as *Elynour Rummynge* shows, there was something in the squalid and the down-at-heel with their coarse energy which fascinated the scholar and tutor of princes.

This interest in the slapdash and confused states of life generally is metrically paralleled by Skelton's rhythmic energy, generated in the Skeltonic line, which he uses to enormous effect in his great satires. The form probably developed from medieval Latin prose, where rhymed ornament enabled parallel structures to be emphasized, though native rhythms may have had a share too. Whatever its origins, Skelton put the form to good use, particularly in the tumbling gaiety and inconsequence of *Elynour Rummynge*, and in his savage onslaughts upon Wolsey in the satires, where the terse stressed lines, with their seemingly everlasting runs of inventive rhyme, jab out like the fists of a boxer, punching his hatred home.

Skelton stands very much at the centre of his own poems, but such appearances are not to be likened to the self-confessions of a Romantic or a contemporary poet; he uses his own *persona* as a foil to other elements in the work, as in *Phyllyp Sparowe*, where, as Stanley Fish shows, he draws a contrast between the innocence of the girl and the 'knowingness' of experience embodied in the figure of the poet himself. Thus he incorporates the Self as a literary device for the purposes of commentary rather than self-revelation.

His chief note is exaggeration; he adores hyperbole, and some remarks by Huizinga are relevant to his art: '. . . mediaeval man always preferred drastic treatment. He was like an invalid who has been treated too long with heroic medicines; only the most powerful stimulants produced an effect on him'. (*The Waning of the Middle Ages*, 1924, p. 198.) Skelton proffered that kind of stimulation. He has notable affinities with Rabelais—humour, inventiveness, a healthy delight in the seamy and the grotesque, a love of parody and ridicule, a preference for shock tactics. But neither of them was artless, brutal or primitive: in Skelton many strengths were fused with a degree of sophistication not available to a less responsible artist. 'A variety of vernacular traditions, a vernacular kind of insight, a metre and a rhythm which had for long had contact with vernacular expression—all these are things that come together in Skelton's verse.' (John Holloway, *Proceedings of the British Academy*, XLIV, 1958, pp. 100–1.)

66. LULLAY, LULLAY, LYKE A CHYLDE

Skelton's only carol is typical in employing parody to realize its satiric intention: taking the form of the dialogue between the Virgin and child as its basis (seen in 'Lullay, lullay, my lityl chyld', p. 48) and using the 'Lullaby' burden, the poet draws an implied contrast between the innocence and harmony of the Biblical scene, and the depravity of this pastoral encounter between drunkard and whore, where the deceit and sexual animalism of the woman are mercilessly exposed.

l.4. ly in your lap: a frequent euphemism for having sexual intercourse (cf. *Hamlet* III. ii. 120).

l.7. Hys hed was hevy: Fish sees here a phallic image, echoed at *l.23*, but the surface meaning is perfectly adequate.

l.9. toke no kepe: 'did not take charge', 'did not pay attention'.

l.10. ba, ba, ba etc.: kisses (cf. *The Wife of Bath's Tale, C.T.,* III. 433, 'let me ba thy cheke!'), cf. French 'baisser'.

l.13. dedely sin: i.e. the sin of fornication.

l.21. a hete: i.e. 'on heat' to make love.

l.25. lust and lykyng: poetic formula for 'pleasure'. (Cf. *Elynour Rummynge, l.222.*) There is a character called 'Lust and Lykynge' in the morality play *Mundus et Infans.*

l.26. blynkerd blowboll: 'short-sighted sot'. There is a sixteenth century popular poem entitled *Colyn Blowbol's Testament.*

l.29. cowardly: 'faint-heartedly, feebly'.

l.30. powle hatchet: the meaning is 'blockhead' but the derivation is obscure; does it suggest that the fool's head (or 'poll') is thick enough to use for chopping wood on?

l.30. blered thyne I: a very common semi-proverbial phrase, meaning 'deceived'.

67. THE AUNCIENT ACQUAINTANCE

Skelton opens this perfect 'custard-pie' poem by employing the heavily embellished diction and panegyric style of the conventional courtly compliment, only to break its elaborate formality at the start of the third stanza, with terms and sentiments of the most uncourtly kind! From this point on, the poem remains set in the colloquial mould, and the lady, her husband, the new lover, the servants are placed at odds with each other, while the former 'lovyng knyght' looks on, his sexual jealousy compensated for by the anarchy which the lady's unbridled lust has released. The impact of the abuse mainly results from Skelton's use of equestrian imagery to describe human activity.

l.7. 'You may be considered as encouraging all manly activity.'

l.8. favorable: 'well-favoured', but also carrying the sense of 'looking favourably on'.

l.11. dame Menolope: Melanippe (occasionally translated as Menalippe) in Greek mythology was the mother of two sons, Aidos and Boiotos, by the sea-god Poseidon. Euripides wrote two plays about her—both now lost—one entitled *Melanippe the Wise.* (I am grateful to Professor R. E. Wycherley for this information.)

l.13. hole delyght: Fish, with transatlantic ingenuity, points out the possibility of a ribald pun here. But the phrase is common.

l.14. your old trew lovyng knyght: presumably the speaker.

ll.15–26. These lines seem addressed to the new lover, the sergeant farrier.

l.15. take up: 'adopt as a partner, take up with'.

l.16. Hys jentyll curtoyl: 'Your knight's noble curtal'—a curtal is a horse with

196

a docked tail, and was often transferred to a slut or a loose woman (O.E.D. meaning 3), by association with short skirts!

l.17. '*Gup, morell, gup!*': 'Gee up, black horse!'

l.18. '*Jayst ye, jenet of Spayne*': 'spring about, jog up and down, small Spanish horse' (cf. *Othello* I. i. *l.*14: 'You'll have gennets for germans').

l.18. *tayll:* often used with deliberate ambiguity for the female sexual organ.

l.19. *haggys:* for Skelton, a general term of abuse for members of both sexes.

l.20. *sergeaunt ferrour:* farrier to the King.

l.21. 'To ride the wild mare' meant to copulate, according to Tilley (M 655).

l.23. I cannot explain this line satisfactorily. 'Kalkyns' or 'calkins' are the turned-down ends of a horse-shoe, and a 'clench' is a nail bent back on itself; 'keylyth' means 'cools'; the allusions are clearly to vigorous sexual activity. Does it mean that the lady digs her nails in and grips the lover as she obtains satisfaction?

l.24. *goyth wyde behynde:* goes astray sexually? *Hewyth:* blushes. *gallyng:* 'blistering, being made sore'.

l.25. *widders:* normally the withers or 'shoulders' of the horse where the saddle rests. Here, since the lover is presumably being warned of the dangers of catching a venereal disease, the reference must be to that part of his anatomy nearest the front of the saddle.

l.25. *wrenche:* 'trick, ruse'.

l.26. *trenche:* a clear sexual reference.

l.27. *jentyll:* presumably ironic, since the husband's conduct is scarcely that of a perfect knight.

l.30. *day wach:* while on guard-duty during the day?

l.32. *clappys:* not, as Fish suggests, V.D., but 'blows'.

l.33. *lepe the hach:* can mean simply to run away, but here in view of the horsing images throughout, it may mean the servants literally leap over the half-door of the stable.

l.34. *conusaunce:* the lord's cognizance or coat of arms worn as a badge on the livery of all his retainers. *a wily py:* perhaps the cognizance is a magpie, proverbial for its sly tricks.

l.36. *counsell:* private advice.

l.36. *cryed at the cros:* proclaimed publicly from the market cross in the town centre.

l.37. The speaker's sympathy with the husband is quite obviously hypocritical.

l.38. *not furst:* cf. the proverb 'I am not the first and shall not be the last'.

68. THE BOKE OF PHYLLYP SPAROWE

This poem on the death of a girl's pet sparrow was written in time for Barclay to refer to it disparagingly in *The Shyp of Folys*, dated 1508. The suggestion that it is merely a kind of comic parody of the Divine Office has been dismissed by Fish, and by I. A. Gordon who, in the *Modern Language Review* 29 (1934), pp. 389–96, demonstrated that Skelton's use of the Roman Catholic Service Book was at least partly serious in intention. It is possible that Skelton was inspired to write this lament by two of Catullus's lyrics on a similar bereavement which befell his mistress Lesbia (*Carmina* II and III). Philip's owner seems to have been Jane Scrope or Scroop, daughter of a family of local gentry, a pupil at the conventual school of Benedictine nuns at Carowe, in the suburbs of Norwich.

l.1. Placebo: in the service of Vespers in the Office for the Dead, the first antiphon which began the service commenced: '*Placebo Domino in regione vivorum*' (Psalm 114.9 in the Vulgate) [*B.C.P.*, Psalm 116.9: 'I will walk before the Lord: in the land of living'].

l.3. Dilexi: 'I am well pleased'–another quotation from Psalm 114 (Vulgate) [*B.C.P.*, Psalm 116.1]; this psalm followed the antiphon.

l.4. Dame Margery: one of the nuns leading the singing?

l.5. Fa, re, my, my: notes of the chant being sung.

l.7. Philip Sparowe: a familiar name given to sparrows, resembling the sound of a chirp 'Phip!'

l.9. Nones Blake: Benedictine nuns (from the colour of their habits).

l.12. bederolles: list of those to be prayed for (Old English 'gebed', prayer).

l.13. Pater noster qui: 'Our Father which . . .'

l.14. Ave Mari: 'Hail Mary' (one of the most common medieval prayers, based on Gabriel's salutation of Mary).

l.15. the corner of a Crede: a fragment of the Creed.

l.21. Pyramus and Thesbe: the story was told by Ovid in his *Metamorphoses* Book IV; Chaucer includes a version in the *Legend of Good Women*.

l.27. Gyb our cat: 'Gilbert' or 'Gib' was a traditional name for a cat. It occurs in *The Romaunt of the Rose*.

l.28. worrowyd: 'worried' i.e. killed by shaking and biting.

l.53. mayden, wydow, and wyfe: a poetic formula (cf. 'The Martyrdom of Becket' [p. 51] *l.35*).

l.57. at me: from my example.

l.64. Heu, heu, mel: 'Woe, woe is me.' The next antiphon from the Vespers in the Office of the Dead.

l.66. Ad Dominum, cum tribularer, clamavi: '*Heu, heu me*' is followed by this psalm, 119 in the Vulgate (*B.C.P.* 120). 'In my distress I cried unto the Lord.'

ll.68–70. Catullus (*Carmina* III. 11–15) also pictures Lesbia's sparrow facing the terrors of Hades.

l.69. marees: waters.

l.70. Acherontes well: Acheron was a river of the underworld.

l.72. Pluto: King of the Underworld.

l.74. foule Alecto: one of the Erinyes or Furies.

l.76. Medusa: one of the three Gorgons, winged female monsters with snakes for hair. Medusa, the only mortal one, whose face turned to stone those looking on it, was killed by Perseus. *mare:* hag, spectre.

l.78. Megera's edders: Megaera, like Alecto, was a Fury. *edders:* adders.

l.83. Proserpina's bowre: Hades. Persephone (Proserpina) was seized by Pluto, and made his consort in the underworld.

ll.85-6. Cerberus was the dog guarding the entrance to Hades, usually represented as having three heads (see *l.91*). Theseus, one of the greatest of Greek heroes, made an expedition to Hades to rescue Proserpina; he was captured, and had to be rescued by Hercules. Hercules was another great Grecian hero, one of whose twelve 'labours' was to kidnap Cerberus and bring him to the upper world.

l.88. famous poetes: did Skelton have anyone specific in mind?

l.92. Jupyter: Jove, king of the gods.

l.95. Dominus: the next antiphon in the Vespers in the Office of the Dead: 'The Lord shall preserve thee from all evil' (Psalm 120 in the Vulgate; *B.C.P.*, Psalm 121.7). The appropriate Psalm follows.

l.97. Levavi oculos meos in montes: 'I lifted up my eyes to the hills', the opening of Psalm 120 (Vulgate), *B.C.P.*, Psalm 121.

ll.98-9. Zenophontes: Xenophon, the Greek soldier and historian (*c.* 430–*c.* 355 B.C.). *Socrates:* the great Greek philosopher (469–399 B.C.).

ll.108-11. Andromach: the grief of Andromache at the killing of Hector during the siege of Troy closes Book XXII of *The Iliad*.

l.114. go: gone.

l.118. kepe his cut: keep his distance, 'stay'.

l.125. Betwene my brestes softe: a similar image appears in Catullus's 'Ad Passerem Lesbiae' (*Carmina* II. 2. *quicum ludere, quem in sinu tenere*).

l.143. Si iniquitates: the next antiphon, a quotation from Psalm 129 (Vulgate), *B.C.P.*, Psalm 130, *l.*3: 'If thou shouldest mark iniquities, O Lord . . .'

l.145. De profundis clamavi: 'Out of the depths have I cried unto thee, O Lord', the opening of Psalm 129 (Vulgate), *B.C.P.*, 130.

ll.148-53. Dame Sulpicia at Rome: Sulpicia was praised for her love poetry by Martial. She was probably the authoress of six short elegies, avowing her passion for a man of her own circle.

74. THE TUNNYNGE OF ELYNOUR RUMMYNGE

With *Phyllyp Sparowe*, *The Tunnynge* is one of Skelton's best-known poems, a tableau of low life which probably did more than any other of his productions to earn Skelton the epithet 'beastly'. It has been suggested that Elinor is intended as an admonitory type-portrait of Gluttony, but Skelton's concern seems to be to build up a graphic picture of the ale-house and its grotesque inhabitants, employing a minimum of moral commentary. The gossips' drinking-bout was a scene which impressed itself on other writers and painters of the time: there is a carol in Balliol MS 354, to which the burden runs:

> Hoow, gossip myne, gossip myne,
> Whan will we go to the wyne?

while Mrs Noah's gossips are a feature of the Chester Play of the Deluge.

l.3. Skelton preserves the minstrel's standard opening. *chyll:* the dialect form of 'shall'.

l.4. *comely:* this seems an odd word to use here and at *l.18.* It corresponds to the modern ironic 'beautifully' (cf. 'fayre' in *l.26*). *gyll:* a 'Jill', a woman.

l.25. 'Like a glutinous rain falling, a gummy slime.'

l.26. *fayre:* 'plainly' (or possibly, as we might say, 'pretty ugly').

l.28. *camously:* concavely.

l.38. *jetty:* part of a building jutting out from the rest, especially an upper storey overhanging the street.

l.40. 'To see what gums she has.'

l.42. *gently:* presumably another ironic epithet.

l.49. *plane:* not the modern plane, but a tool like a plasterer's trowel used by plumbers and bricklayers to smooth off their work.

l.52. *jolly fet:* possibly from French 'jolivet'.

l.53. *flocket:* a loose gown with long sleeves (from Old French 'floquet', a tufted, shaggy cloth).

l.54. *gray russet rocket:* 'russet' is a coarse homespun woollen cloth; 'rocket' is 'rochet', an outer garment, usually a smock or mantle.

l.55. *cocket:* usually 'simper de cocket', a flirt (cf. coquette). Tilley under 'simper the cocket' (S 462) cites Skelton.

l.56. *huke:* a cape or cloak with a hood.

l.70. *kyrtel:* a gown, skirt or outer petticoat *Brystow red:* dyed red. (Apparently, Bristol water allowed red dye to take most satisfactorily.)

l.72. *sowe:* a bar of metal. Chaucer makes the same joke about the Wife of Bath's head-gear. (*C.T.* I. 453–5.)

l.75. *whym wham:* something whimsical, fantastic.

l.76. *trym tram:* neat ornament (cf. nick-nack).

l.78. *Egyptian:* gipsy.

l.86. *blanket hose:* hose of undyed wool.

l.87. *falowe:* possibly ploughland, but more probably uncultivated land left to lie 'fallow' for a year.

l.88. *talowe:* suet, or candle-grease.

l.90. *baudeth:* befouls.

l.96. *Sothray:* Surrey.

l.98. *Lederhede:* Leatherhead.

l.99. *tonnysh gyb:* 'a beery cat'. 'Tonnysh' derives from 'tun', a beer or wine cask, or the vat where the ale is brewed. (For 'gyb' see *Phyllyp Sparowe l*.27 and note.)

l.103. *port-sale:* should this be 'pot-sale'?

l.105. *swynkers:* I think 'labourers' here, though it can mean 'deep drinkers'.

l.109. 'Render themselves penniless.'

l.110. *'Now away the mare':* a popular song. (It also crops up in Skelton's play, *Magyfycence*.)

l.116. *styll:* this word can mean 'silent, motionless, secretly', the latter seems likeliest in this context: Elinor's customers are not very silent or motionless. The view that 'styll' refers to the distilling apparatus is possible, though *O.E.D.* gives the earliest usage in this sense as 1533.

l.123. *dagged:* be-mired, mud-spattered.

l.126. *tytters:* Skelton's own word? It must be analogous to 'tatters'.

l.137. *It . . . it:* perhaps these should both be altered to 'that'.

l.139. *A sorte:* a set, a collection of foul sluts.

l.142. *skewed as:* squinting like.

l.143. *sho clout:* a rag for cleaning shoes.

l.145. *herelace:* a hair-band.

l.148. *unlust:* unpleasantness, repulsiveness.

l.149. *strawry:* not found in the *O.E.D.* Does it mean 'as if they've just got out of the straw'?

l.150. *cawry-mawry:* a rough kind of coarse material (referred to in *Piers Plowman*, 'A' text, V. 62).

l.151. *tegges:* literally 'female sheep', but often applied contemptuously to a woman.

l.153. *lewde sorte:* 'low set'.

l.159. *To Mawte and to Molde:* to Maud and to Molly?

l.161. *thyder commy:* come thither.

l.163. *shreud aray:* 'an evil state of affairs'; in modern slang, a 'bad show'. 'Aray' can mean an argument or strife.

l.167. *hym that me bought:* Common expression for Christ.

l.169. The sense is a little obscure here, but Elinor seems to break off from refusing her customers credit, to deal with the hogs which break into the assembly.

l.171. *draffe:* hog-wash i.e. coarse liquor and brewer's grains, which goes into the swill-tub.

l.174. *hye dese:* the dais, high table.

l.177. *wrygges:* twists, turns, wriggles.

l.178. *frigges:* rubs.

ll.185–6. The exact sense escapes me here. The general sentiment is 'Devil take the animal! May it never thrive!'

*l.*189. *patch:* 'in so foul a spot as that'.

*l.*190. *mashfat:* the vat, where the 'mash' was prepared. 'Mash' was a mixture of malt and hot water, producing the 'wort', which, after fermentation, became beer (see 'mashe bolle', *l.*196).

*l.*192. *ale joust:* joist, a beam running across the room where the open casks of ale are kept.

*l.*194. *tunnes:* casks, barrels.

*l.*204. *Gossyp:* female companion, crony.

*l.*206. *flowre:* froth, make a head.

*l.*212. 'If you can stand it.'

*l.*222. *lust and . . . lykyng:* stock phrase; see *Lullay, lullay, lyke a Chyld* (p. 66), *l.*25, and note.

*ll.*223–4. *whytyng:* a term of affection, like *mullyng* (usually of a woman), *mytyng* (usually of a child), and *nobbes*.

*l.*225. *conny:* literally 'coney, rabbit'.

*l.*227. *Bas:* kiss.

*l.*228. *good:* goods.

*l.*229. *falyre fonny:* 'falyre' is not in the *O.E.D.* Probably 'fellow'. A 'fon' is a fool; 'fonny' presumably 'foolish'.

*l.*230. *dronny:* 'dronnish' means 'sluggish, inactive' and 'dronny' probably means the same.

81. COLYN CLOUTE

Colyn Cloute is the second of Skelton's major satires, being composed in the spring or summer of 1522, after *Speke Parrot*, and before *Why Come Ye Nat to Court?* Though the satire is not specifically levelled at Wolsey, his figure looms large over the general picture of ecclesiastical incompetence and irregularity, which Colin draws as he claims to report 'what people are saying' up and down the country.

*l.*4. *shake oute:* display, demonstrate before you.

*l.*5. *connyng bagge:* store of knowledge, learning.

*l.*6. *hagge:* Skeltonic usage.

*ll.*7–10. Conventional modest disclaimer required by the dictates of rhetorical practice.

*l.*11. 'If you "go along with it".'

*l.*20. *blother:* blether, talk rubbish, babble foolishly.

*l.*21. *tone . . . tother:* the one . . . the other. *ayenste:* I have restored this alternative reading; Dyce reads 'agayng'.

*l.*23. *in hoder moder:* in 'hugger-mugger' i.e. 'secretly, in concealment, clandestinely'.

*l.*31. *sely:* in this context, 'simple, innocent, harmless'.

202

ll.36–8. 'And as for their skill (or learning?) – only sour looks and play-acting.' They use their knowledge to cheat people.

l.37. *mummynge:* possibly 'silence' (cf. 'keeping mum') but probably 'acting a part'.

l.43. *forked cap:* the bishop's mitre.

ll.44–5. 'Indeed they are too bad even to admit it, accursed as they all are!'

l.48. *matters . . . rawe:* 'how they are ignorant of the way to manage affairs'.

l.50. *Jacke and Gyll:* men and women.

l.51. *byll:* a formal petition submitted by a member of the public asking for the redress of a stated grievance.

l.53. *For other mennes skyll:* 'before other men's expertise (or powers of judgement)' (i.e. they ignore the legal opinions of others).

l.55. *leve theyr owne causes:* neglect their proper interests, i.e. church affairs (to meddle in civil matters).

l.56. *provynciall cure:* the bishop's see, though strictly, a 'province' was the area of jurisdiction of an archbishop or metropolitan. (For 'cure' see Glossary.)

ll.58–9. 'They hardly concern themselves at all with the rightful legal claims of the Church.'

l.60. ire *and* venire: 'to go and come'.

l.61. *solfa so alamyre:* 'solfa' is presumably to sing; *A la mi re* was a note in the medieval scale or gamut, which occurred in both mean and high octave ranges (see C. Parrish, *A Dictionary of Musical Terms*, Glencoe, U.S.A., 1963). Perhaps Skelton intended to convey the idea of the clergy having an idle time, or it may be a phrase of deliberate nonsense to indicate that more serious offences are being drowned by the music.

l.62. *premenyre:* During the later Middle Ages, Papacy and English crown often clashed over their respective areas of authority, especially the control of property, and appointments to benefices. The Statute of Praemunire was passed in 1393 to strengthen the king's power to proceed against subjects who defied the royal authority when Crown and Papacy were in opposition. The Statute came to be invoked against the English clergy at the time of the Reformation on the grounds that their loyalty to the Pope had trespassed on the King's rights: Wolsey was himself charged under its provisions when he fell from power in 1529, and the whole body of English clerics had to buy pardon when indicted under the terms of the Statute in 1530. Its use is here anticipated by Skelton.

l.63. *set afyre:* set in motion, invoked.

ll.66–8. Possibly this means 'They have formulae to explain away anomalies of doctrine or behaviour, treating them as if they did not exist'. There is an attractive alternative, put to me by Mr G. A. Usher, that 'spirituall con-tradictions' may signify the prohibitions sometimes placed on ecclesiastical courts by the Crown, preventing them from hearing cases thought to be better

suited to civil courts. The meaning might then be that the bishops have claims
or titles to countermand the prohibitions placed on them, considering such
commands to be mere fictions.

l.77. But slumbre forth: they sleep out of their diocese. (Absenteeism and
pluralism were common at this period.)

l.96. reason: line of argument, explanation.

l.99. out of measure: innumerable, excessive numbers, beyond all moderation.

l.106. Aaron and Ure: Aaron was Moses' lieutenant in Egypt (see Exodus).
'Ure' is probably the prophet in Jeremiah xxvi whose denunciation of King
Jehoiakim led to his flight to Egypt, where he was seized and slain.

ll.117-8. The fable of the mice deciding who should hang a bell round the
cat's neck to warn them of its approach is a well-known one (see Tilley B 277).
It is alluded to in *Piers Plowman*, 'B' text, *ll.146-209.*

l.120. deuz decke: a card game, presumably played with two packs.

l.121. made for the becke: made to bow down to authority, 'Yes-men'.

ll.126-8. 'Thomas puts his hand to bolder deeds, he scorns defeat, scorns
insults, no injury breaks Thomas.' This quotation forms lines 6–8 of the
Antiphon 'Studens livor Thomae supplicio' from the office of St Thomas of
Canterbury (Lauds); see *Analecta Hymnica*, xiii. 238. I am grateful to Professor
G. T. Shepherd for this information.

l.135. Sho the mockysshe mare: See *The auncient acquaintance* (p. 67, *l.21* and
note), though the sense here seems to be rather that of belling the cat: 'let's
see who dares to catch the offender' (see note to *ll.117-8* above). It may be an
allusion to a rough Christmas game.

l.137. not worth a leke: proverbial.

ll.138-9. Either 'it is bold to seek to defend the Church' or 'Courage is too
sick to defend the church'.

ll.140-4. A typical disclaimer: Colin (and Skelton) are only referring to what
other people say!

ll.145-6. usque ad montem Sare: a reference from Joshuah xv. 10. 'And the
border compassed from Ba-a-lah westward unto mount Seir': 'men, even as
far away as Mount Seir, say you couldn't get any worse than you are'.

l.147. parkes: parks were enclosed areas of land, specifically leased for the
purpose of preserving beasts of the chase, for hunting.

l.148. hauke on hobby larkes: this reference has been complicated by the fact
that Wolsey had a mistress called Joan Larke, who bore him two children.
But Skelton may simply mean that the clergy hunt larks on the wing ('hauke')
with small hawks called 'hobbies' (cf. *Magnyfycence*, *l.1358*: 'An hoby can
make larkys to dare' where 'dare' means 'petrify into stillness'). 'wanton
warkes' (*l.149*) does not necessarily imply sexual activity. (See, too, the
following note.)

l.150. Whan the nyght darkes: one of the earliest Laws of the Forest was that no hunting should take place during the hours of darkness. See the Assize of the Forrest (1184), Clause 16.

l.152. The gray gose for to sho: Proverbial for spending one's time on an unnecessary labour. (See Tilley G 354.)

ll.155–6. sell/The grace of the Holy Gost: a reference to the sale of indulgences pardons, etc. (cf. the activities of Chaucer's Pardoner).

ll.159–60. eate/In Lenton season fleshe mete: possibly an allusion to Wolsey's suspension of certain regulations about fasting during Lent 1522 (see Heiserman, p. 194).

l.164. Saltfysshe, stocfysshe: fish cured in salt; fish, usually cod, cured by being split open and dried in the sun till hard.

l.165. werynge: 'wearing' i.e. employment, use.

l.168. loke to: expect to.

l.170. gorge not endewed: throat not 'endowed', supplied with.

l.172. a stewed cocke: in the *Interlude of the Four Elements,* 'a stewed hen' is used to mean a whore, and I think this must be the meaning here, in view of the lines which follow, 'stewed' probably punning on the sense of 'stew' 'a brothel'; 'cocke' is possibly related to 'cocket' a form of 'coquette'.

l.173. whate is a clocke: 'what goes on'?

l.174. surfled: stained?

l.175. wodicocke: a fool, a dupe. Or a euphemism for the female organ?

l.176. gyve orders: hold ordinations.

l.178. Sitientes: the Saturday before Passion Sunday was known as 'Sitientes Saturday' from the first word of the Introit of the Mass for the Sunday: 'Sitientes, venite ad aquas, dicit Dominus' (A.V., Isaiah lv. 1, 'Ho, everyone that thirsteth . . .'). It was a favourite day for ordination in the medieval church. (I am grateful to Mr J. B. Bednall for this information.)

ll.179–83. insufficientes: lacking; this and the following references are keywords used by the bishop at ordination and on visitations. *parum sapientes:* 'not wise enough'. *nihil intelligentes:* 'stupid'. *valde negligentes* 'extremely negligent'. *nullum sensum habentes:* 'having no sense'.

l.186. Dominus vobiscum: 'The Lord be with you.' The priest's traditional greeting. Skelton's point is that once they have become priests, the clergy throw discretion to the winds.

l.191. The Lord's Prayer, the *Ave Maria,* and the Creed.

l.192. Construe: interpret as.

l.194. Mattyns: probably the service preceding the first Mass on Sundays.

l.197. prymes and houres: the 'hours' of the Church were Mattins (with lauds), Prime, Terce, Sext, Nones, Vespers, Compline.

l.202. vagabundus: 'vagabonds, loafers'.

l.203. totus mundus: 'the whole world'.

l.204. Laetabundus: 'we will rejoice'.

l.205. ale stake: a pole was often displayed at the door of a tavern as a sign.
l.206. hake and make: O.E.D. suggests 'hake' may mean an idle woman from the Scots or Northern dialect, 'hake', 'to wander about idly'. 'Make' means 'mate, partner'.
l.207. A reference to Christ's breaking of the bread at the Last Supper.
l.209. the good wyfe: priest's concubine. At this period, clerical celibacy seems to have been laxly enforced, and the offence overlooked on payment of a fine.
l.210. theyr apostles lyfe: Skelton is more concerned about the way priests treat their duties as successors of the apostles, than their domestic arrangements.
ll.211–13. 'With those very people who live in towns is a wife or a maid-servant.'
ll.216–17. stylla: still, quiet. *wylla:* desire.
l.218. Paternoster: Our Father: *pekes:* fools: i.e. 'clerical clowns'.

87. TO MAYSTRES ISABELL PENNELL

During the time that Skelton was working on *The Garlande of Laurell*, he resided at Sheriff Hutton Castle, Yorkshire, as a member of the Countess of Surrey's household. The complete poem makes use of the dream-vision frame-work, to allow the poet to overhear Fame demanding of Pallas whether Skelton's literary achievements fit him for a place in her palace. His claim is eventually upheld on the testimony of Gower, Chaucer and Lydgate! Eventually conducted into the Countess's chamber, he finds her ladies busily engaged in embroidering a garland for their newly honoured author; in return, Skelton interpolates eleven short charming compliments to his admirers, of which this gay, tender lyric associating Isabell with the most fragrant scents of a summer garden, is one.

l.3. godely: goodly.
l.5. Reflaring rosabell: odorous lovely rose. (This appears to be a unique example of the word 'rosabell'.)
l.6. flagrant: fragrant. *camamell:* camomile, a sweet-smelling, daisy-like flower used in medicine, and in the Middle Ages, often strewn on the floor as a covering.
l.7. rosary: usually a rose-bed, but here a rose-bush or tree.
l.8. rosemary: an aromatic evergreen shrub, with a blue flower and a fresh pungent scent, much used in cooking, perfumery and medicine.
l.9. praty: dialect form of 'pretty'.
l.10. nepte: Nepeta Cataria or cat-mint. Its American name is 'Cat-nip'.
l.11. jeloffer: the 'gillyflower', a generic name given to clove-scented flowers (Old French 'gilofre' means 'clove'), applied especially to pinks, carnations, wall-flowers and stocks.
l.13. Enuwyd: freshly put on.
l.20. Of womanhode the lure: 'the most alluring of women'.

ALEXANDER BARCLAY

(c. 1476–1552)

LIFE
Barclay's birthplace is unknown, though he was probably a Scot. Since his
will describes him as a Doctor of Divinity, he possibly took a first degree at
Oxford or Cambridge, but he also seems to have studied abroad. He took
Holy Orders on his return, being ordained by Thomas Cornish, suffragan
bishop of Bath and Wells, who found him a place as Chaplain to the College
of St Mary Ottery in Devon, of which Cornish was Warden. Barclay's duties
included acting as librarian and instructor to the choir boys, but he found
time to translate (or rather adapt for English readers), Sebastian Brant's
allegorical satire, *Das Narrenschiff* (1494), which Richard Pynson published in
1509 as *The Shyp of folys*. By this time Barclay had probably left Devon to
join the Benedictine order, becoming a monk at Ely monastery, where the
remainder of his literary composition was done.

His *Egloges*, written c. 1513–14, though based on foreign models, make use
of English materials, and allude to national and local personalities, including
More's patron, Cardinal Morton (Bishop of Ely 1479–86), John Colet, and
Skelton, whose work seems to have offended Barclay's aesthetic, if not his
moral, susceptibilities. In the years up to 1524 Barclay published further
translations from Latin (including a good prose version of Sallust's *Jugurthine
War*, dedicated to Thomas, Duke of Norfolk, father of Surrey the poet), and
a book on learning French. In April 1520 he was summoned to France to the
celebrated meeting between Francis I and Henry VIII at 'the Field of the
Cloth of Gold', 'to devise histoires and convenient raisons to florisshe the
buildings and banquet house withal', in other words, to provide expository
verse texts or 'scriptures' accompanying the elaborate decorations at Guisnes–
but there is no evidence that Barclay complied.

Soon after this, he exchanged the Benedictine order for the stricter discipline
of the Franciscans at Canterbury, only to become a temporary convert to
Lutheran doctrines, which forced him to flee abroad during the 1520s. How-
ever, he had recanted his heresy and admitted his errors by the time of the
suppression of the monasteries and the breach with Rome, since, as if to atone
for his former apostasy, Barclay retained both the garb and the orthodox

beliefs of his order for a number of years, and in a letter of October 1538 Latimer warns Cromwell of the poet's reactionary activities in Cornwall and Devon. Eventually he appears to have conformed; at all events, in 1546, he was presented to livings in Essex and Somerset, and in April 1552 was made Rector of All Hallows, Lombard Street. However, he died shortly after taking up the post, and his burial is recorded at Croydon on 10th June 1552.

POETRY

Opinions on Barclay range from C. S. Lewis's 'With Alexander Barclay . . . we touch rock bottom . . . his poetry has no intrinsic value' to Derek Pearsall's observation that 'his tough, homespun language . . . seems to possess potentialities of development . . . realized in Barclay's five Eclogues. Barclay's language has an immediacy which marks the final eclipse of the narrower aureate tradition'. Admittedly, his translation of Brant's *Narrenschiff* is a hit-or-miss affair, and retains its interest today chiefly for its picture of the times, rather than for anything intrinsically literary, but Barclay has a certain power when he writes on traditional themes like female frailty, or universal mortality. But the Eclogues are better than Lewis's curt dismissal suggests: Barclay and the humanists may have misunderstood the nature of true pastoral, laying too much stress on its polemical and satirical aspects, but it is unfortunate to belittle the way the poet 'naturalizes' Mantuan and Aeneas Sylvius, and to criticize his humanist impulse because it manifested itself in a medieval guise. Barclay's use of the couplet to exploit a contrast is excellent, and there is a colloquial integrity and a natural force about his best work that anticipates men like Gascoigne, and parts of *The Shepheardes Calender*.

89. EGLOGE V

Barclay based his *Egloges* on the pastorals of Aeneas Sylvius Piccolomini (Pope Pius II), and those of Mantuan: this is a free adaptation of Mantuan's Sixth, in which Cornix and Fulica dispute on the relative merits of town and country life. Barclay naturalizes the Italian's picture of the winter countryside, giving it a distinctly Northern flavour. The game of football and the comments on it remind us that it was often a very rough affair, (even) by comparison with today; Thomas Elyot in the *Boke of the Governor* (1531) calls it 'nothyng but beastely fury and extreme violence wherof procedeth hurte . . .'

(The scansion presents a problem: See Introduction, pp. 8–11.)

l.9. Mably: Common English form of Mabel.
ll.11–12. grewell: a kind of soup made by boiling oatmeal etc. in water or milk. *pulment:* a kind of pulse, 'pease-pudding', a pottage made of peas, beans, leeks etc. *frument:* 'furmety', husked wheat boiled in milk and seasoned with cinnamon and sugar. *Lent:* when no meat could be eaten, of course.

l.28. *top:* one of the oldest of toys, known to Plato, Aristophanes, Homer and Virgil. In medieval and Elizabethan England, a large village top was often kept, so that people could keep warm in winter by playing with it.

l.34. *peason:* the old plural form, 'peas'.

l.43. *Overcommeth:* a singular verb with a plural subject (and vice versa) is quite common in sixteenth-century English.

l.47. *domage:* old form of 'damage'. 'We exert ourselves in such petty matters to our own disadvantage' (i.e. by sustaining an injury at football).

STEPHEN HAWES

(c. 1475–?1523)

LIFE

It has been conjectured that Hawes was a native of Suffolk, educated at Oxford, and well-travelled by early Tudor standards; he undoubtedly entered Henry VII's household, rising to become a Groom of the Chamber. His name appears in a list of court payments for 1506 as receiving ten shillings for composing a 'ballet' (a slight lyric poem), though he himself condemned the fashion for 'balades of fervent amite'. About 1504 his allegorical poem *The Example of Vertu* appeared, and in January 1509, Wynkyn de Worde published its most famous successor, *The Passetyme of Pleasure*, which Hawes dedicated to the king. At the accession of Henry VIII in April 1509, the poet commemorated his coronation with *A Joyfull Medytacion to All Englande*; in the same year he published *The Convercyon of Swerers*. The exact date of his death is unknown.

POETRY

Hawes's chief poems, *The Example of Vertu* and *The Passetyme of Pleasure*, illustrate how the taste for allegorical verse lingered on into the sixteenth century, and how effete the tradition was by the time it was abandoned. *The Passetyme* vaguely anticipates *The Faerie Queene* in its attempt to bring together the allegorical dream-vision, elements from popular chivalrous romances, and moral and educational ideals derived from humanist theories. In his poem of nearly 6,000 lines, Hawes describes how the knightly hero, Graunde Amour, wins the love of La Bell Pucell in the approved manner, by defeating vice in its various guises, but the main didactic interest lies in the hero's preparations for his task at the hands of the Seven Liberal Arts in the Tower of Doctrine, and King Melezyus's instructions on the principles of chivalry. Graunde Amour's adventures in arms are mostly standard sensational stuff, and more promising are his encounters with Godfrey Gobelyve, a repulsive, loud-mouthed dwarf, an ugly misogynist whose mocking cynicism about women forms a comic contrast to the knightly reverence. But Hawes employs him without subtlety, and we soon tire of his antics and lewdness.

Hawes's imaginative faculty was large, but his literary talent was limited: the victim of his rhyme-scheme, he is too pedestrian and unselective, over-zealous to follow Lydgate and fit out his homely thinking in rhetorical finery which it wears uncomfortably; too frequently he is prone to provide earnest, literal explanations, a habit which conflicts with his love of wonders and marvels. But just occasionally (as C. S. Lewis shows in *The Allegory of Love*) he catches fire, and produces a memorable cluster of lines, of which the best-known example must suffice:

> After the day there cometh the derke nyght,
> For though the day be never so longe
> At last the belles ryngeth to evensonge.

91. THE PASSETYME OF PLEASURE

This snippet of Hawes's lengthy poem illustrates his style at its usual level; it is essentially a rhetorical manner, partly derived from Lydgate, to whom Hawes pays tribute in the course of the work. At this point in the poem, Graund Amoure, the knightly lover, has overcome all his enemies and now returns to La Bell Pucell to claim her hand in marriage: what may seem to the modern reader excessive reference to the lady's generosity must be regarded as the essence of the courtly love relationship.

l.2. Countenaunce: an allegorical personification of Continentia, continence or self-restraint.

l.3. basse courte: the lower courtyard of a castle (cf. French 'basse cour').

l.4. a conduyte head: a water-spout.

l.8. basse toure: lower tower.

l.10. fanes: pennants, flags, or weather vanes.

ll.20–1. Hawes strikes the typical note of medieval moralizing: 'Sic transit gloria mundi'.

l.23. La Belle Pucell: derived from French 'pucelle', a young girl, a maiden. Used specifically of Joan of Arc (cf. *1 Henry VI*).

l.26. dyde me duty: 'paid my respects'.

l.36. whyte as ony lyly: a stock epithet, but welcome here for its simplicity.

l.38. knottes kerved: carved ornaments, 'bosses'. *craftely:* skilfully.

l.42. The syege of Troye: possibly inspired by Lydgate's *Troy Book*, though the poetic device of introducing illustrative tapestries can be found in the *Aeneid*, and *The Knight's Tale* of Chaucer.

l.44. geometry: geometrical patterns.

l.45. for the nones: 'for the occasion'; or possibly a tag to fill the line.

l.46. mysty: musty?

l.52. flagraunte: fragrant (cf. 'To Maystres Isabell Pennell', p. 87, *l.6*).

*l.*53. *perturbacyon:* anything to perturb one.
*l.*54. *operacyon:* full effect produced.
*l.*56. 'And tinted, adorned with sapphires and many turquoises.'
*l.*58. *the syege of Thebes:* possibly indebted to Lydgate's poem on the subject.
*l.*59. *depured:* purified, clear.

TUDOR COURT SONG-BOOKS

Virtually all that exists of early Tudor song is contained in three manuscripts in the British Museum, Additional MSS 5465, 5665, and 31922, which have been brilliantly edited and 'placed' by Dr John Stevens (see *Guide to Further Reading*, p. 21). Together they comprise about 180 songs and instrumental pieces, mostly by Tudor court composers including Henry VIII himself. The topics covered are typical: a large group of moral and religious pieces is surpassed by an even greater predominance of love songs, topical and political pieces, inevitable when one recalls the audience for whom the songs were composed. Within these broad categories, the range is wide: the Fayrfax MS (Add. 5465) includes devotional hymns such as 'Woffully araid' (sometimes attributed to Skelton), and a high proportion of formal love complaints, alongside Skelton's rumbustious 'Manerly Margery, milk and ale' and sundry other 'low' pieces. The Ritson MS (Add. 5665) is a similar mixture, with a bias towards more simplified popular-sounding songs, while Add. 31922 specializes in secular pieces, chiefly songs of love and conviviality. All three manuscripts may be taken as indicating courtly tastes in song between about 1500 and 1520, and serve as a timely reminder that we cannot insist too dogmatically on a distinction between 'courtly' and 'popular' lyrics, at least, not as far as their potential audience is in question.

94. UP Y AROSE IN VERNO TEMPORE

This song, from Add. MS 5665 (Stevens No. R. 18) is in the traditions of both *chanson d'aventure* and the *chanson de jeune fille*, mentioned earlier (pp. 181, 189). Again, it is a cleric (*l.*10) who is blamed for the girl's condition, and the tone is sympathetic, rather than callous. The poem is an example of the macaronic method, half the line being in English, the other half in Latin.

The phrases in Latin run as follows:

*l.*1. in spring time.
*l.*2. under a certain tree.
*l.*3. in her heart.
*l.*4. a child stir.
*l.*5. of former times (*plesers:* those who gave me pleasure).
*l.*6. I was wont to play.

l.7. deride me.
l.8. I begin to weep.
l.9. to my parents.
l.10. a certain clerk (*Bycause:* inasmuch as).
l.11. with rods and cudgels.
l.12. in the presence of everyone.
l.13. what shall I do?
l.14. or kill it?
l.15. to what place shall I flee?
l.16. and life everlasting.

94. BENEDICITE! WHATE DREMYD I THIS NYGHT?
From Add. MS 5465 (Stevens No. F. 12). A love lyric of curious power, almost apocalyptic in its imagery, with the unexplicable intensity of the best popular poetry. It is of interest too, in that Sir Thomas More translated it into a Latin epigram, *Dii melius* (see *Modern Language Notes*, 63 (1948), p. 542). There is a totally unremarkable second verse, possibly by another hand, which I have omitted here.

l.1. Benedicite!: a common expression of surprise: 'Bless me!'
l.2. *up so downe:* upside down.

95. WESTRON WYND, WHEN WYLL THOW BLOW
'There is almost everything in it—weather, distance, longing, passion, and sober home-felt reality' (C. S. Lewis).
This quatrain sounds like a popular song, comparable to the equally passionate cry heard in the burden of the earliest secular carol preserved in English:

> Blou northerne wynd!
> Sent thou me my suetyng,

found in Harley MS 2253 (G. L. Brook, edn. No. 14). The same theme, recurs in folk-songs, e.g. 'Blow the wind southerly' and 'Bring back my bonny to me', the narrator in 'Westron wynd' being also female, with a lover away overseas (cf. Surrey's poem, 'O happy dames' (p. 112) for another treatment; and Tennyson's 'Sweet and Low'). The tune of 'Westron wynd' was utilized by three early Tudor composers as the basis for a setting of the Mass (see Stevens, pp. 236–7).

l.2. *smalle rayne:* several critics have commented on the felicity of this epithet in conjuring up the fine rain of the British Isles.

SIR THOMAS WYATT

(1503–42)

LIFE

Son of Sir Henry Wyatt, supporter and councillor of both Henry VII and VIII, Wyatt was born at his father's castle of Allington in Kent, and came to court possibly after a Cambridge education. In about 1520 he married Elizabeth Brooke, daughter of Lord Cobham; their son, Thomas the younger, led the celebrated rebellion against Mary I in 1554, for which he was beheaded. The elder Wyatt repudiated his wife for adultery after a few years' marriage.

Wyatt won a reputation for courage, shrewdness, wit, and literary talent at court; several times he travelled abroad, visiting Italy with Sir John Russell in 1527, where he was briefly captured by the Spaniards, and may have been first attracted by Italian poetry. At the end of the year he presented to Catherine of Aragon his prose version of Plutarch's *De Tranquillitate Animi*. At some point during these years, he had been involved with Catherine's successor as Queen of England; though some of the evidence pointing to an intimate relationship between Wyatt and Anne Boleyn can be disregarded, their names are too often found connected for us to regard every piece of testimony as groundless gossip. There may be some truth in the story that Wyatt warned Henry against Anne; at all events, Wyatt, who acted as Chief Ewer at Anne's coronation on 1st June 1533, was arrested in May 1536 and imprisoned in the Tower along with Anne and her alleged lovers.

However, Wyatt's fortunes generally prospered: Marshal of Calais from 1528–32, he was knighted on Easter Day 1535, made Sheriff of Kent the following year, and in April 1537, left England as Ambassador to the court of Emperor Charles V. His task was to improve relations between the Imperial Court and England following Henry's divorce and the repudiation of Papal authority, yet at the same time to prevent Charles making an alliance with France and the Pope against the English. Though personally Wyatt gained Charles's respect, his master's diplomatic aims were unrealistic, and the poet grew weary and discouraged, as his letters home make clear. He owed much to the friendly interest of Thomas Cromwell, who kept an eye on his chaotic finances, and defended his efforts to serve Henry VIII's interests. When Bishop Bonner and Simon Heynes arrived at Nice in April 1538 as special

ambassadors to 'observe' the encounter between Charles and Francis I,
Wyatt's outspokenness and animosity alienated Bonner to the point where he
complained to the King about his ambassador's behaviour, though Cromwell's
support carried Wyatt through this crisis.

In May 1540, Cromwell was arrested and executed at Tyburn on 28th July,
the day Henry married Catherine Howard, and among Cromwell's papers
was found Bonner's 'charge-sheet' concerning Wyatt's conduct in Spain in
1539; on 17th January Wyatt was arrested once more, and placed in the
Tower. He prepared a detailed and determined defence, but was probably
saved from his master's wrath by the intercession of Queen Catherine. He was
soon at liberty; in April he was captaining a troop defending Calais; in 1542
he was made Knight of the Shire for Kent, and Chief Steward of the Manor
of Maidstone.

Early in October 1542, hastening to meet the Spanish Ambassador at
Falmouth and accompany him to London, Wyatt contracted a fever of which
he died; he was buried in Sherborne Abbey, Dorset.

POETRY

'In the latter end of the same kings raigne sprong up a new company of
courtly makers, of whom Sir *Thomas Wyat* th'elder & *Henry* Earle of Surrey
were the two chieftaines, who having travailed into Italie, and there tasted
the sweete and stately measures and stile of the Italian Poesie . . . they greatly
pollished our rude & homely maner of vulgar Poesie, from that it had bene
before, and for that cause may justly be sayd the first reformers of English
meetre and stile.'

Puttenham's famous tribute of the 1580s was probably deserved, but it
focussed attention on only one aspect of Wyatt's work, the translations from
Italian which have such a prominent place in the selection of poems published
by Tottel in 1557. Little importance is attached to his work with the indigenous
lyric, or his satires, which have native as well as continental roots: only in this
century has it been possible to view Wyatt's all-round achievement in some-
thing like its proper completeness.

Wyatt was not only a pioneer; he also used the long-familiar forms and
attitudes of native love poetry. His triumph was to take over the conventions
of haughty lady and pleading suitor, vows of fidelity and cries of unappeased
longing, and inject a new intensity into them. At his best, he discovers new
variations on the old stereotyped attitudes, chiefly because he rejects the
troubadour and Petrarchan convention that love is a ceaseless masculine
aspiration towards an idealized female, and insists instead on a conception
involving a mutual moral obligation between lovers. Many of his poems
reflect on the instability of the courtly love relationship, which breeds that
sense of disillusion and haunting melancholy which pervades so many of his

lyrics, giving them their distinctive rueful tone. Idealization of woman is rare in Wyatt: so is the traditional manly subservience. Wyatt frequently rebels against the code which demands male sacrifice on the altar of female beauty, since too many women are not worthy of such self-immolation. The spare diction and accomplished rhythms of his finest lyrics reinforce the directness of his approach and the plainness with which he speaks.

His sonnets and satires are also considerable achievements: if the former lack the polish of Surrey's, they include one or two brilliant adaptations of the Petrarchan model to suit Wyatt's different philosophy of love and more argumentative temperament, while the satires are most successful reconstructions of materials adopted from a wide variety of sources, bound together by a genuinely personal and conversational format, which compensates for the somewhat anonymous quality of many of Wyatt's lyrics.

Viewed as a whole, Wyatt's complete achievement is considerable, and his poetic stock stands higher today than at almost any time since his death.

96. FAREWELL, ALL MY WELLFARE

Wyatt here adopts the character of the seduced maiden found in other pieces of the period, but infuses it with sympathy for the girl's plight, laying stress on the ethical breach implied by the man's infidelity, and the eternal female desire for security in love, which this relationship did not respect.

l.1. Farewell, all my wellfare: a typical play on words, for which Wyatt has a taste. The line 'Adew, all my welfare' occurs in a song 'Hey nony nony nony nony no' in the court song-book, Add. MS 31922. (See Stevens, No. H. 31.)

l.2. My shue is trode awry: proverbial phrase for being seduced (Tilley, S 373).

l.3. karke and care: alliterative cliché frequently found in medieval verse.

l.6. shyffte: 'expedient, trick, resource'.

l.9. pretence: 'intention, design' (not used here with the modern meaning).

l.17. dowtles: used with more force than it is today: 'with no doubt at all'.

l.22. feythe to borow: gave his word as a surety. This usage is found frequently in *T. & C.* and elsewhere.

l.24. And he forsworne: cf. *The Legend of Good Women* F. 666: 'Ye men that falsly sweren many an oth'.

l.28. 'to hinder you from progressing as swiftly in a love affair as he did'.

l.30. fayn: feign.

97. WHAT MENYTHE THYS

The poet here exploits the theme of 'love's contrarities', popularized by Petrarch, though the citing of paradoxes in connection with sexual attraction can be traced back to earliest times. W. H. Wiatt in *Renaissance News* 11 (1958) suggested a possible source for this poem in Ovid's *Amores*, I. ii, *ll.*1–4: ('How comes it that my couch seems hard to me, my covers won't stay in place on the bed, that I've passed the whole night without sleep, and the weary bones of my twisted body ache?')

The hard bed, dishevelled bed-clothes, sleepless nights, and the aching body are commonplaces, but Wiatt sees significance in the face that the torments follow the same order in both poems, and his theory should be considered in the light of a possible Ovidian source for 'They fle from me' (p. 103), though in both cases, Wyatt may simply have been drawing unconsciously on his recollections of Ovid, rather than modelling himself on the Roman poet.

*l.*10. *For hete and cold I burne and shake:* a typical Petrarchan image, though similar examples in *T. & C.* and the anonymous lyrics suggest that Wyatt need not have turned to the Italians for this type of imagery.

*l.*13. *A mornynges:* in the mornings.

*l.*14. *gysse:* mode of behaviour.

*l.*15. *devysse:* deliberate, try to work out.

*l.*19. *The cold blood forsakythe my face:* a traditional image of medieval love poetry.

98. ONS IN YOUR GRACE

A lyric, from the Blage manuscript, which demonstrates Wyatt's ability to adopt a simple idiomatic phrase as a refrain, and through successive repetitions, to charge it with significances unrealized at the start of the poem.

*l.*3. *tornyd my case:* changed my condition.

*l.*16. *knyt the knot:* one of Wyatt's favourite images.

*l.*18. 'Though you pretend the oath is now forgotten.'

*ll.*23–4. 'And though I've satisfied you well enough for you to claim that you've been adequately repaid (for your loving remarks).'

*l.*29. 'Saying they no longer apply to me.'

*l.*32. Death as a result of unrequited love is a tedious convention of Western love poetry: for one connection see De Rougemont's *Passion and Society*.

100. QUONDAM WAS I

Wyatt's commentary on the fickleness of women is extensive, repetitive, and not always successful, but here, addressing the favoured rival, he embodies the general moral in a particular example, and achieves a Donne-like blend of mockery and regret.

*l.*1. *Quondam:* at a certain time, once (cf. the first line of the preceding poem).

*l.*3. *trad the tras:* an alliterative cliché of the period; 'been through the experience'.

*l.*9. *laughte . . . smyl:* a neat contrast between the spontaneous total sincerity of laughter and the guarded ambiguity of a smile.

*l.*12. *kysses many whon:* 'many a kiss'.
*l.*14. *the moo:* 'more of the same kind'.

100. I LOVE LOVYD

An attractive expression of the paradox of a love reciprocated, yet frustrated by the antipathy of the unseen enemies of any courtly love affair, whose prototype is found in the *losengiers*, the 'tale-bearers' of troubadour verse. Some of the oxymorons have a Petrarchan ring, but the issues are material ones, and the whole poem is set on a more mundane level than its Italian parallels.

*l.*1. *I love lovyd:* cf. the opening of a song in Add. MS 5465, the Fayrfax MS, one of the song-books used at Henry VIII's court (Stevens, No. F. 21): 'I love, loved'. Also one in Add. MS 31922 (Stevens, No. H. 108): 'I love unloved'.
*l.*4. The MS reads 'will', to stress Wyatt's pun on 'well' and 'will'.
*l.*19. 'Since of all misfortunes, we alone suffer this particular one.'
*l.*23. *greve:* grief.

101. MY LUTE AWAKE!

One of the most celebrated of Wyatt's lyrics, 'My lute awake' exhibits a wider range of imagery than is usual with him, and the poet rarely attains to the intensity of expression and tragic simplicity of stanzas 6 and 7. The revolt against the dictates of *amour courtois* which commanded the male to serve faithfully despite his mistress's indifference, is typical.

*l.*6. *ere:* ear.
*l.*7. 'As soon as lead can engrave marble'; this stanza and its successor employ many of the conventional images of love poetry.
*l.*17. *love's shot:* Cupid with his bow and arrow was supposed responsible for people falling in love.
*l.*26. *wethered:* withered, though possibly the modern meaning of 'weathered' applies too.

103. THEY FLE FROM ME

This famous lyric has attracted much critical attention in recent years; leaving aside biographical content, which can never be firmly ascertained, the chief points of interest have been the interpretation of the imagery, and the poem's possible source. The most plausible explanation of the first stanza is that Wyatt is thinking of the manner in which a falcon was trained for the hunting-field, by familiarizing it with human contact until it subordinated its own will to the falconer's. He recalls how formerly the birds trusted him, 'stalking' about his room 'with naked fote' (i.e. without jesses), sacrificing their freedom to eat from the poet's hand: now they have reverted to their former 'wild' state, as has Wyatt's former mistress. (See Ann Berthoff, 'The Falconer's Dream of Trust': Wyatt's 'They Fle from Me', *The Sewanee Review*, 71 (1963), pp. 477–94. But cf. R. L. Greene, *Bucknell Review* 12 (1964), pp. 17–30.)

Interest in discovering a source for 'They fle from me' is partly occasioned by the unusually sensuous quality of the poem, by comparison with most of Wyatt's other work. Ovid's *Amores* has been suggested as a likely stimulus to his creative imagination here, and C. E. Nelson ('A Note on Wyatt and Ovid', *Modern Language Review* 58 (1963), pp. 60–3) cites two passages in Book I. v and Book III. vi, in which Ovid depicts Corinna, which may have contributed to Wyatt's description of the girl in stanza 2. He may well have used these hints, for certainly there is nothing to parallel such a picture of female seductiveness elsewhere in his writings.

l.1. They fle from me: this vivid phrase is also used by Charles d'Orleans in describing his sorrows: 'They fle fro me, they dar not onys abide' (*l.*1347).

l.6. bred at my hand: a satiric poem in MS Eng. poet e.1., describing female types, has the line, 'Some wil tak bred at a man's hand'.

l.8. Thancked be fortune: a common enough expression, though Wyatt could have found it used several times by Chaucer, e.g. *The Knight's Tale*, *C.T.* I. 925; *T. & C.* IV. 2.

l.12. armes long and small: long slender arms were part of the medieval ideal of female beauty (cf. Charles d'Orleans's 'long smal armys twayne', *l.*4138).

l.14. A most beautiful impression of the girl's hesitant forwardness is conveyed here.

l.15. It was no dreme: Wyatt is possibly thinking here of the erotic dream convention found in some late medieval poems.

l.19. newfangilnes: fickleness, cf. *The Squire's Tale*, *C.T.* V. 610–11:

> Men loven of propre kinde newfangelnesse
> As briddes doon that men in cages fede

a simile which may have a bearing on the genesis of the whole poem.

l.20. kyndely: a play on words (1) 'kindly' (used ironically), (2) 'by kind' i.e. 'by nature, naturally' (she's reverted to type, a 'natural being' no longer 'tame').

103. MY GALY CHARGED WITH FORGETFULNES

A moderately successful rendering of Petrarch's sonnet 189, 'Passa la nave mia colma d'oblio'. Wyatt retains the shape and ideas of his original, allowing the flow of analogies between sea-voyage and emotional disturbance to control the poetic structure.

However, he does not reproduce Petrarch's metrical scheme of ABBA ABBA CDE CDE or the 'Shakespearean' form, preferring the less satisfying compromise, ABBA ABBA CDD CEE. He does, however, seem to view

the sestet as a unit, not as a quatrain and a couplet, though here the first pair
of rhymes isolate them a little.

*l.*3. *myn ennemy:* Love.

*l.*5. *owre:* translates Petrarch's 'remo', an oar. But some commentators suggest
the meaning 'hour'.

*l.*6. 'as if death were preferable to survival in such circumstances'.

*l.*8. *sighes:* the wind is composed of sighs and fear.

*l.*10. *wered:* worn.

*l.*11. *Wrethed:* woven, twisted.

*l.*12. *The stars be hid that led me to this pain:* a notable single line, not found in
Petrarch.

*l.*13. *confort:* some editors read 'consort' here.

104. FAREWELL, LOVE, AND ALL THY LAWES FOREVER

An original sonnet on the 'rebel lover' theme, which Wyatt infuses with
his own particular brand of masculine pride and integrity.

*l.*3. *Senec:* Seneca, Latin author and Stoic philosopher (*c.* 4 B.C.–A.D. 65).
P'ato: Greek thinker and teacher (*c.* 429–347 B.C.), who immortalized the
work of Socrates (469–399 B.C.).

*l.*4. 'To apply my intelligence to acheiving perfect happiness' (Wyatt often
uses 'wealth' to imply a state of contentment and harmony).

*l.*8. *libertie:* freedom from the entanglements of love.

*l.*14. *rotten boughes to clyme:* a proverbial phrase meaning to undertake a risky
task (Tilley B 557). Wyatt uses the image elsewhere, and his work is one of
the earliest contexts in which it occurs.

104. YOU THAT IN LOVE FINDE LUCKE

In this original sonnet, Wyatt portrays himself as one whose experiences of
live have exploded the elaborate 'make-believe' of *amour courtois*, juxtaposing
sad but concrete memories of previous danger and disappointment to the
dubious success of a romantic encounter on May morning, one of the key
'events' in the Lover's calendar. The poem abounds in Chaucerian echoes.

*l.*2. *lust and joyful jolitie:* cf. *Complaint unto Pity*, *l.*39: 'And fresshe Beautee,
Lust, and Jolyte'.

*l.*3. *Do away your sluggardie!:* cf. *The Knight's Tale*, *C.T.* I. 1042: 'For May
wole have no slogardie a-nyght'.

*l.*4. *do May some observance!:* cf. *T. & C.* II. 112: 'And lat us don to May
some observaunce'.

*l.*6. *happs most unhappy:* a typical Wyatt pun, which increases the tension
between the language of youthful idealism and the disillusioned tones of
experience.

l.8. *As oon whome love list litil to avaunce:* cf. *T. & C.* I. 518: 'Of hem that Love list febly for to avaunce', a line echoed in *The Complaint of the Black Knight*, *l*.354.

l.9. *Sephame:* W. H. Wiatt (*Notes and Queries* 197, June 1952) identifies 'Sephame' with Edward Sepham, M.A., a lecturer in logic at Oxford, though his astrological skill is not on record outside Wyatt's poem.

l.10. *the ruler of the May:* Venus was supposed to govern the sign of Taurus.

ll.12–13. Wyatt was imprisoned in May 1534 and in May 1536, and he may be referring to these 'mishaps' here, though Chaucer is also found alluding to May as a time of misfortune in *The Boke of the Duchesse, T. & C., The Knight's Tale* etc.

105. DYVERS DOTHE USE, AS I HAVE HARD AND KNO

Another original sonnet in rebellious mood, though the poet here adopts a superior pose and accepts female fraility as part of the nature of things, to which the only mature reaction is an amused cynicism.

l.1. *Dyvers dothe use:* 'various men are accustomed'.

l.13. *of kinde:* natural, by nature.

l.14. *That often chaunge doth plese a woman's minde:* proverbial (see Tilley W 673, which does not cite Wyatt).

105. WHOSO LIST TO HOUNTE

Wyatt's most celebrated sonnet, partly because of its traditional association with the figure of Anne Boleyn, with whom Wyatt is generally agreed to have been on intimate terms. (Kenneth Muir explores the evidence fully in his *Life and Letters of Sir Thomas Wyatt*.) Although he bases his poem on a Petrarchan original, 'Una candida cerva sopra l'erba' (*In Vita* 190), Wyatt deliberately destroys the reverential atmosphere and mystical purity of the Italian's vision, notably by his substitution of the flirtatious courtly 'hind' for Petrarch's gentle milk-white hart, and the pack of eager suitors for the awed observer. (See also Introduction, p. 18.)

l.4. *theim:* them.

l.8. *Sins in a nett I seke to hold the wynde:* proverbial. (See Tilley W 416.)

l.9. *put him owte of dowbte:* a common phrase, but it does occur in the English translation of *Le Roman de la Rose*, *l*.2102: 'And I hadde putte hym out of doute.' (See context.)

l.13. *Noli me tangere:* traditionally Christ's words to Mary Magdalene after his resurrection (A.V., John xx. 17). Wyatt took the phrase and the diamond-studded collar from Petrarch.

l.13. *Cesar's I ame:* Petrarch indicates by this phrase that Laura belongs to

God and will therefore enjoy only a short earthly life before she returns to his keeping; Wyatt may be assumed to be referring to Henry VIII.

106. TAGUS, FAREWELL

Wyatt was recalled to England from Spain in April 1539, and began his journey home in June; Muir suggests the poem was written in May. The piece appears in the Egerton MS in Wyatt's own hand, headed 'In Spayn': its biographical content and patriotic tone make it an unusual example of Wyatt's art.

*l.*1. *Tagus:* one of the most important rivers of Spain and Portugal, flowing roughly west from near Madrid, through Toledo, over the border, entering the sea near Lisbon where its estuary forms an important harbour.

*ll.*1–2. Wyatt is undoubtedly recalling Boethius' *De Consolatione Philosophiae* Book III, Metrum 10, though not necessarily Chaucer's translation (*Boece*): 'Alle the thinges that the ryver Tagus yveth yow with his goldene gravelis'.

*l.*2. *alredy tryd:* already sifted from the dross.

*l.*3. *Tems:* Thames.

*l.*5. *the town which Brutus sowght by drems:* London. Brutus, the great-grandson of Aeneas, was said to have landed at Totnes in Devon with a band of Trojan followers, and founded his capital of Troia Nova or Trinovantium on the banks of the Thames. Cf. *A Myrrour for Magistrates* (1587 edn.). Tragedy 26 (Julius Caesar):

> Of *Priames* bloud wee ar, from *Greece* we *Trojanes* came,
> As *Brutus* brought us thence, and gave this land his name.
>
> (*ll.* 110–11).

*l.*6. i.e. the Thames encloses London in her 'embrace'.

106. SYGHES AR MY FOODE

Another personal poem, inspired by one of Wyatt's spells in prison, possibly that of 1541. It is addressed to Sir Francis Bryan, a prominent courtier of the day (see notes to 'A spending hand' (p. 108).

*l.*6. *assaulteth:* I have rejected the reading 'assaulted'.

*ll.*7–8. A proverb which may be traced back to the *sententiae* of Publilius Syrus (*c.* 43 B.C.) No. 196: *Etiam sanato vulnere cicatrix manet* ('Even when the wound heals the scar remains'), cf. Tilley W 929.

107. STOND WHOSO LIST

Wyatt was heavily indebted to Seneca, the Stoic Roman thinker and dramatist, for his own philosophy of life and this poem shows the debt most openly, based as it is on a passage in Seneca's tragedy *Thyestes* (*ll.*391–403). It forms a memorable expression of the perils of public service and the consolations of obscurity, a note re-echoed in the Satires; the diction is colloquial and vigorous, adding new intensity to the Senecan commonplaces.

l.3. use me quyet: emphatic; '*I* will practise living a placid existence'.
l.4. brackishe: literally 'salty', therefore 'leaving a nasty taste in the mouth'.
l.7. after the common trace: in keeping with general human experience.
l.8. by the croppe: a stock expression, meaning 'by the throat'.
l.10. dazed: 'stunned, stupefied'. *dreadfull:* 'full of dread'. The alliteration contributes powerfully to the effect.

107. WHO LYST HIS WELTHE AND EAS RETAYNE

Like the preceding, this poem reveals a debt to Seneca, its refrain taken from a line in *Phaedra* (*l.*1140), part of a chorus lamenting that Fortune's fury is unleashed chiefly against the great, while it spares the humble. Here Wyatt appears to be describing his experiences while in the Tower in May 1536, at the time when Anne Boleyn and her alleged lovers were executed there: the exact reasons for Wyatt's arrest at this time are still obscure, but evidently he felt sufficiently implicated to express his disillusion with courtly ambition.

l.2. 'let him keep himself obscure and anonymous'.
ll.3–4. 'Do not press forward too fast to enter the gate, the return through which is caused by the contempt of others.'
ll.6–7. Something of a commonplace. Wyatt probably took it from the same chorus in Seneca:

> The highest mountain tops catch every wind that blows . . .
> green valleys rarely feel the thunder's stroke

it also appears in Horace, *Odes* II. 10. 9–12.
l.22. 'Being quick-witted does not advance one's defence very speedily.'
l.24. geve God the sterne: Wyatt uses a similar image in a letter to his son from Paris, 15th April 1537 (Muir, *Life and Letters*, p. 39): '(God's) punischment is first the withdrawing of his favour and grace, and in leving his hand to rule the sterne, to let the ship runne without guyde to your owne distruction . . .', cf. also Skelton's *The Bowge of Courte, l.*250: 'Holde up the helme, loke up, and lete God stere'.

108. A SPENDING HAND THAT ALWAY POWRETH OWTE

It is now generally accepted that Wyatt's three satires in *terza rima* are among his finest works, combining classical taste and temper, with the best features of English native diction and homely traditions of aphoristic philosophizing. Successfully 'naturalizing' his materials, chiefly borrowed from Alamanni and Horace, he shows himself a pioneer in the art of 'imitation' (in which he was followed by Surrey, Donne, and Jonson) whereby modern instances are utilized to illustrate the moral observations of the original. Late seventeenth- and eighteenth-century literature is full of examples, one of the best being Dr Johnson's version of Juvenal, *The Vanity of Human Wishes*.

The poem is addressed to Sir Francis Bryan, one of Wyatt's contemporaries at court and a favourite of Henry VIII, frequently beating him in games of skill and chance; he appeared with him in feats of arms during court festivities, losing an eye in a joust on Shrove Tuesday 1526. He was twice married, first to the widow of John Fortescue (a fact Wyatt may allude to in *l*.60), and later to the Countess of Ormond: during the infancy of Prince Edward (later Edward VI), Bryan and his wife were in charge of his household. It is difficult to judge whether Wyatt is touching on certain of Bryan's personal characteristics in the satire, or whether he should be viewed as a virtually anonymous 'foil' to the poet.

The whole satire is a fluent exercise in sustained irony; Wyatt may have learnt the technique from Horace's *Satire* II. 5, in which Tiresias offers Ulysses mock-serious advice on repairing his fortunes by obtaining a legacy, but the details and tone are very much his own. Horace is subtler, but the directness and intensity, even at times the savagery, of the English transcend the comparison, and make Wyatt's poem peculiarly personal to him, reminding us that the voice of experience lies behind it.

ll.1–2. *A spending hand*: I have been unable to trace this proverb elsewhere though Wyatt's use here indicates that it was a familiar one. Miss Thomson suggests that the poet is here mocking the contemporary love of proverbial wisdom, though he indulged in it himself.

ll.3–4. *And on the stone* etc.: Cited by Tilley S 885.

l.16. *noppy*: an epithet commonly applied to ale (cf. *The Tunnynge of Elynour Rummynge*, *l*.102).

l.16. *for the noyns*: possibly 'heady enough to suit the occasion'.

ll.18–21. 'That's the way swine grunt in the sty, chew the turds formed on the ground, and slaver over pearls (cf. A.V. Matthew vii. 6), with their heads still in the trough, so (in the same way) a donkey is incapable of appreciating harp-music'. The use of 'then' = 'so' is odd; Tottel reads 'so'.

l.21. *Then of the harp*: cf. *T. & C.* I. 731–5:

> Or artow lik an asse to the harpe,
> That hereth sown whan men the strynges plye,
> But in his mynde of that no melodie
> May sinken hym to gladen, for that he
> So dul ys of his bestialite?

l.22. *So sackes of durt*: 'That's how those dung-bags (the monks) grow fat in their monasteries.' Wyatt is traditionally an ardent supporter of the Reformation. 'Durt' means ordure.

*l.*31. *intend:* assert.

*l.*34. *it is boeth welth and ese:* i.e. it is wealth and ease to flee truth.

*l.*36. *Full nere that wynd:* i.e. truth is almost impermissible in society today.

*l.*36. *misese:* poverty, misery.

*ll.*37-9. *Use vertu as it goeth nowadayes:* cf. Wyatt's letter to his son, 15th April 1537 (Muir, *Life and Letters*, p. 38). 'And here I call not honestye that men comenly cal honestye . . .'

*l.*44. *as to a dogge a chese:* probably proverbial, though I have not met it elsewhere. Does it mean 'only lend something to someone who has no use for it'?

*l.*45. *a kant:* a portion; i.e. 'make sure you charge interest of half again'.

*l.*47. *Kittson:* Nott suggests an allusion to Sir Thomas Kittson, Sheriff of London 1533: Rollins refers to a London bookseller, Anthony Kitson.

*ll.*51-8. The poem resembles Horace's Satire II. 5, most closely at this point.

*l.*65. *Let the old mule byte upon the bridill:* proverbial (Tilley B 670).

*l.*69. *myddell:* 'waist', here used with the meaning of the modern 'figure'.

*l.*75. *Pandare:* Pandarus, a clear allusion to *T. & C.*

*l.*78. *Be next thyself, for frendshipp beres no prise:* 'Look after Number One, since friendship carries no prizes with it.'

*l.*91. *coyne to kepe as water in a syve:* proverbial (Tilley W 111).

HENRY HOWARD,
EARL OF SURREY

(1517–47)

LIFE

Grandson to the victor of Flodden Field (1513), Henry Howard was the eldest son of Thomas, created Duke of Norfolk in 1524, when his son received the courtesy title of Earl of Surrey. The Howards were one of the most powerful and influential families in England, prominent Roman Catholics, who claimed descent from Edward the Confessor, and Surrey received a sound education in the humanities: when in his early teens, he is said to have made translations from Italian and French. At the age of thirteen, he became companion to Henry VIII's illegitimate son, Henry Fitzroy, Duke of Richmond, and they were educated together as intimate friends, in 1532 travelling with the King to France, where they remained with the court of Francis I for nearly a year, and where Surrey was subject to strong Italian literary influences. In the same year, Surrey married Lady Frances Vere, daughter of the Earl of Oxford, though they did not live together till 1535; by her, the poet had five children.

During the years of court service that followed, Surrey helped his father to put down the Pilgrimage of Grace in 1536 (his confinement to Windsor in 1537 resulted from striking Sir Edward Seymour for suggesting that the suppression had been half-heartedly performed), attended the trial of Anne Boleyn (at which his father presided) and the execution of his cousin Catherine Howard, helped to overthrow Cromwell, and served in various military campaigns in Scotland and France, being created a Knight of the Garter in 1541. A haughty pride seems to have been the dominant feature of Surrey's temperament; alluded to in 1539 as 'the most foolish proud boy that is in England', he was imprisoned in February 1542 for quarrelling with another courtier, while the next year saw him again in prison, for hooliganism in the London streets and eating meat in Lent. In 1544 he began to build himself a splendid neo-classical mansion near Norwich, but in the following year he was serving abroad, being Marshal of the Field at the unsuccessful siege of Montreuil in September, and later in command of Boulogne, where he was reprimanded for exposing himself to unnecessary danger; he was recalled to England in March 1546.

With the last illness of Henry VIII, the Howards were felt to be too close to the throne for the comfort of others, especially the aspiring Seymour family, whom they had antagonized. In December 1546 Surrey was arrested on charges of treason (including that of quartering the arms of Edward the Confessor with his own), his previous rashness and present defiance standing him little chance of acquittal. On 19th January 1547, Surrey was executed on Tower Hill, dying only a week before his sovereign.

POETRY

Surrey enjoyed his highest renown in the eighteenth and nineteenth centuries, when his poetry, often assumed to pre-date Wyatt's, was praised for its superior metrical regularity, polished elegance, and clarity of diction and syntax by readers who found Wyatt awkward, lawless, idiosyncratic, and even incompetent. In the last few decades a reverse tendency has shown itself, so that Surrey is now condemned as effete, mechanical and artificial, his smooth rhythms appearing monotonous, his finely turned phrases 'literary'. No doubt the contemporary preference for Wyatt will abate somewhat, but it is unlikely that critical discussion will again centre around any battle for poetic supremacy: Wyatt and Surrey are now recognized as belonging to very dissimilar schools of poetry.

Surrey can now be seen as the first major English poet working in the spirit of classical humanism, a neo-classical writer attempting to convey in his native tongue something of the weight, dignity, poise, ease, felicity of diction, 'measure' and harmony of the Latin poets. This is particularly evident in Surrey's version of Books II and IV of Virgil's *Aeneid*, where, if some have found his inversions and metrical accuracy repellent, resulting in a loss of linguistic vigour, others have praised them as assisting Surrey to reproduce the effects of his original. The classical virtues of balance and polish are not confined to Surrey's translations alone: in many original works, for example the poem on Wyatt's death (p. 116), he creates a memorable English work in an almost Roman style, and his best writing is found almost entirely outside the dominant medieval genres of love-complaint, devotional lyric, and chivalrous romance: his powers of invention are slight, and he is happiest on real-life topics involving marital love or masculine comradeship. Even in the hallowed form of the Petrarchan sonnet, he is most at ease when he can escape its traditional sentiments, and turn to domestic or political themes: 'Set me wheras the sonne' is a poor thing beside 'Th'Assyryans' king'.

Surrey's verse may not generate the excitement we receive from the dynamic speaking voice of Wyatt; the tension of interior conflict is often missing, and the surprises are fewer, but at the same time, Surrey's achievement is not simply of mere historical importance, a vague indication of what late Elizabethan verse might flower into. At his greatest, he combines impeccable technical skill with the ability to coin lasting phrases and crystallize human moods and states of mind; he produced poetry that is not only worth consideration by virtue of its content, but also a pleasure to contemplate, by virtue of the classic grace of its design.

III. WHEN RAGYNG LOVE WITH EXTREME PAYNE

Turning to this delicate love poem by Surrey from the work of Wyatt, one is soon aware of Surrey's more classical sense of balance and restraint, his greater fluidity and control, though one may miss the greater intensity and immediacy of feeling and language of the older poet. The initial letters of the stanzas form the word 'W-I-A-T-T', and it is possible that Surrey devised the poem as a compliment to the older poet, though such letters often occur quite naturally at the openings of stanzas (cf. 'I that Ulysses' yeres have spent', p. 124).

ll.1–6. Surrey here uses many stock Petrarchan images of a lover's woes.
ll.7–18. The economy with which the Trojan War is depicted is typical of Surrey's classical temperament; the imagery reinforces, but does not overwhelm, the central situation.
l.11. *Agamemnon's daughter:* Iphigenia, daughter of Clytemnestra and Agamemnon king of Mycenae, was sacrificed to appease the wrath of the goddess Diana, so that the Greek fleet might leave Aulis to sail for Troy. At the last moment, Diana spared Iphigenia's life. On his return Agamemnon paid for his crimes at the hands of his wife.
l.18. *Helene:* wife of Menelaus of Sparta; her flight with Paris, a Trojan prince, led to the great expedition to Troy to recover her.
l.28. *draweth in ure:* 'comes into existence', literally 'use'.
l.30. *fare:* two meanings are available here, 'food' or 'journey'. Since Surrey's classical analogy concerns a voyage, I incline to the second interpretation.

112. SET ME WHERAS THE SONNE DOTHE PERCHE THE GRENE

Translated from Petrarch's sonnet 'Pommi ove 'l sole occide i fiori e l'erbe' (*In Vita* 145), which may owe a debt in its turn to some lines of Horace (*Odes* I. 22. 17–24). Surrey follows Petrarch's sense fairly accurately, echoing his neatly paired antitheses, but cannot resist substituting Wyatt's wry note of resigned frustration for Petrarch's proud claim of enduring fidelity. Surrey also modifies the Italian's rhyme-scheme producing the classic English form of the sonnet known as the Shakespearean.

l.11. *Thrawle, or at large:* ' a slave or at liberty'.
l.14. Petrarch stresses that he has already 'sighed for' Laura fifteen years; Surrey prefers to hint that some redress might be proferred him.

This piece was probably written for the Countess of Surrey, from whom Surrey was separated while on military duties in France, 1545–6; it owes something to Serafino's *Epistola* VI, which in turn derives from Ovid's *Heroides*, a collection of fictional letters by the heroines of antiquity. The poem is a fine example of Surrey's delicacy and poise, while the dramatic core and the way in which the strong sense of actuality modifies the conventional phraseology of love poetry are in the best traditions of the English lyric.

l.7. help to fill my moorning voyce: 'join my lamentations, and so make them louder'.

ll.8–14. The imagery may owe something to Petrarch's 'Passa la nave' (*In Vita* 189), translated by Wyatt as 'My galy charged with forgetfulnes' (p. 103).

l.10. governance: keeping control.

l.14. avail: profit, advantage.

l.22. in armes acrosse: i.e. embracing each other.

l.23. Rejoyce: enjoy, or give pleasure to.

ll.24–8. These lines owe something to Serafino, and to Vergil's but the wry wit of the last line is original to Surrey.

l.33. This line too is closely based on Serafino. *my swete fo:* cf. *T. & C.* V. 228: 'Criseyde, my swete fo'.

l.42. This line anticipates Sidney's attempts in *Astrophel and Stella* to reproduce abrupt changes of thought with greater vernacular realism.

114. WHEN WINDESOR WALLES SUSTAINED MY WEARIED ARME

Some of Surrey's best verse is devoted to the celebration of male comradeship rather than heterosexual relations, and in this sonnet, it is his memories of a happy childhood spent partly at Windsor as companion to Henry Fitzroy, that provide the contrast with his present misfortune, presumably his imprisonment in the castle in 1537 for striking a fellow-courtier within the precincts of the Court. (See also the notes to the next poem.)

ll.1–2. Surrey depicts himself in a typical attitude of thought, leaning his elbow on the castle walls, cupping his chin in his hand.

l.3. green with warm: a rare usage, 'green with warmth'.

l.4. Veare: Ver, the Spring.

l.5. the weddyd birds so late: the recently married birds. Surrey also alludes, in another poem, 'When somer tok in hand', to 'the new betrothed birds'; their function is partly conventional.

l.7. joily woes: 'jolly woes', an oxymoron typical of the Petrarchan love tradition. Cf. *T. & C.* II. 1099: 'I have a joly wo, a lusty sorwe'.

l.7. the hateles shorte debate: 'brief friendly rivalry'.

*l.*11. *smoky sighes:* 'misty, steaming sighs', cf. Petrarch's sonnet *In Morte* 288. 1. 'I'ho pien di suspir quest' aere tutto'. Emrys Jones parallels Wyatt's 'Lik as the pilgryme' (Muir, CVIII, 414), 'a smoky rayne', and *T. & C.* III. 628: 'that smoky reyn'. (See also 'The smoky sighes, the bitter teares' (p. 127).)

114. SO CREWELL PRISON HOWE COULD BETYDE, ALAS
Presumably written at the same period as the previous sonnet, 'So crewell prison' is a more direct evocation of Surrey's youthful days, and a more poignant memorial to his childhood companion. Henry Fitzroy, born in 1519, was Henry VIII's bastard son by Elizabeth Blount, and created Duke of Richmond in 1525; in 1533 he married Surrey's sister Mary and died of consumption in 1536.

Surrey's poem, apart from its interest as an attractive description of noble life in the Tudor period, is a skilful exercise in rhetorical techniques: *enumeratio*, by which a whole complex of related illustrations is built up, and *parison*, a contrast between past and present. It is worth remarking that the stanza-form is that of Gray's *Elegy*.

*l.*1. 'Alas! How could such a cruel prison as proud Windsor befall me?'
*l.*3. *childishe:* possibly simply 'youthful' but the word 'Childe' to signify a youth awaiting knighthood may be pertinent here.
*l.*4. *Priam's sonnes:* according to Homer, Priam had fifty sons, including Paris and Hector.
*l.*6. *courtes:* courtyards.
*l.*7. *maydens' towre:* part of the castle where the ladies of the court had their apartments.
*l.*8. *easye:* light, insignificant.
*l.*9. *sales:* halls, rooms.
*l.*11. *tygers:* often introduced into love poetry of the period as types of unfeeling savagery.
*l.*13. *palme playe:* a kind of tennis where the ball is hit with the palm of the hand. (Fr. 'jeu de la paume'.) *dispoyled:* 'changed' for the game (cf. the modern soccer player's 'strip').
*l.*16. *leddes:* the 'leads' of the flat roof, or possibly the leaded window-panes.
*l.*17. *graveld ground:* the space between the lists, spread with gravel, for tilting. *sleves tyed on the helme:* a lady's favour was often worn on a knight's helmet during joust or tournament.
*l.*19. 'With expressions suggesting that one of us would surely destroy the other.'
*l.*21. *rewthe:* sorrow (figurative).
*l.*26. *pleasaunt playnt:* 'pleasing complaint', typical oxymoron in love verse.

l.30. raynes avald: reins slackened. *ybrethed:* exercised.

l.32. chase . . . à force: an old hunting term ('chasse à forcer') for running a quarry down, as distinct from shooting it as it moves ('chasse à tirer').

l.38. dyvers chaung of playe: various changes of activity, or, possibly, of jest.

ll.41–4. This stanza employs many of the stock images of grief and distress.

l.44. upsupped: 'swallowed up, consumed'. 'As soon as sobbing sighs have swallowed up my tears (and caused them to stop) . . .'

l.45. O place of blisse: there is a three-stanza poem in Add. MS 17492 ('The Devonshire MS') attributed to Wyatt by Muir (Muir CLXXXVII) which begins 'The restfull place, revyver of my smarte', of which another version in the Egerton MS begins, 'O restfull place, reneewer of my smart'. It is likely that Surrey knew this lyric, which is actually an expanded version of Petrarch, *In Vita* 198.

l.46. 'Tell me where my noble companion is.'

l.51. fredome: 'nobility, generosity'.

ll.53–4. 'By remembering my greater grief (the loss of my boyhood friend) I cast out the lesser sorrow (of being imprisoned).'

116. WYATT RESTETH HERE, THAT QUICK COULD NEVER REST

Sir Thomas Wyatt died early in October 1542, and was buried in Sherborne Abbey (where the first line of Surrey's tribute is now engraved on a memorial stone); Surrey's epitaph appears to have been published by the end of the year. Jones remarks that it is 'arguably Surrey's best poem'; it certainly makes clear the admiration which the younger poet had for a writer fourteen years his senior, and despite the eulogistic tone, reinforces the impression of Wyatt's quizzical, restless personality which emerges from his own letters and non-amatory poems. The terse, epigrammatic style Surrey employs here was deemed to be the fittest mode for epitaphs, and the blend of laconic, elliptical, senatorial gravity and 'wit', looks forward to the seventeenth century and the Augustans.

l.1. H. H. Hudson (*Modern Language Notes* 45 (1930), p. 543) observes that this line translates an epitaph on Jacopo Trivulzio (*d.* 1518), an Italian soldier Camden renders it as

> *Hic mortuus requiescit semel,*
> *Qui vivus requievit nunquam*

l.2. disdayn: the contempt of others. In particular, Bishop Bonner and Simon Heynes, who in 1541 had Wyatt impeached before the Privy Council, and imprisoned. (Cf. also *ll.*4 and 30.)

l.4. envy: malice.

l.5. misteries: hidden meanings i.e. deep, profound thoughts.

l.6. The images of forge, hammer, and anvil are very common in sixteenth-century descriptions of the creative process.

l.7. *where that:* where.

ll.9–10. 'Where both sterness and mildness grew, to scorn vice and rejoice in virtue.'

l.13. It would be interesting to know if this is merely conventional tribute, or whether Surrey had some specific aspect of Wyatt's literary achievement in view.

l.14. A conventional flattering comparison throughout fifteenth-and sixteenth-century writing.

l.15. 'Uncompleted for lack of time' or possibly 'because of what time brought about ' (i.e. Wyatt's untimely death).

l.21. *none affect:* no passion.

ll.25–6. A standard portrayal of an honest councillor (cf. Wyatt's first satire, Muir CV. 19–21):

> My Poynz, I cannot frame my tonge to fayne,
> To cloke the trothe for praisse withowt desart,
> Of them that lyst all vice for to retayne.

l.27. *loft:* elated. *represt:* 'kept down'.

l.29. *corps:* the body, living or dead.

l.32. A conventional compliment.

ll.34–5. Surrey refers here to Wyatt's translation of the seven Penitential Psalms (Muir CVIII).

118. TH' ASSYRYANS' KING

Surrey is here found drawing on classical mythology once more for a leading image. Sardanaphalus, the effeminate king of Assyria, was alleged to have burnt himself and his household to death while under siege, and became commonly cited as an example of royal degeneracy, for instance in Gower's *Confessio Amantis* VII, and Lydgate's *The Fall of Princes* II. Actually the historical Sardanaphalus (the great Assyrian monarch of the seventh century B.C., Assur-bani-pal) scared his rebellious half-brother into this form of suicide at the siege of Babylon in 648 B.C. The aggressive tone, which stands out despite the elegant precision of the phrasing, has led some commentators to assert that Surrey is here directing his attack against Henry VIII, but M. Bryn Davies (*Huntington Library Quarterly* 23, 1959–60) suggests that it may also have been prompted by the poet's self-disgust at not dying a hero's death in the English retreat of January 1545/6 at Boulogne.

ll.1–4. 'Vanquyshed' governs both subordinate clauses.

l.6. *targe:* target, shield.

l.8. *charge:* burden, weight, responsibility. (Used here both literally and figuratively.)

Translating from the *Odes* of Horace II. 10, Surrey aims here for the concision and density of the original, in which the Latin poet recommends to Licinus, brother-in-law of his patron Maecenas, the ideal way of life, which for Horace lies in pursuing 'the golden mean'. Classical verses on 'right conduct' attracted many Renaissance writers, and Sir Philip Sidney made a version of this Ode, beginning 'You better sure shall live' (Ringler edn., pp. 142–3).

The 'Thomas' addressed is probably Thomas Clere, Surrey's squire, who died on 14th April 1545, as a result of a wound received at the siege of Montreuil in September 1544 when saving the poet's life. He was related to the Boleyn family. Another possible candidate is Thomas Ratcliffe, third Earl of Sussex, who also served with Surrey in France, and is addressed in another poem, 'My Ratclif, when thy rechlesse youth offendes'.

l.1. compasse: boundary, limit. The stress is on the second syllable.
l.6. advisdly: advisedly, wisely.
ll.9–11. See note to 'Who lyst his welthe and eas retayne' (p. 107, *ll.6–7*).
l.10. falne: the old third person plural indicative of 'fall'. 'Lofty turrets fall with a more violent impact.'
ll.15–20. 'At certain times Apollo stops frowning and, unbending his bow, sings to the harp; in straitened circumstances put on a bold front, and when the favouring winds fill your billowing sails, be prudent and take in a reef.'
l.20. ryft: a reef (nautical), part of the sail that can be reduced in area by rolling it up. *Hast is wast:* an English proverb, the sense of which is not found in Horace. (Tilley H 189.) It is typical of the Tudor translators from the classics that they should render classical notions with traditional native expressions.
l.20. profe: experience.

119. CERTAIN BOKES OF VIRGILES AENAEIS TURNED INTO ENGLISH METRE...

'Every school-boy knows' that Surrey's translation of Books Two and Four of Virgil's *Aeneid* is the earliest blank-verse poetry published in English; Book Four exists in three versions, the earliest dated 1554, while there is only one version of the second Book, that published with Book Four by Tottel in 1557. Tottel's text, which is followed here, is the best and most complete version extant. For observations on Surrey's blank verse, the reader must consult Emrys Jones' first-rate introduction to his edition of the poems.

The lines printed here translate *Aeneid* IV. 584–629. I have made reference to Professor R. G. Austin's excellent edition of Book IV (O.U.P. 1955) in composing many of my notes.

*ll.*1–3. The general nature of Surrey's indebtedness to Gavin Douglas's translation can be suggested by a comparison between their versions of these lines:

> Be this Aurora, leifand the purpour bed
> Of hir lord Titan, heth the erd ourspred
> With new days licht, and quhen the queyn
> The first grekyng of the day hes seyn
> And fra hir hie wyndoys gan espy . . .
>
> (Book IV. C xi, *ll.*1–5)

(see Jones' edition, and F. H. Ridley, 'Surrey's Debt to Gavin Douglas', *P.M.L.A.* 76 (1961). The text can be found on pp. 67–9 of David Coldwell's *Selections from Gavin Douglas*, Oxford, 1964.

*l.*3. *by her windowes:* the Latin has *e speculis*, 'from her watch-tower'; Surrey's version has a more homely, less heroic touch. So too 'the peping day' to render *primum albescere lucem* ('the first light grow white').

*l.*4. *splaid:* spread, displayed. (The Trojans have ceased to row, and now hoist sail.)

*ll.*8–9. The repetition of 'thus' in these lines is clumsy, and illustrates Surrey's difficulties in rendering the elliptical nature of the original.

*l.*9. *and scorne:* the Latin reads *inluserit*–'Shall he have made a mockery of us?'

*l.*12. *the rode:* roadstead, harbour. *some:* Tottel reads 'sone'.

*l.*12. *warpe:* tow, move by hauling on a rope. (Classical scholars differ about the reading at this point in Virgil's text, but whether *diripient* ('fall upon', scramble for') or *deripient* ('tear away') is preferred, there is no doubt that Dido is calling for violent activity from her people).

*l.*13. Surrey omits Dido's *date tela* 'issue weapons'.

*ll.*15–16. Modern editions of Virgil read *infelix Dido, nunc te facta impia tangunt*, 'unhappy, Dido, do your godless deeds come home to you now?' Surrey's rendering is based on the earlier reading of *fata* for *facta*.

*ll.*17–18. Surrey's translation obscures the sense here. Dido says that she should have been aware of the impiety of what she was doing when she made over her power to Aeneas. Compare Dryden's version:

> Then, when I gave my person and my throne,
> This hate, this rage, had been more timely shown   (*ll.*855–6)

*l.*18. *right hand:* translates the Latin *dextra*, which is equivalent to *fides*, 'faith'.

*l.*19. *countrie godes:* in Latin *Penates*, 'household gods'. Tottel reads 'goodes'.

*l.*23. *Ascanius:* Aeneas's son, rescued from the ruins of Troy by his father.

*l.*24. *his father's bord:* Dido is suggesting that she should have revenged herself on Aeneas as, for example, Atreus in Greek mythology served Thyestes, by killing his sons and serving them to their father as a meal.

*l.*27. *myselfe must die:* Surrey renders the Latin into the present tense.

*l.*28. *into that navy:* Virgil has *castra*, the stockade round the ships.

l.32. Sunne, with thy beames: Dido now proceeds to denounce Aeneas and his race, and by so cursing, makes her story part of the history of Rome. The invocation to the sun is a standard literary convention of the classical period; Milton utilized it at the opening of Book IV of *Paradise Lost*.

l.33. Surrey omits to assign to Juno any responsibility for Dido's sufferings, as Virgil does, calling her *interpres*, intermediary between Dido and Aeneas, as goddess of marriage.

ll.34-5. Proserpine: Persephone, borne off by Pluto (or Hades) to become Queen of the Underworld. Surrey substitutes her for the Latin *Hecate*, the goddess of the underworld, associated with black magic and sorcery, and whose devotees often congregated at cross-roads to worship and sacrifice dog's flesh to her.

l.36. Infernal furies: Latin *Dirae*. The Furies, or *Erinyes*, were the spirits of vengeance in the ancient world, summoned up by the curses of those whose kindred had been injured to punish the guilty.

l.39. Withdraw from me: Surrey has the older reading *avertite*, where modern editors print *advertite*. Dido asks for the gods to take note of her ills since they merit divine concern. The older version suggests that the gods should punish the wicked (not Dido), whose conduct justifies the exercise of divine powers.

l.40. cf. Douglas's line: 'And thir our prayeris accept, we you beseik' (*l.59*).

ll.44-53. The terms of Dido's curse were all fulfilled: Aeneas fought to establish himself on Italian soil and never returned to Troy, he had to abandon his son Ascanius or 'Julus', beseech help from Evander, and witness the deaths of many of his Trojan supporters; he is reputed to have reigned only few years before being killed; Servius says his body was never found.

l.46. hardy nacions: Virgil speaks of a single nation, the Rutuli, with whom Aeneas was in conflict after his landing in Italy, and who, according to Livy, eventually slew him.

l.48. rashed: dragged.

l.50. Tottel reads 'giltlesh'.

l.51. hard condicions of peace: the Rutuli and Trojans made a pact agreeing that the two races might mingle, but that the name of Troy should be lost.

l.52. 'May he never enjoy his kingdom nor the happiness of a long life.'

l.53. Surrey ends the curse on an Alexandrine, with a line almost the equal of Virgil's famous original *sed cadat ante diem mediaque inhumatus harena*. To the ancients, dying in one's prime and unburied was the most dreadful earthly fate conceivable (cf. Sophocles's *Antigone*). *ungraved:* 'unburied' (the first use cited by *O.E.D.*).

l.54. require: insist upon.

l.55. Tirians: Tottel reads 'Trians'. Carthage was founded by exiles, under Elissa, daughter of the Tyrian King. Dido's flight from Tyre to Carthage following the murder of her husband Sichaeus, is related in Book I of the *Aeneid*.

l.56. cinders: Latin *cineri*, of which 'ashes' would be a happier rendering. 'rewarde', however, is neat and economical, as is Surrey's treatment of the next line.

l.58. some wreaker may there spring: imperative in the Latin: 'Arise from my bones, some avenger!' The reference is to Hannibal; Dido is here presaging the three Punic Wars between Rome and Carthage, 264–146 B.C.

l.61. cf. Douglas 'Thir costis mot be to tharis contrar ay' (*l.91*).

GEORGE BOLEYN,
VISCOUNT ROCHFORD

(*c.* 1505–36)

LIFE

The earlier part of Rochford's life is less well chronicled than its gloomy end; as only son of Sir Thomas Boleyn, head of the wealthy commercial family whose fortunes soared highest during Anne's brief period as Queen (1533–6), George Boleyn first appears as one of those young pleasure-seeking aristocrats who made up the livelier section of the Tudor court in the 1520s and 30s. He, like Sir Francis Bryan and to a lesser extent, Wyatt, shared Henry's leisure pastimes of bowls, tennis, jousting, hunting, gambling, and making love, music and poetry. In later life he seems to have supplemented this earlier reputation as a playboy; created Viscount Rochford in 1529, he became a trusted ambassador abroad, and behaved with considerable courage, defiance and dignity during his arrest, imprisonment, trial and execution in May 1536, when he was said to be implicated in his sister the Queen's alleged adultery. In his speech from the scaffold on 17th May, he besought his hearers to 'trust not on the vanitie of the worlde, and especially in the flateringe of the courte'. Whatever the facts of Anne's supposed guilt, it seems unlikely that Rochford was involved in his sister's marital infidelities.

POETRY

Rochford is traditionally one of the gentleman-poets of the early Tudor court, frequently associated with *Tottel's Miscellany* though none of its anonymous contributions has ever been convincingly proved his. John Bale names him as the author of 'most elegant poems of various kinds, in the English tongue' and Anne Boleyn, while in the Tower, may have alluded to her brother's skill as a maker of 'balettes' in a casual conversation, unfortunately only surviving now in a mutilated form.

'O Death, Rocke mee Asleepe' has been frequently accepted as Rochford's work, and certainly it is very appropriate to his situation in 1536. Hebel and Hudson (*Poetry of the English Renaissance*, rev. edn. 1957, p. 920) prefer the claims of Richard Edwards, basing their opinion on Gascoigne's reference to a piece Edwards wrote in sickness called 'Soul-knell' which they identify as this lyric. If 'O Death, Rocke mee Asleepe' is by Edwards, it is very unlike his other extant works, which are mostly moralistic and reflective, and phrases like 'guiltlesse Ghost' and 'alone in prison in stronge' sound more suited to a condemned prisoner than a sick man. Pistol alludes to it in *2 Henry IV*, II. iv. 210: 'Then death rock me asleep, abridge my doleful days!'

The text is transcribed from folio 107v of British Museum Add. MS 26737, which includes Edwards's 'In goinge to my naked bed', a point which may seem significant to those who support Edwards's claims as author of the present poem.

122. O DEATH, ROCKE MEE ASLEEPE

l.4. carefull: full of care.
l.17. Woe worth: a curse on.

TOTTEL'S MISCELLANY

This important anthology, which introduced the work of poets such as Wyatt and Surrey to a general public, was published 'to the honor of the English tong, and for profit of the studious of Englishe eloquence', under the title *Songes and Sonettes*, by Richard Tottel, a London printer, on 5th June 1557. It contained forty poems by Surrey, and nearly a hundred by Wyatt, besides a number by 'Uncertain Auctours', of which only a handful can now be identified. One named contributor, Nicholas Grimald, Chaplain to Bishop Ridley, is usually claimed as the editor of the miscellany, partly because the very consistent alterations carried out on the poems in the interests of metrical regularity bear the stamp of an educated humanist, tidying up the rougher native rhythms to comply with classical principles.

It would be hard to exaggerate the influence of the collection: it ensured that 'the honorable stile of the noble earle of Surrey, and the weightinesse of the depewitted sir Thomas Wyat the elders verse' remained current into the Elizabethan period, though its example was not always beneficial. Predominantly courtly in tone, and amatory in subject, chiefly compiled from private manuscripts of the aristocracy (Tottel asks the ordinary reader to respect 'the statelinesse of stile removed from the rude skill of common eares'), its traditionalism was leavened by fashionable novelties stemming from Petrarch and neo-classical influences. There was a high quota of sententious verse too, in the native moralistic vein, though the underlying ideals are now less overtly Christian.

The vogue *Tottel's Miscellany* enjoyed was enormous: it went through nine editions by 1587, and became part of the popular consciousness: the foolish suitor Slender, in *The Merry Wives of Windsor*, seeking to impress Anne Page, cries 'I had rather than forty shillings I had my Book of Songs and Sonnets here!' (I. i. 205–6).

Thomas, 2nd Baron Vaux of Harowden, the only identified contributor (apart from Wyatt and Surrey) whose work I have selected, was born in 1510 and became a prominent member of Henry VIII's court, being created a Knight of the Bath in 1533; for a time he was captain of the isle of Jersey. He died in 1556.

The first two stanzas, with their burden of classical reference, might suggest Surrey as the possible author, especially as a copy of the poem found in Harley MS 78 (fol. 30v) has 'H.S.' written in the margin alongside it, but the tone of the whole is very unlike the urbane Surrey's. The initial letters make an anagram of 'WIATT', which may be an indication of the author's identity, a compliment or a coincidence; two other anonymous poems in *Tottel's Miscellany* (Rollins edn., Nos. 225, 296) also contain the same anagram, as does Surrey's 'When ragyng love' (p. 111). If the poem *is* Wyatt's, its attitudes could be paralleled from pieces like 'Farewell, Love, and all thy lawes forever' (p. 104).

l.3. folly I have ment: I have been striving after something foolish.
l.5. Troylous' case: originally the poet thought his mistress as faithful as Ulysses' wife Penelope, but she has proved as fickle as Cressida, while he, like Troilus, is constant, but deceived and deserted. (Another indication of the popularity of Chaucer's poem in the early Tudor period.)
l.11. Scilla to Caribidis: Charybdis was a treacherous whirlpool on the coast of Sicily in the straits of Messina; opposite lay the cave of Scylla, a monster who devoured sailors venturing too near the shore.
ll.15–17. These homely images are very characteristic of Wyatt's bitter jests about the fates of over-trusting lovers.
l.22. streame and winde: cf. Tilley W 429 'Sail with wind and tide'.
l.27. stedy stone, no ground of glasse: a secure footing, not a slippery surface.
l.28. sure to save: certain to be safe.

125. THE AGED LOVER RENOUNCETH LOVE

This melancholy lyric, which preserves many of the medieval attitudes to age, sin and death's terrors, is familiar to many through its appearance in a garbled version in the graveyard scene of *Hamlet*, where it is sung by the Gravedigger (*Hamlet* V. 1. 69ff.); it was registered for publication as a ballad in 1563–4, and one of the pieces in *A Gorgious Gallery of Gallant Inventions* (1578) is set 'to the Tune of I lothe that I did love'. Gascoigne in his Preface to the *Posies* (1575) says that Vaux's poem 'was thought by some to be made upon his death bed', and Harley MS 1703 has a version whose title claims it was written 'in time of the noble Queene Marye' which dates it 1553–8. (Vaux died in October 1556.)

l.7. tract of time: course of time.
l.10. his clowche: The original reads 'cowche' which subsequent editions printed as 'crutch' or 'crowch'. I have preferred to substitute 'clowche' or 'clutch', the reading which appears in *Hamlet*, and received the support of Bishop Percy in his *Reliques* (1765).

l.11. lusty life: some versions substitute 'youth' for 'life' as making better sense, but it destroys the alliteration, and is unnecessary if 'life' is taken to mean 'vitality, animation'.

l.20. leave of: leave off.

l.23. hedge him: intrude himself, thrust in.

l.25. harbinger of death: sickness as the traditional emissary of death is a common figure. (Cf. Donne, *Holy Sonnets*, IV. 2. '. . . sicknesse, deaths herald, and champion'.)

l.29. Dothe: a singular verb with a plural subject is very common at this time. *provide:* i.e. 'Provide for myself'.

l.37. My kepers knit the knot: Percy saw an allusion to Ecclesiastes xii. 3: 'the keepers of the house shall tremble', but 'keepers' means nurses who look after the sick, and the sense is 'my nurses keep me under restraint'.

l.49. her bande: her band of followers, i.e. women.

l.51. lande: the land of death, from which man emerges and to which he must return.

127. THE LOVER ACCUSING HYS LOVE FOR HER UNFAITHFULNESSE
Another poem using classical legend and allusion, in the 'rebel lover' idiom popularized by Wyatt. There is a lengthy discussion of the metre of its opening lines in *The Arte of English Poesie* (1589).

l.11. leve me off: the first edn. prints 'oft'.

ll.28–30. a tree of holly etc.: cf. Brian Melbancke's *Philotimus* (1583): 'The Hollin tree beareth barke, and berries, the one kills birds, the other feedes them'. But did Melbancke derive his information solely from this poem? (See the next note.)

ll.33–6. Adrianus: a similar story is told, not of Adrianus, but of Zeuxis or Zeuxippus, of Heraclea in South Italy (*c.* 450–370 B.C.), who is mentioned in Plato's *Protagoras* as just having come to Athens. But Melbancke (*op. cit.*) also cites Adrianus ('Adrianus painted grapes so artificially, that birds becked at them, neither could any descerne them, but with diligent marking'), but then he may have followed *Tottel's Miscellany* blindly.

l.44. commodious: agreeable.

ll.45–8. Naulus' hate: Nauplius, king of Euboea, whose son, Palamedes, wrongly accused of treason, was stoned to death by Agamemnon, Diomedes and Odysseus, took his revenge on the Greek fleet as it sailed home from Troy, by placing lights on the rocky promontory of Caphareus in the south of his kingdom, so wrecking many ships. (See Propertius, *Elegies* IV. i. 113–16.)

129. UPON THE DEATH OF SIR ANTONY DENNY
One is tempted to ascribe this poem to Surrey: it has his wit, elegance, and

poise, but Denny died two years after Surrey was executed; indeed, it has been suggested that Denny had a hand in bringing about Surrey's demise, since as a Secretary of State, he was responsible for affixing the stamp of royal approval to official documents during Henry's later life, and may have been bribed by Surrey's enemies to endorse the death sentence on the poet. Denny was born in 1501, was a member of the Privy Council, an ardent supporter of the Reformation, and a favourite of his sovereign, whose will he helped to execute, serving as a councillor to the young Edward VI. He died in October 1549, and is praised by John Cheke and Roger Ascham; Surrey mentions him in 'When rechles youthe in an unquiet brest' (Jones edn., No. 36).

l.8. quite: set free.
l.9. corps: body, living or dead.

THOMAS SACKVILLE,
EARL OF DORSET

(1536–1608)

LIFE

Sackville, son of a successful Sussex businessman, studied at Oxford and then at the Inner Temple, to which he was admitted in 1555, the year of his marriage to Cecily Barker, a Privy Councillor's daughter. In 1561 his blank-verse tragedy, *Gorboduc*, written in collaboration with Thomas Norton, was performed at the Inner Temple, and later before the Queen at Greenwich; Sackville wrote nearly all of the last two acts, and the first scene. *Gorboduc* is an important landmark in the development of Elizabethan tragedy, deriving in large measure from the plays of Seneca, and its use of blank verse for drama showed the way to men such as Kyd and Marlowe.

In 1558 Sackville began his public career as M.P. for Westmorland, later serving for East Grinstead, and Aylesbury. He went abroad to France and Italy in 1563-4, became one of the Queen's favourite companions, and in 1567, the year after his father's death, was created Baron Buckhurst. He was frequently employed on diplomatic missions, participating in the negotiations involved in Elizabeth's proposed marriage to the Duke of Anjou, in 1571. Having become a Privy Councillor in 1585, he was selected in December 1586 to convey the death sentence to Mary Queen of Scots; he was frequently involved in diplomatic missions to the Netherlands during their struggle against the Spanish, though in 1587 his attempts to act in furtherance of England's constantly changing policies incurred Leicester's enmity and the Queen's rebuke; however Sackville was soon restored to favour. Honours soon came to him in endless succession: the Garter in 1589, the Chancellorship of Oxford University in 1591; in 1599 he succeeded Burghley as Lord High Treasurer; in 1601 it was Sackville who passed sentence on the Earl of Essex. After the accession of James I, Sackville was made Earl of Dorset in 1604, and negotiated a peace with Spain. On 19th April 1608, while attending a meeting of the Privy Council, he died 'in a manner unperceived on as though he had slumbered'.

POETRY

All Sackville's literary compositions belong to his earliest years: his *Induction* and the *Complaynt of Henrye Duke of Buckingham* were contributed to the second edition of *A Myrrour for Magistrates*, compiled by William Baldwin. Baldwin's task had been to prepare, with the aid of 'seven gifted men', a continuation of Lydgate's *Fall of Princes*, incorporating the life-stories 'of suche as Fortune had dalyed with here in this ylande: whiche might be as a myrrour for al men as well noble as others, to shewe the slyppery deceytes of the wavering lady, and the due rewarde of all kinde of vices . . .' beginning with the reign of Richard II. By the second edition of 1563, twenty-seven 'tragedies' had been added, down to the end of Richard III's reign, drawing mainly on the moral lessons of the Wars of the Roses. The aim of the work was in accordance with the Tudor view of history as a guide-book for the present to learn from: 'For here as in a loking glas, you shall see (if any vice be in you) howe the like hath bene punished in other heretofore, whereby admonished, I trust it will be a good occasion to move you to the soner amendment.'

Sackville's *Induction* seems to have been originally intended as a general preface to a series of 'tragedies' of his own devising, and does not, strictly considered, fit into Baldwin's scheme; stylistically too, it is much more deeply steeped in classical lore (particularly in its debts to Virgil), than are the other contributions. It has been over-praised, but it is a remarkable independent achievement, not only because of its statuesque gravity and dignified melancholy, but for its fluency and finish at a time when poetry tended to be deficient in such respects. Its nature may be conservative, its total impact more Gothic than anything, but it shows how the new learning could be reconciled with the earlier tradition.

130. THE INDUCTION TO A MYRROUR FOR MAGISTRATES

Sackville relates his encounter with the goddess Sorrow at twilight on a blustery autumn evening, and how she offers to accompany him to the Underworld and let him hear the laments of former great ones, now brought low by the cruelty of Fortune. This extract begins as they elude Cerberus, and reach the borders of Hell (lines 204–280).

After his descriptions of the evening, the stellar landscape, and the encounter with Sorrow, Sackville comes to rely very much on Virgil's account of Aeneas' descent into the Underworld in Book VI of the *Aeneid*, but where Virgil is content simply to cite the allegorical figures his hero meets, Sackville expands the Roman poet's catalogue into brief portraits, some of which (like those of Revenge and 'Greedy Care') are in the medieval descriptive manner found in *Piers Plowman*, and bequeathed to Spenser's *Faerie Queene* (cf. the pictures of the Seven Deadly Sins (I. iv. 18–35) or the Seasons and the Months (Mutability Cantos, VII. 28–43).

l.2. orewhelmde: 'so overhung as to be almost covered'.

l.7. Averne: Averno, a lake in a volcanic region of S. Italy, 'Avernus' to the Romans, traditionally the entrance to the Underworld.

l.9. swelth: foul, troubled water.

ll.10–12. cf. Virgil, *Aeneid* VI. 237–41: 'There was a deep cave, gaping vast and wide, rugged, and sheltered by a black lake and gloomy forests, over which no winged creature could fly unharmed, such a foul exhalation steamed up from those black jaws into the dome of the sky.'

l.12. savours: smells.

l.14. dreadfull: full of dread.

l.16. Remorse: Sackville decreases the number of Virgil's personifications, and alters the order of their presentation.

l.16. besprent: sprinkled.

l.20. thoughtful: as in Lydgate's *Life of our Lady, l.1,* 'sorrowful, troubled'.

l.25. tedious: painful.

l.33. staring of his heare: 'with his hair on end'.

l.34. Stoynde: astounded, stunned.

l.34. shade: shadow.

l.40. frets: becomes eaten away. *so farforth:* to such an extent.

l.47. fet: fetched, 'heaved'.

l.50. sumdeale pyned: somewhat wasted away.

l.54. pieced: mended. *cloutes:* patches of cloth.

l.55. skrip: a scrip was a small bag or satchel, often carried by beggars, pilgrims and shepherds.

l.61. the bare: the (bare) flesh.

l.70. tawed: 'flayed'. Leather was said to be 'tawed' when it had been softened by beating.

ARTHUR GOLDING

(1536–1606)

LIFE

Golding, born of a well-to-do Essex family (his father being an auditor of the exchequer, and a half-sister becoming Countess of Oxford, and a Lady-in-Waiting to Queen Elizabeth), had strongly Protestant, even Puritan sympathies, and he may have left Jesus College, Cambridge, when Mary came to the throne in 1553. For a time he lived at Cecil's house in the Strand, acting as adviser to his nephew, Edward de Vere, but his main activity in later life was as a prolific translator from French and Latin. In addition to his celebrated version of Ovid's *Metamorphoses*, he left behind over thirty works, including versions of Caesar's *Gallic Wars* and Calvin's *Sermons*, and some pieces of graphic reporting, especially a description of the London earthquake of 1580, which he attributes to the sinfulness of the time. He also completed his friend Sidney's translation of de Mornay, *A Woorke concerning the Trewnesse of the Christian Religion*.

Golding inherited a considerable amount of property, and his latter years were overshadowed by litigation and financial embarrassment: indeed, he was compelled to pass some time in the Fleet prison, and died still owing large sums.

POETRY

Opinions of Golding's version of Ovid range from Ezra Pound's tribute, 'possibly the most beautiful book in the language', to F. O. Matthiesen's complaint that it fails to suggest the qualities of the original, while possessing no exceptional poetic merit to compensate us. Undoubtedly Golding misses all the Roman poet's urbanity and polished wit, but as C. S. Lewis remarks, the *Metamorphoses*, unlike Ovid's other productions, can always be read for the pure story, and this the Englishman preserves in his trotting fourteen-syllable couplets, despite his tortuous style and slightly helpless air of a man being carried rapidly along by his metre and material. His artlessness and remorseless rhythm are off-set by the relish and verve of his language, a mixture of oddities and archaisms, with a flavour all its own, though our pleasure is often at Golding's expense when meeting inversions like

247

She staide without, for to the house in enter might she not
(which, to do him credit, is an extreme sample!), or passages where Golding's
metre forces him to drag out an expression to several times the original's
length. We may also find amusement in Golding's earnest assurance that
Ovid's poem is to be recommended for its morality:

Considring what a sea of goodes and Jewelles thou shalt fynd,
Not more delyghtfull to the eare than frutefull to the mynd.

Yet Golding was a pioneer, and his *Metamorphoses* was the standard version
for the Elizabethans, including Shakespeare, who may have poked fun at
Golding in the interlude of Pyramus and Thisbe in *A Midsummer Night's
Dream*, but whose laughter is surely affectionate.

133. THE XV BOOKES OF P. OVIDIUS NASO, ENTYTULED
     METAMORPHOSIS

These lines translate Ovid's Eighth Book, *ll*.620–720, recounting the story
of Baucis and Philemon, of which Dryden included a version in his *Fables
Ancient and Modern* (1700), calling it a 'good natur'd story' and adding, 'I see
Baucis and Philemon as perfectly before me, as if some ancient Painter had
drawn them'. The homely rusticity of the tale suits Golding's muse, and he
makes something of his own from Ovid's materials.

In the source, Theseus, after taking part in the boar hunt in Calydon, is
returning to Athens, when he finds his path blocked by the river Achelous
in spate; he accepts the hospitality of the river-god, along with some com-
panions. Pirithous, one of them, is sceptical of the gods' powers, and the
following tale is told by Lelex, the hero of Troezen, to persuade him to alter
his mind.

l.1. *Phrygie:* Phyrgia, the country of Pelops. *Teyle:* a linden tree.

l.3. *Pithey:* Pittheus, king of Troezen, son of Pelops.

l.6. *Moorecocks:* male red grouse. *Cootes:* originally any swimming or diving
birds, often guillemots, then applied to Bald Coots.

l.7. *Jove and Mercurie:* visits to earth by these particular Olympians were
traditional (see Plautus' *Amphitryo*). Ovid is more elaborate than Golding,
calling Mercury 'Atlas's grandson, he who carried the caduceus, his wings
laid aside'.

l.11. *pelting:* paltry, insignificant (cf. *Richard II*, II. i. 59–60: '. . . (England)
is now leased out . . . Like to a tenement, or pelting farm'.).

l.12. *fennish:* from the fens.

l.18. *It skilles not:* it does not matter.

l.29. *Skillet:* a small metal cooking pot used for boiling and stewing, with a
long handle and usually three or four short legs.

l.30. *Coleworts:* cabbage or kale.

248

*l.*36. *spirget:* a peg for hanging things on.

*l.*39. *Sallow wood:* wood from a low shrubby kind of willow.

*l.*49. *Pallas' fruite:* olives. *with double colour stripte:* picked when half green, half black.

*l.*50. *Cornels:* a kind of cherry. *Endive:* a type of chicory, whose leaves can be used for salads.

*l.*51. *soote:* fresh, not salted.

*l.*52. *reare rosted:* slightly underdone.

*ll.*53–4. *same Selfe:* self-same.

*l.*54. *Mazers:* drinking bowls made from very hard 'mazer' or maple wood.

*l.*57. *hedg wyne:* a third-rate, inferior wine. (Miss Vivien Cook informs me that Thomas Nashe speaks of 'hedge-wine and lean mutton' (*Works*, ed. McKerrow, I. 376.30) the *O.E.D.* taking this as its earliest example of the combination.)

*l.*59. *Mawnd:* a woven basket, often of wicker, with a handle each side.

*l.*62. *overmore:* moreover, furthermore.

*l.*71. *wyght:* swift. Ovid's word is 'celer', which confirms that Golding did not mean 'white'.

*l.*81. *flyghtshot:* a bow-shot.

*l.*88. *eyther fold:* each side of a double door.

*l.*102. *They told the fortune:* they recounted the fate.

*ll.*106–7. *eche of them did take/Theyr leave of other:* Nims is rather severe on the pun 'leave/leaf', claiming that it weakens the conclusion; was it deliberate, or careless, on Golding's part?

*l.*108. *park:* enclosed piece of land (cf. *l.*2: 'within a wall').

BARNABY GOOGE

(1504–94)

LIFE

Googe, whose name is also spelt Goche, Goghe, and Gouche, was the son of
the Recorder of Lincoln, and a kinsman of William Cecil, later Lord
Burghley; by his early twenties, he had attended Cambridge and Oxford
Universities, been a law student at Staple Inn, and travelled in Spain and
Italy. His first published work was a translation of a long-winded Latin work
of religious didacticism, *Zodiacus Vitae* by Palingenius, of which part appeared
in 1560, the whole in 1565. The eclogues, for which he is best known, were
completed in 1561, when Googe departed for Spain, and they appeared, along
with some of his other verses, as *Eglogs, Epytaphes and Sonettes*, in 1563, the
poet claiming that his friend Laurence Blunderston, a student of Gray's Inn,
was solely responsible for their publication. About this time he was made one
of Queen Elizabeth's gentlemen-pensioners, and in the same year Cecil
involved himself in Googe's courtship of Mary Darrell, the daughter of a
Kentish landowner, whose family appear to have hoped to find her a more
lucrative match elsewhere. In 1564 Googe married the girl of his choice.

Further translations appeared in the 1560s and 70s, several of them inveighing
ardently against the wickedness of the Papacy; his version of Thomas
Kirchmeyer's *Regni Papistici* (*The Popish Kingdome*) was dedicated to Cecil.
From February to July 1574 Googe was in Ireland, on government service
for his illustrious kinsman, and he returned there in 1582 as Provost Marshal
to the Presidency Court of Connaught, an uncongenial post to which he was
probably compelled for financial reasons, but from which he sought speedy
release, which was granted in April 1585.

Googe died about 7th February 1594; he left a large family, one son
becoming a Fellow of All Souls', Oxford, another Master of Magdalene
College, Cambridge.

POETRY

Googe does not command quite so high a place in mid-century verse as
Sackville or Gascoigne, but his work demands careful consideration. His verse
is obviously the work of a writer steeped in *Tottel's Miscellany*, and Googe's
love for 'fourteeners' and 'Poulter's Measure' does not encourage exploration,

but his epitaphs, tributes, and moralizing poems sometimes attain a very high standard of lucidity and a memorable economy. The *Eclogs* may disappoint readers who hope to find Spenser more worthily anticipated, though Googe also employs rough dialect, and a romantic narrative framework, but pieces like *Of Money*, *Of Nicholas Grimald*, and *To Mayster Henry Cobham* are good examples of unsophisticated, direct unpretentiousness, preserving the medieval homiletic strain, while tempering it with a classical restraint.

137. TO MASTER HENRYE COBHAM

Henry Brooke (1538–1605?) who always subscribed himself, and was known as 'Henry Cobham', was a member of the important Brooke family, Lords of Cobham, near Rochester in Kent, into which the elder Wyatt married: he was a distinguished diplomat, and was knighted in Kenilworth in 1575, serving as Ambassador in Paris from 1579 to 1583.

Googe's lines in praise of the 'golden mean' and rural tranquillity read like a translation, analagous to Surrey's version of Horace (p. 118) but I have been unable to trace a source.

*l.*10. *gawne:* 'gape, yawn'. Its use appears to be peculiar to Googe.

*l.*11. *Cayser:* Caesar.

*l.*13. *what he once sayde:* it is tempting to suggest that Googe is alluding to Wyatt as he reveals himself in his satires. The pun in 'Courte not in any case' (*l.*14) is consonant with Wyatt's reputation for wit.

*ll.*17–18. These are humanist commonplaces (cf. Barclay etc.).

*l.*21. Bacchus *hath no place:* i.e. 'drunkenness is not allowed'.

*l.*22. Venus *hath defecte:* 'there's no promiscuous love-making'.

*l.*23. Thraso: a boastful army officer featured in Terence's comedy *The Eunuch*; the braggart soldier was a traditional element in early Greek comedy.

*l.*24. Gnatoes *secte:* Gnatho is the parasite or 'hanger-on' in *The Eunuch*.

138. GOYNG TOWARDES SPAYNE

Googe travelled to Spain in the winter of 1561/2, arriving back in 1562/3. The two following poems were inspired by his departure and return.

'Goyng towardes Spayne' is a fourteen-line poem in rhymed couplets known as 'fourteeners' (except *l.*1 which is irregular), and heavy with alliteration. It is printed in the original edition in half-lines, to fit the small pages, though the division may tell us something about Googe's conception of the metre.

*l.*1. Brutus: see note to *l.*5 of 'Tagus, farewell' (p. 106).

*l.*7. *pynch:* constrain.

139. COMMYNGE HOMEWARDE OUT OF SPAYNE

Probably suggested by Wyatt's 'Tagus, farewell' (p. 106).

GEORGE TURBERVILE

(c. 1540–c. 1595)

LIFE

Readers of Hardy will recognize the variant form of Turbervile's family name: he was born in Whitchurch, Dorset, second son to Nicholas Turbervile, and in 1554 proceeded to Winchester as a scholar, and then to New College, Oxford, where he became a perpetual fellow in 1561. Passing to one of the inns of court, he started to acquire a reputation as a poet and man of affairs. In June 1568 he accompanied Thomas Randolph on a special mission to the court of Ivan the Terrible at Moscow; three verse-letters describing his experiences survive from a larger body of work.

Turbervile's output was extremely varied: in 1567, in addition to *Epitaphs, Epigrams, Songs and Sonnets* (translations and original pieces), he published versions of Ovid's *Heroides* and Mantuan's eclogues; then followed *A Plaine Path to Perfect Vertue* (a translation from Latin) in 1568, *The Booke of Faulconrie or Hauking* and *The Noble Arte of Venerie or Hunting* (both prose compilations) in 1575, and *Tragical Tales*, which are verse translations from Italian, chiefly Boccaccio, supplemented by a section of sonnets and epitaphs. But his contemporary popularity was soon eclipsed by changes in literary fashion.

POETRY

Not even his warmest advocate would claim Turbervile as a major poet: opinions only differ as to the size of his minority. Many of his verses are inspired by the 'Tottel poets', notably Wyatt, adding little to the stock of Petrarchan clichés and attitudes, but his non-amorous pieces (chiefly 'Epitaphs' and 'Epigrams') indicate that his work is not merely derivative. He is one of the few pre-Spenserian poets to manifest that serious interest in trifles which distinguishes many seventeenth-century poets, and his attempts at neatness and wit are occasionally of the same order. He exploits paradox, he aims at clarity and pithiness, he essays the classical epigram: if he lacks the intellectual pressure and verbal energy to anticipate Donne, and the moral strength and elegance to foreshadow Jonson, Turbervile can faintly hint at the coming greatness of both.

140. AN EPITAPH OF MAISTER WIN DROWNED IN THE SEA

I have been unable to trace 'Maister Win'; he was possibly from the celebrated Welsh family of Wynn, possibly either an Oxford contemporary of Turbervile's or an Inn of Court acquaintance. (The collection from which the poem is taken also includes an elegy on the death of Arthur Brooke, author of the poem *The Tragicale Historye of Romeus and Juliet* (which Shakespeare must have known), who was drowned in 1563.) It follows a recognized rhetorical mode, that of the *ethopoeia* or direct address to the reader, and its attitudes are purely conventional, but it has a Renaissance polish, sophistication and elegance of construction which carry it beyond its medieval legacy, especially in its urbane and graceful conclusion.

*l.*3. *Recline:* incline.
*l.*22. See note to 'The lover disceived by his love', *l.*11.
*l.*24. *a livesman:* a living being.
*ll.*27–8. *well-renowmed Fame:* the typical Renaissance consolation for untimely death (cf. *Love's Labour Lost*, I. i. *ll.*1–15).

141. TO HIS LOVE THAT SENT HIM A RING
Turbervile here anticipates the argumentative, dramatic, impassioned tone of the best later Elizabethans, notably Sidney with his vehement self-contradictions and inexorable logic; indeed, in Turbervile and Gascoigne, the essential continuity between Wyatt, Sidney, and the Metaphysicals is maintained. However, the debate between Reason and Love is a hoary one, and all Turbervile's poetic energy and gift for self-dramatization are needed to sustain the reader's interest.

Sentimental love 'posies' in rings are satirized by Jaques in *As You Like It* (III. ii. 288–90): 'You are full of pretty answers: have you not been acquainted with gold-smiths' wives and conned them out of rings?'

*l.*6. Reason *and* Love: cf. *A Midsummer Night's Dream*, III. i. 151: '. . . reason and love keep little company together nowadays'.

141. TO AN OLDE GENTLEWOMAN
Turbervile's epigrams are interesting forerunners of a form which came to maturity in England in the seventeenth and eighteenth centuries, although his wit is often too heavy and his technique too rough to do justice to this neat, delicate genre. This example is adapted from the Greek Anthology, Book XI. 408, a satiric epigram by Lucian; the metre is 'Poulter's Measure', but I have retained the divided lines of the 1570 text, as closer in spirit to the original.

*l.*10. *cranck and curious:* conceited and fussy.
*l.*11. *Trulles:* technically 'harlots', but it probably means simply 'wenches'.

GEORGE GASCOIGNE

(c. 1538–1577)

Gascoigne's career fluctuates between extremes of good fortune and disastrous failure: the elder son of Sir John Gascoigne, of Cardington, Yorkshire, he probably attended Trinity College, Cambridge, and began to study law at Gray's Inn in 1555. He spent some time abroad, became M.P. for Bedford in 1558, and served as the Queen's Almoner at Elizabeth's coronation in January 1559. In his efforts to gain preferment at court, Gascoigne plunged deeply into debt, a situation not eased by the costly legal actions he incurred by marrying Elizabeth Breton, a widow apparently contracted elsewhere, in 1561; this indiscretion (with others) may have cost him his courtly success: it also made him step-father to Nicholas Breton, a popular author of a later period. For a while Gascoigne retired to his diminished estates, then returned to his studies at Gray's Inn, where he appears to have spent as much time in literary activities as legal ones, for in 1566 his prose comedy *The Supposes*, adapted from Ariosto, and *Jocasta*, a neo-classical tragedy in the Senecan manner, adapted with a fellow student from Dolce's *Giocasta*, were performed at Gray's Inn. Some of Shakespeare's ideas for *The Taming of the Shrew* were gleaned from *The Supposes*.

With the death of his father in 1568, Gascoigne inherited a considerable fortune, but he squandered it so quickly that by April 1570 he was in Bedford Gaol for debt, and in 1572 his creditors prevented him from taking his seat in Parliament. He sought to improve his fortunes by serving as a soldier in the Netherlands in 1572, and again from 1573–4, when he was captured and repatriated. *A Hundreth sundrie Flowres* consisting of verses and prose pieces by himself (including the prose tale, *The Adventures of Master F. J.*), and probably others, with editorial matter suggesting that Gascoigne was sole author, was published in 1573 during his absence. On his return, a revised version was issued, entitled *The Posies*, which incorporates *Certayne Notes of Instruction*, an intriguing and valuable essay on poetic composition.

In the same year (1575) Leicester sought his assistance in devising entertainments for the Queen during her visit to Kenilworth that summer, and a further offering by Gascoigne greeted her Majesty at Woodstock. On New Year's

Day 1576, he presented her with a copy, asking at the same time that he should be found employment in the royal service. His plea was attended to, and later in the year he was sent to the Netherlands as an English agent; a spectator of the fall of Antwerp in November, he published his racy account, *The Spoyle of Antwerpe*, in London before the month's end, a graphic description of war's horrors, on which he had expressed his view already in a long semi-biographical poem, *The Fruites of Warre*. While abroad, he also composed four poems on the vanity of human life; these he presented to the Queen on New Year's Day, 1577. He died at Stamford, Lincolnshire, on 7th October 1577. One of his patrons was Lord Grey of Wilton (under whom Spenser was shortly to serve in Ireland), to whom Gascoigne addressed his confession, *Gascoigne's Woodmanship*, and dedicated *The Fruites of Warre*, and his satire *The Steele Glas* (1576), the first original blank-verse poem in English.

POETRY

Gascoigne is either dismissed as a mere imitator of the stylistic hyperboles and rhetorical lamentations of the worst parts of *Tottel's Miscellany*, or praised because a few hints in his verse suggest that the 'Golden' years of Elizabethan poetry are about to dawn. But at his best, Gascoigne transcends the talents of the average miscellany poet, and we gravely misunderstand him if we only respond to the isolated anticipations of Spenser or the madrigalists in his work. The keys to his quality are found not so much in his 'grace and melody' as in his strong masculine diction, his re-infusion of drama into the lyric, his self-awareness and humanity, and the way he illustrates a Wyatt-like seriousness and integrity in less stringent language and through wider-ranging imagery. The poem which begins:

> Give me my Lute, in bed now as I lie,
> And lock the doores of mine unluckie bower

tells us almost everything about the transition from early to late Tudor verse, and only its length prevented my using it here. This piece, *The Arraignment of a Lover*, *The Divorce of a Lover*, *Gascoigne's Good Morrow* and *The Praise of Phillip Sparrowe* will all repay study, but he deserves even higher praise for reflective poems, such as *Gascoigne's Woodmanship*, *The Green Knight's Farewell to Fansie*, *The Councell given to Master Bartholomew Withipoll, 1572*, concerned with large moral, social and personal questions which form part of an older didactic pattern, and where poetic technique is subordinated to the dissemination of an ethic based on a settled but broadly sympathetic view of human life.

143. A SONET WRITTEN IN PRAYSE OF THE BROWNE BEAUTIE

This sonnet, which unlike many of its predecessors which employed the title, really *is* a sonnet, is from among the 'Hearbes' in Gascoigne's *Posies* of

1575, a revised reissue of *A Hundreth sundrie Flowres* of 1573. The mood reminds one of Donne's delight in defending seemingly indefensible propositions, especially when we remember that the Elizabethan ideal of female beauty was fair and fresh-complexioned. Ovid is also found praising tanned skins in the *Ars Amatoria*. Gascoigne's panegyric conveys something of the back-handed compliment Donne paid Magdalen Herbert in 'The Autumnal': I have no suggestion as to who Mistress E. P. was, unless the title should read 'E. B.', referring to Gascoigne's wife, Elizabeth Breton.

l.6. Pallas' pooles: the eyes.
l.11. 'had I wist': a very common proverb (cf. Tilley H 8, 9, 10).

143. THE LULLABIE OF A LOVER
Gascoigne's most celebrated poem, this lyric employs the lullaby theme and refrain for adult purposes, as does Skelton in 'Lullay, lullay, lyke a chylde' (p. 66). Gascoigne adapts the lullaby to the medieval *topos* of advancing years and approaching death, already heard in Vaux's 'I lothe that I did love' but with no trace of melancholy. He sings his declining faculties to rest, with the amused air of a content and mellowed philanderer.

l.4. As womanly as can the best: Donald Peterson stresses the irony here; the speaker's declining sexual prowess makes him effeminate.
l.7. wanton: here 'playful'.
l.15. courage: sexual vigour.
l.16. beguile: divert attention from something painful.
l.17. my gazing eyes: Gascoigne now follows standard Renaissance sex psychology. The Elizabethans believed that love, contracted through the eyes, stimulated the passions, in alliance with the fancy, to gain control of the will, overthrow it, and achieve physical satisfaction.
l.26. reigne: rein.
ll.33/4. my loving boye,/My little Robyn: the male organ.
l.42. my ware: a common euphemism for the male organ (cf. 'We ben chapmen', p. 64, *l.6*).
l.48. In the edition of 1573 the line reads 'Remember Gascoigne's lullaby'.

145. MAGNUM VECTIGAL PARCIMONIA
This 'theme', 'Thrift is a great revenue', was one of those supplied to Gascoigne by various of his contemporaries at Gray's Inn when he decided to resume studies there in about 1564; the friend who supplied it, John Vaughan, could have found it in the works of Cicero, *Paradoxa* VI. iii. 49. (*Non intelligunt homines quam magnum vectigal sit parsimonia.*) Vaughan was no

doubt glancing at Gascoigne's own far from frugal habits up to that point, and it is ironic that the poet, as rejoinder, should write a classic defence of the 'plain living and high thinking' school of sixteenth-century thought. The tone is very often closely akin to that of Wyatt's satires.

l.1. *spend and God will send:* characteristically, Gascoigne renders the Latin by a parallel native proverb (see *O.D.E.P.*, p. 613).

l.3. *wallet:* a bag for provisions, a knapsack, especially a beggar's pack.

ll.8–9. *he that list with lavish hand to linke:* 'he who spends a pound with the same abandon as he spends a penny'.

l.10. *shrinke:* draw back his head (in shame).

l.11. *Dainties:* choice foods.

l.12. *clouts upon their knee:* patches on the knees of their tights.

l.13. *goonhole grotes:* coins. 'Goonhole' is possibly the corruption of a foreign name (the 'gunhole' is an embrasure or port-hole for a gun in the side of a ship); a groat was worth about 4d.

l.16. *rappes a royall on his cappe:* 'smacks a gold coin on his cap'. (The 'rial', a gold coin originally worth 10/-, was first issued in 1465 by Edward IV.)

l.23. *angells:* the old English coin, originally the 'angel-noble', bore the device of the Archangel Michael and the dragon.

l.25. *lacke his grace:* i.e. go without meals. (Possibly a play on the sense in *l*.21.)

l.26. *For haggard hawkes mislike an emptie hand:* proverbial. Cf. *The Wife of Bath's Prologue*, *C.T.*, III. 415: 'With empty hand men may none haukes lure'. *haggard:* hawks caught wild with their adult plumage already developed.

ll.27–8. 'Some patronize the clothier's stall constantly until they have bled their property white to pay for silken suits.'

l.30. *Davie Debet:* the personification of debt, or the bailiffs. (Melbancke, in *Philotimus* (1583), speaks of 'Davie debt'.) *parler:* in great houses, a small room set apart from the hall, for private conversation.

l.36. *a stand of ale:* an ale barrel. (*ll*.36–7. 'Get your stomach accustomed to beer before wine-merchants book your order for Madeira'.)

l.37. *Malmesey:* a strong sweet wine from Malvesia on the East coast of the Peleponnesus.

l.38. *for shifte:* a play on (1) a change of clothes; (2) an expedient.

l.39. *teynter hokes:* the 'tenter' was a wooden frame on which cloth was stretched with hooks after being milled, so that it could set or dry evenly. Hence to be 'on tenters, on tenter-hooks'; as here, 'suffering from a sense of strain'.

l.41. *princkt with plumes:* 'dolled-up' with ornamental feathers. *plummes:* tit-bits, 'perks'.

l.42. *hooches:* the huche was a chest or coffer for storing belongings.

l.47. *soft fire makes sweet malte:* proverbial (*O.D.E.P.*, p. 602).

l.48. *No haste but good:* proverbial (*O.D.E.P.*, p. 280, 'No haste but good speed').

l.49. *Bought witte is deare etc.:* proverbial (*O.D.E.P.*, p. 58).

l.50. *Repentaunce commes to late:* proverbial (*O.D.E.P.*, p. 539).

A HANDEFULL
OF PLEASANT DELITES

(1566)

Probably the second poetical miscellany of the sixteenth century, *A Handefull* was first printed in 1566, as *Very pleasant sonettes*, though the only known edition is dated 1584. Unlike *Tottel's Miscellany*, whose success doubtless inspired its appearance, it consists of anonymous ballads, formerly broadsides sold in the streets, collected and printed by a specialist in this field, Richard Jones. The dominant tone of the collection is less classical in spirit and less exotic in tone than Tottel's, and its chief potential audience is obviously regarded as less educated. Many poems are alive with contemporary detail, employing much proverbial material, and since they are primarily for singing, the verses have a popular lilt.

147. FAIN WOLD I HAVE A PRETIE THING

A slight but spritely song, on the frustrations of wooing, in which the singer lightly ridicules male inexpertise at present-giving, and woman's insatiable expectations. The tune to which the song is to be sung, 'Lustie Gallant', is still extant.

l.7. to make adventure: to venture, take a risk.
l.14. where gases be not geason: where there is no lack of gazes.
l.22. Silkie wives: to aid the scansion, we should perhaps read 'Silke wives'.
l.25. Silke in Cheape: Cheapside was famous for its textiles (cf. *London Lickpenny, ll.75–6*).
l.29. Gravers: engravers. *showes:* objects displayed.
l.31. Shemsters: sempstresses. *sowes:* another example of a singular verb for a plural subject, common in the sixteenth century.
l.38. my good willing misseth: my excellent intentions fail to accomplish.

149. THE LOVER COMPARETH HIMSELF TO THE PAINFUL FALCONER

This hearty love-song, because of its jaunty rhythm, unabashed refrain, and extrovert sentiments, is in cheerful contrast to the many mournful pieces which take desertion and deceit as their theme. Like many poems of the period, it employs hawking terminology extensively.

l.5. sound of bell: falcons wore bells on their jesses to indicate their whereabouts.

l.7. Wo, ho! a call commonly used by the falconer to call the falcon back to the lure. (Cf. *Hamlet* I. v. 115: 'Hillo, ho, ho, boy! come, bird, come'.)

l.9. in finest sort: in the best manner possible. *Lure:* a dummy bird used in training and in the field. (See note to *The Dance of Death*, p. 167, *l.*39.)

l.11. gorged: satiated, glutted.

l.13. bending eies: eyes looking towards him as if 'bending' down to the lure.

l.36. stoup unto his Lure: in training, the hawk has to be taught to 'stoop' or plunge from a height on to the lure, so it may later swoop down on to its prey in the same manner.

l.37. hood: used in taming and training the hawk, and sometimes when flying it.

THE PARADYSE
OF DAYNTY DEVISES

(1576)

The most popular miscellany issued in Elizabeth's reign, running into ten editions between 1576 and 1608, *The Paradyse* was 'devised and written for the most part' by Richard Edwards (*c.* 1523–66), Master of the Children of the Chapel Royal, a musician and dramatist, responsible for two plays chosen for 'command performance', *Damon and Pithias* (1564) and *Palamon and Arcite* (1566). Edwards probably had no thought of publishing his collection of pieces by himself and 'sundry learned Gentlemen, both of honor, and woorshippe', but his manuscript fell into the hands of a publisher after his death. Among the authors represented (many are anonymous) are Jasper Heywood, the English translator of Seneca; Vaux, who appears in *Tottel's Miscellany* (see p. 125); William Hunnis, and Edward, Earl of Oxford.

Hunnis (*c.* 1530–97) was a Gentleman of the Chapel Royal under Edward VI, but was deprived of his post for his part in a Protestant conspiracy against Mary I, and sent to the Tower. His place was restored under Elizabeth, for in 1566 he succeeded Edwards as Master of the Children. He wrote several literary works, chiefly devotional, and is assigned fourteen lyrics in *The Paradyse*, though one is certainly Wyatt's.

Edward de Vere, 17th Earl of Oxford, probable author of eight poems in the volume, was born in 1550, possibly tutored in Cecil's house by Arthur Golding (see p. 246), married Cecil's elder daughter in 1571, and became one of Elizabeth's favourite courtiers, although his violent temper caused him to misuse his wife, and insult Sidney (even, it was rumoured, plot to have him murdered). Oxford served in the Netherlands and against the Armada, but retired from public life in 1592, though his duties as Lord Great Chamberlain involved him in the trial of Essex in 1601, and James I's coronation in 1603. He died in 1604.

Oxford was a celebrated poet and patron in his own day, and in our time, claims have been made for him as the author of Shakespeare's plays. For some years he maintained a private company of players, 'the Erle of Oxforde his servauntes', and John Lyly, Oxford's secretary for a time, wrote some of his plays for the troupe. Spenser's dedicatory sonnets to *The Faerie Queene* include one to Oxford.

The Paradyse, unlike Tottel's collection, prefers the admonitory to the amatory, and *sententiae* to sonnets; the choice of poems bears the mark of Edward's somewhat sober personality, and the contents do not compare favourably with the innocent cheerfulness of many of the songs in *A Handefull*: there is often little attempt to render the inculcation of prudence and virtue attractive.

151. DONEC ERIS FELIX MULTOS NUMERABIS AMICOS

A typical piece of early Elizabethan didactic verse, but notable for the brevity and intensity of the comparison. The title is taken from Ovid's *Tristia* I. ix. 5–6, which Thomas Elyot in *The Book Named The Governor* (1531) translates as

Whiles fortune the favoureth frendes thou hast plentie,
The tyme beinge troublous thou arte alone

Title: I have amended *admissus* to the correct form *admissas*.

l.1. Kite: a bird of prey of the hawk type, formerly common in Britain and well-known as a scavenger.
l.3. tiring: term given to the way in which a bird of prey tore its food; a hawk was said to be 'tiring' when it tore at a tough morsel, given to exercise the beak on. *talentes:* talons, claws.
l.6. all to pull: pull quite apart.
l.13. true intent: honest intentions.

152. NO PAINES COMPARABLE TO HIS ATTEMPT

This lyric only appears in the first edition of 1576; in the later known editions another poem with the same title is inserted. Its tone is again didactic, but the lively impression of, and compassion for, a sea-faring life reanimate the stale analogy between amorous misadventure and nautical hazards.

l.5. A bedlesse borde: 'a table, but no bed', or perhaps 'a mere plank, not a proper bed to sleep on'. (Or is Hunnis thinking of a corpse carried on a plank?)
l.9. oft tyme: the text reads 'tymes'; I have altered it in the interests of the rhyme.
l.10. No nere: i.e. 'he shouts "No nearer" when the Master blows "How?" on his whistle'. (See *The Tempest* I. i. 6–7.)
l.12. 'Immediately ruin has overcome the ship.'
l.17. game: proceeding, undertaking.

152. THE JUDGEMENT OF DESIRE

Another poem which only occurs in the 1576 edition; there is another copy in Rawlinson Poet. MS 85, entitled 'Desire' but with no refrain. It is an unusually light-hearted treatment of the subject, and though courtly, in some measure recalls the un-literary gaiety of the best medieval lyrics. The refrain phrase has a Provençal flavour, but I have not found one to correspond with it, though Mr J. H. Watkins has drawn my attention to the use of phrases like 'dorenlet' in the refrains of Old French *pastourelles*.

l.5. Aurora: the goddess of the dawn.
l.6. Thetis: used here, as elsewhere, for the ocean. *gilt:* possibly a pun?
l.17. saied me no naie: did not deny me.
l.22. answered than: the text reads 'answered me', but the rhyme requires 'than'.

153. BETHINKING HYMSELF OF HIS ENDE

A very similar poem to Vaux's 'I lothe that I did love', illustrating how the Renaissance continues medieval literary themes, e.g. *Sic transit gloria mundi*. It first appears in the edition of 1578.

l.1. postyng horsse: at certain roadside inns called post-houses, horses were kept for the use of travellers or riders carrying letters.
l.4. erthe: The printed text reads 'eithe'.
l.8. As shaft: text reads 'shafts', but I have amended it to conform with the singular subject of the simile; I have retained the plural 'birds', however, as Elizabethan usage often ignored concordance between subject and verb.
l.14. Winter weareth: 'winter wears on'.

EDMUND SPENSER

(c. 1552–1599)

LIFE

Spenser's origins were humble, though recent scholars have argued against an impoverished background: his father was a free journeyman (a self-employed craftsman) of the Merchant Taylors' Company, from East Smithfield, and Spenser attended Merchant Taylors' School, then under the distinguished educationalist, Richard Mulcaster. In 1569 Spenser published translations from Marot and Du Bellay in *A Theatre for Voluptuous Worldlings*, an anthology edited by a Protestant refugee from the Netherlands. In the same year he proceeded to Pembroke Hall, Cambridge, as a sizar; there he formed a lasting friendship with Gabriel Harvey, a young Fellow of Pembroke, and a scholar of some note, though the passage of time has given him the reputation of a pedant and a bore. Harvey's exchanges on making English verse conform to the rules of classical prosody are preserved: both made experiments with Latin metres.

Spenser may have remained at Cambridge after receiving his M.A. in June 1576, or perhaps went North, but he soon reappears, in London, where Harvey introduced him into the Earl of Leicester's circle, where he met Leicester's nephew, Philip Sidney. He was first employed, as a secretary, by John Young, Bishop of Rochester, and then joined Leicester's entourage, serving his master in various capacities, dividing his time between Leicester House and Sidney's residence at Penshurst, Kent. In Sidney, with whom he was soon 'in some use of familiarity', Spenser found an enlightened and informed ally and patron, and when *The Shepheardes Calender* appeared in December 1579, it was dedicated to 'the Noble and Vertuous Gentleman most worthy of all titles both of learning and chevalrie, M. Philip Sidney'.

The remainder of Spenser's career may be summarized:

August 1580.	Takes up appointment as Secretary to Lord Grey of Wilton, the new Lord Deputy of Ireland. Holds various posts there.
1589.	Clerk of the Council for Munster. Friendship with Raleigh. Leaves Ireland for London in Raleigh's company.

1590.	Publishes Books I–III of *The Faerie Queene*, dedicating it to Queen Elizabeth.
1591.	Receives a pension of £50 a year. Returns to Ireland. Ponsonby publishes his *Complaints*.
June 1594.	Marriage with Elizabeth Boyle, of Kilcolnan. Resigns Clerkship in same year.
1595.	*Colin Clout's Come Home Again*, and *Astrophell* published.
Winter 1595–6.	Second visit to London, to arrange for publication of Books I–VI of *The Faerie Queene*. Returns to Ireland, 1597.
September 1598.	Recommended as High Sheriff of Cork.
October 1598.	Tyrone sends expedition into Munster; Kilcolnan sacked and burnt down. Spenser and family escape.
December 1598.	Spenser carried dispatches from Ireland to the Privy Council in London, and presents them. Taken ill soon after.
13th January 1599.	Spenser dies. Buried near Chaucer in Westminster Abbey, the Earl of Essex defraying the funeral expenses.

POETRY

The Shepheardes Calender, though never published under Spenser's name during his lifetime, was the first work he presented to the world, and moreover, being issued with introduction, glossary and notes like an established Latin text, its form accentuated its claim to public attention. The classical apparatus was his publisher's accompaniment to a virtuoso performance by an astonishing new poet, and Spenser provided such a demonstration of versatility and technique that one might be forgiven for regarding the work as nothing more than a collection of experiments, or suggesting that this writer is already too conscious of his own abilities. C. S. Lewis is not alone in finding it all a little dull. Yet it is quite clearly a step forward in poetic time, a tribute to, and yet a break with, the past, a confident assumption of independence and autonomy by a Renaissance poet. James Russell Lowell commended the eclogues as showing 'a sense of style in its larger meaning hitherto displayed by no English poet since Chaucer . . . here was a new language, a choice and arrangement of words, a variety, elasticity and harmony of verse most grateful to the ears of men . . .' Moreover, Spenser's linguistic freedom, despite Sidney's strictures, permitting him to blend a basically normal diction with dialect, archaic and obsolescent terms, and words made to sound antique, 'went far toward establishing the adequacy of our language as an instrument of thought and expression, and its capability of unfolding the resources and displaying worthily the inventiveness of the highest poetic art'. (Hubbard.)

Nor was Spenser unaware that he was enrolling himself in a lengthy pastoral brotherhood; indeed, he borrows something from all his predecessors in the eclogue, yet adds novel features of his own designing. At the same time, none of the earlier poets had offered such a wide metrical range for inspection, Spenser employing thirteen different stanza-forms, from the rugged, pseudo-medieval couplets of *February* to Cuddie's sophisticated sestina in *August*, or the complex ten-line stanzas of Colin's funeral elegy in *November*. The young poet is demonstrating what voices are at his command.

Modern readers may find the metrical agility empty cleverness, the rustic dialect mere clowning, and the topical allusions to bishops and statesmen irksome and remote; one cannot 'immerse oneself' in *The Shepheardes Calender* – it is too much like a sales catalogue of poetic goods perhaps – but one surely responds to the seasonal descriptions, the reckless display of sheer poetic talent and enthusiasm, the impulse that drives the poet on to his confident declaration of faith in 'divine poesy', and above all, to the authority and assurance of this clear, new voice.

155. THE SHEPHEARDES CALENDER: OCTOBER

The October Eclogue has often been declared the focal-point of the whole *Shepheardes Calender* sequence, and certainly, with its classic expression of the functions of poetry and the poet, and its finely balanced debate-structure, it deserves high praise. It is the most self-conscious of the Eclogues, and as W. A. Nelson points out, while Cuddie's part is chiefly based on Mantuan, Piers speaks largely with Spenser's own voice, rejecting worldly fame for the knowledge that the poet shares in the divine task of inspiring mankind to virtuous action. Here Spenser not only gives expression to the Renaissance doctrine that a writer receives his inspiration directly from God, and shares something of the Creator's power, but also proudly asserts his own claim to the noble title of 'poet'.

l.1. *Pierce:* generally taken as Spenser himself, or at least in one of his aspects.
l.1. *Cuddie:* Paul E. McLane (*Journal of English & Germanic Philology*, 56, 1955) argues convincingly that Cuddie is Sir Edward Dyer (*d*. 1607), a poet friend of Sidney. Others have canvassed the claims of E. K. himself, and Fulke Greville.
l.3. *Phoebus' race:* the course of a day when the sun crosses the heavens.
l.5. *bydding base:* prisoner's base (a kind of 'He'), or more probably, a poetic contest. (Mantuan's original reference is to wrestling.)
ll.11–12. The grasshopper has always been proverbial for improvidence. *ligge so layd:* 'subdued'; 'lye so faynt and unlustye' (E. K.).
l.13. *dapper:* 'prettye' (E. K.).
l.14. *fry:* 'Frye is a bold Metaphore, forced from the spawning fishes. For the multitude of young fish be called the frye' (E. K.).

l.15. *what I the bett forthy:* 'how much better-off am I as a result?'

l.17. *I beate the bush* etc.: a very common proverb.

l.23. *pricke them forth:* 'inspire then onwards with pleasure at your poetic style'.

l.24. 'To which you were pleased to lure back their strayed desires.'

l.25. *in frame:* in order.

l.27. *their soule of sence bereave:* E. K. compares the classic view of the similar effects of music.

ll.28–30. An allusion of Orpheus, a Thracian hero, who attempted to rescue his dead wife, Eurydice, from Hades, by the power of his music. He succeeded in charming the infernal gods into releasing her, but broke their condition that he should not look back at her until they were in the Upper World again.

ll.31–2. *the Peacock's spotted traine:* Argus, an all-seeing, never-sleeping creature with many eyes, was appointed by Juno to guard Io, whom Jove loved and transformed into a cow. Argus was killed by Hermes, and as a reward for his fidelity, Juno caused his eyes to be placed in the peacock's tail. The story is told in Book I of Ovid's *Metamorphoses*.

l.36. *Sike words bene wynd:* a very common proverbial image. (Tilley cites eighteen examples.)

ll.37–54. Piers' advice and Cuddie's reply follow Mantuan substantially, but *ll*.38–48 appear to forecast Spenser's own ambitions accurately.

l.40. *weld:* bear. *awful:* full of awe.

l.41. *doubted:* redoubtable. *woundlesse:* unmarked, since peace had endured so long (cf. 'unbruzed, *l*.42).

l.45. *Elisa:* Queen Elizabeth.

l.46. *bigger:* more powerful.

l.47. *the worthy whome shee loveth best:* E. K. 'guesses' Robert Dudley, Earl of Leicester (1533?–1588), Elizabeth's favourite, though at this time in disgrace due to his secret marriage to the Earl of Essex's widow. Spenser's reference shows his temerity and also the strength of his friendship with Leicester.

l.48. *the white beare:* Leicester's cognizance was a white bear guarding a ragged staff.

ll.49–54. Not in Mantuan.

l.52. *the Myller's rownde:* a country dance.

l.53. *All were Elisa,* etc. 'Although, were Elisa to be a member of this same ring of dancers . . .'

ll.55–60. *Tityrus:* an allusion to Vergil, who after his pastorals, the *Bucolica*, turned to epic poetry in the *Aeneid*.

l.56. *Mecoenas:* Vergil's patron, Maecenas, brought him to the notice of the Emperor Augustus Caesar.

l.58. *timely eare:* corn in season.

*l.*62. *Augustus:* Gaius Julius Caesar Octavius (63 B.C.–A.D. 14), created first Emperor of Rome in 27 B.C.

*l.*65. 'He sheweth the cause, why Poetes were wont to be had in such honor of noble men; that is, that by them their worthines and valor shold through theyr famous Posies be commended to al posterities' (E. K.). *dering doe:* 'in manhoode and chevalrie' (E. K.).

*l.*66. *of hem:* by them (i.e. the men of valour).

*l.*67. '. . . he sheweth the cause of contempt of Poetry to be idlenesse and basenesse of mynd' (E. K.). *for age:* as a result of growing old.

*l.*70. *put in preace:* exert themselves, compete.

*l.*72. *coupe:* coop, cage, prison.

*ll.*75–7. *Or . . or:* either . . . or. *fayne:* conceal, disguise.

*l.*76. Alliteration was often used to characterize the crudity of versification at the time:

> You that do Dictionarie's methode bring
> Into your rimes, running in ratling rowes
>
> (Sidney, *Astrophel and Stella*, xv. 5–6)

*l.*78. *Tom Piper:* the village musician who plays for the local morris dancers.

*l.*84. *whence thou camst:* Spenser follows the Renaissance belief in poetry as an art with divine origins and affinities, advocated by Sidney among others.

*l.*86. *sore:* soar.

*l.*87. *peeced pyneons:* imperfect wings. *in plight:* in condition, 'trim'.

*l.*88. *Colin:* Colin Clout, presumed to be Spenser himself. 'Only Colin is fit to attempt such a famous enterprise . . .'

*l.*90. *soote as Swanne:* 'The comparison seemeth to be strange: for the swanne hath ever wonne small commendation for her swete singing: but it is sayd of the learned that the swan a little before hir death, singeth most pleasantly . . .' (E. K.).

*l.*91. *fon:* fool (i.e. Cuddie).

*ll.*91–5. Piers' defence of love is very much on neo-Platonic lines: earthly shapes are but pallid reflections of ideal forms, and it is man's duty to aspire to heavenly virtue and beauty by contemplating their imperfect earthly counterparts, including 'falling in love' with them: in this way, man's spiritual part, his soul, is preserved untainted by the grosser bodily element in his make-up. This, followed by Cuddie's reply, that love is a tyrant and a distraction to a man of intellect, renders this part of the poem a rehearsal of the theme of *Love's Labour's Lost*.

*l.*95. *caytive corage:* 'base and abject mind' (E. K.).

*l.*100. E. K. says this line is in imitation of Mantuan, but then quotes a line not actually his!

*l.*102. *Unwisely weaves that takes two webbes in hand:* this has a proverbial ring, but does not seem to occur elsewhere.

l.105. E. K. compares Horace, *Epistles* I. 5. 19: 'What man has a bowl of wine failed to make eloquent?'

l.106. *Bacchus' fruite:* the grape. *Phoebus:* Apollo was considered the poet of the gods.

l.110. 'He seemeth here to be ravished with a Poetical furie. For (if one rightly mark) the numbers rise so ful, and the verse growth so big, that it seemeth he hath forgot the meanenesse of shepheads state and stile' (E. K.).

l.111. *wild Yvie:* ivy was dedicated to Bacchus, and wrapped about the thyrsus, the rod carried by Bacchus's devotees, the Maenads.

l.113. *buskin:* 'It was the maner of Poetes and plaiers in tragedies to were buskins, as also in Comedies to use stockes and light shoes. So that the buskin in Poetry is used for tragical matter . . .' (E. K.).

l.114. *queint Bellona:* Minerva, the goddess of war.

l.119. *bellies layd:* given birth.

l.121. *Cuddies Embleme:* taken from Ovid's *Fasti* VI. 5: *Est Deus in nobis, agitaote calescimus illo* (There is a god within us, and through his stimulus, we grow warm').

'Hereby is meant, as also in the whole course of this Aeglogue, that Poetry is a divine instinct and unnatural rage passing the reache of comen reason' (E. K.).

Commentators have suggested that, Piers having no 'embleme', Spenser really intended to assign the first part of this quotation to him.

GLOSSARY

This glossary lists the more common words occurring in the text; explanations of more unusual or obscure words and phrases will be found in the notes.

A

Abowtyn, about
Abreyde, start up, awake
Abye, pay for
Abytt, abide
Acate, purchases, purchasing
Accompt, account
Adawe, subdue
Adue, adieu, farewell
Advert, consider
Affect(s), affections, passions
Affie, trust, pledge
Afraye, frighten, startle, disturb
Ake, ache
Algate, anyway
Also, so
And, if
Ankir, recluse, hermit
Apayd, repaid, satisfied
Apeche, impeach, accuse, delay
Appare, grow worse, deteriorate
Arn, are
As(s)ay, try, make trial of, test, afflict
Asofte, soften
Asor, azure
Astate, estate
Aswage, abate, appease, soften

A-sythe, reparation, amends
Atempre, mild, temperate
Ateynte, attained, achieved, discovered
Aumber, amber
Aunter, altar
Autumpne, autumn
Avantage, advantage, benefit, profit
Avise, take thought to, give thought to
Avisynes, premeditation, deliberation
Avoyde (*adj.*), free, clear
Axe, ask
Aye, always, ever
Ayen(-s), against, towards facing, near
Ayer, Ayre, air

B

Bable, toy, bauble
Bagge, purse
Baier, bier
Bale, torment, woe, evil, grief, misery
Balke, beam
Bame, Baume, balm

270

Ban, curse, swear
Bane, destruction, death
Bard (*vb*), barred
Barke, speak angrily
Bayte, allure
Be, by
Beck (*vb*), nod, bow
Becke (*noun*), nod, bow
Bede, bed
Bedight, equipped, afflicted
Behight, promised
Behove (*noun*), behoof, benefit, use
Bemys, beams
Bent, set, bound
Berayne, rain upon, water
Bern, bear, carry
Beshrewd, accursed
Best (*noun*), beast
Bet, better
Betyde, happen, befall
Bey, buy
Blandyshyng, flattering
Ble, face, features
Blen(ne), blend
Blo, livid, blue-black
Bolle, bowl
Bon, bone
Boote, remedy, relief, profit, use
Bost, boast
Bote, boat
Boundes, boundaries, limits
Bow(e)r, dwelling arbour, boudoir
Bowsy, bloated with drink
Boysteous, rough, violent
Braule, squabble, clamour
Braynpan, head
Brede, breed, be pregnant
(On) Brede, abroad
Brer, briar
Brese, bruise
Brest, burst, break
Brid(d), bird

Brittil, inconstant, fickle
Broke, Brooke, endure, suffer
Brood, broad, wide
Brotilnesse, brittleness, mortality
Budget, pouch, bag
But, unless, except for

C

Can (*vb*), know
Canker, disease
Capon, Capoun, cock fattened for the table
Cark(e) (*noun*), trouble, grief, sorrow; (*vb*) grieve, mourn, be troubled
Carren, dead, putrifying, rotten
Cates, dainties, delicacies
Celestyne, celestial, heavenly
Chare (*adj*), careful; (*noun*) chariot, cart
Charged, filled
Charme, play
Chast (*vb*), chastise, punish, chasten
Chaw, chew
Chayse (*noun*), pursuit
Che, she
Checke, rebuke, censure
Cheere, fare, hospitality
Chepe (*noun*), bargain
Chere, Cheare, expression, face, mood, manner, aspect
Cheyre, cherry
Child, noble youth
Chippe, ship
Chocke, choke
Chorle, churl, fellow
Claryon, shrill trumpet
Cleped, called
Clerk, cleric, man in Holy Orders
Clifted, cleft
Clives, Clyves, cliffs
Cloisterer, dweller in an abbey

Clotte, sod of earth

Clowne, simpleton, rustic

Combred, encumbered

Concourse, course, result

Connyng(e) (*noun*), skill, knowledge, cunning

Constraine, force

Contraryous, adverse, opposed, repugnant

Cook, cock

Copen, buy

Corage, heart, spirit, zeal, vitality

Corp(e)s, body (live or dead), frame

Cosse, kiss

Cost(es), coast(s)

Costey, to coast, skirt

Cote, cottage, shelter

Coye, coy, reserved

Crabbed, perverse, cross, 'crabby'

Croft, small field

Cuntre, region, district

Cure (*vb*), protect; (*noun*) care, protection, concern, spiritual charge of parishioners, hence parish or sometimes larger unit i.e. a see

(Of) Custume, habitually

D

Dalyaunce, dalliance, love-making

Dame, lady, mistress of the house, mother

Darke, darken

Dart(e), Dert(e), javelin, spear

Deburse, disburse, pay out

Deme, judge

Dent, blow, stroke

Deprave, vilify, disparage

Derk(e), dark

Device, Devyse, plan, contrivance, invention, design

Devors, separation

Devysse, contrived, imagined, arranged

Diere, deer

Dight, set to, applied

Discride, descried, saw

Dispoyled, stripped, undressed, 'changed'

Dome (*adj*), dumb; (*noun*) judgement, opinion

Dout(e), Dowte, doubt, dread, fear

Dowe, dove

Dowtles(s), undoubtedly

Drede, doubt, denial

Drench(ed), drown(ed)

Dreryhed, melancholy, depression

Dresse, prepare, make ready, direct

Dul(l)(e), heavy, sad, depressing, listless

Durst, dare

Dyntes, blows

E

Ear, Er, ere, before

Eft(e), again, afterwards

Eke, also

Eld, old age

Emysperye, hemisphere

Enchase, drive away, pursue

Encombrement, incumbrance

Endyte, impose, set down in writing

Enou, enough

Ensure, assure

Entent, intention, purpose, attention, heed, meaning

Entere, devoted

Equipage, equipment, retinue

Erst, first, formerly

Eschaunge, change

Everyliche, always, continually

272

Ewes, eaves
Eynen, eye

F

Fadir, father
Falshed, falsehood, deception
Faute, fault
Fe, reward, wealth
Feer, Fere, mate, companion, friend
Feise, goods, money, inherited estates
Fell(e), fierce, cruel, savage
Femel, female
Ferd, frightened
Fervour, intense heat
Fet, fetched, heaved
Feturs, features
Feyre, fair
Flete, float, flow
Fleych, meat
Fole, fool
For, because
Fordoe, destroy, kill
Forslepid, slept heavily
Frame (*vb*), set, prepare, form
Freat, Frete, destroy, consume
Freight, fraught, filled, loaded
Fro, from
Fyne, finish, end, terminate
(Y-) Fyned, refined, purified
Fyt, feet

G

Gan, began
Gaynward, towards, facing
Geere, furnishings
Gest (*noun*), guest; (*vb*) jest; guessed
Get, jet
Giglot, wanton woman
Ginnes, traps
Gise, mode, fashion

Gite, Gyte, dress, gown
Giust, joust
Gladde (*vb*), gladden
Glased, glazed
Glayre, slime
Gle(e)de, rot-hot coal
Glome, frown
Glosing, flattering
Goed, good
Gose, goose
Gost, spirit
Gostly, Goostly, spiritual
Gowndy, bleary, full of matter
Gras, grace
Grave (*vb*), engrave
Gren, green
Gressop, grasshopper
Grete, cry out
Groyn, groan, grunt
Grutche, grumble, growse
Gryll, fierce, rough, savage
Guye, guide, manage, direct

H

Habitacle, habitation, dwelling
Haboundaunce, Habundance, plenty, prosperity, abundance
Halse, embrace
Halt (*vb*), hold, keep, restrain
Hap(e)(-pe), fortune, chance, luck
Happs, occurrences
Hard (*vb*), heard
Hardely, surely, by all means, confidently, boldly
Haut, haughty, proud, 'high and mighty'
Hayl, haul, tug
Hayt, hath
He, they
Heedes, heads
Heery, hairy
Hem, them

273

Hens, hence
Hent, caught, seized
Her (*vb*), hear
Her, Here, her, their
Here (*noun*), hair
Hertly, hearty
Hete, offer
Hette, heat
Hilld, held
Hode, hood
Hole, whole
Holtes, woods, copses
Hom, home
Hove, linger
Huckels, hips
Hy, hasten, hurry
Hyndes, servants

I

Ich, I (dialect form)
Idell, idle
Ilk, same
Iwys, indeed

J

Jelawsy, jealousy
Jape, jest, joke
Jelyf, jelly
Jet, strut about

K

Karke (*vb*), grieve, mourn
Kechone, kitchen
Keke, kick
Kepe (*noun*), heed, guard, care
Kerved, carved
Kest, Kyst, cast, threw
(Of) (By) Kinde, Kynde, by
nature
Knackes, trinkets, knick-knacks
Kno, know
Knockels, knuckles

Knols, tolls, rings
Koggh, cough
Kus, kiss

L

Lade (*vb*), lead
Lat(e), let
Laurer, laurel
Layd, faint, subdued
Lede (*noun*), lead (metal)
Lefe, Lief, dear, beloved, precious
Leman, Lemman, lover (either
sex)
Lene, lend
Lenger, longer
Lere (*noun*), skin, complexion
Les, Lesyng, lie, falsehood
Lese, lose
Let(-e)(-te) (*vb*), hinder, obstruct,
prevent, delay (*noun*) hindrance,
delay
Leve (*vb*), live; (*noun*) leave,
permission
Lever(e), dearer, rather
Lewde, vile, nasty
Liff, life
Ligge (*vb*), lie
Light, Lyghth, happy, joyful,
swift, nimble
List, Lyst, desire, choose, be
pleased to
Listy, see **Lusty**
Lodmanage, navigation, pilotage
Loken, locked, set
Longe (*vb*), belong
Lore, teachings, lessons, doctrine,
creed, counsel
Lowre, scowl, look dark, lour
Luggard, sluggard
Lust (*noun*), pleasure
Lusty, happy, pleasant, vigorous
Lynne (*vb*), cease

274

M

Madly, in a foolish manner
Mak(-e) (*Plural* **Makis**), mate, partner
Manace, menace
Mas, Mass
Maungy, mangy
May, maiden, young girl
Mead(d)(e), meadow
Mede, reward, meed
Medle, Medyll, meddle, mix, mingle, have sexual intercourse
Mell, as for **Medle**
Melwell, cod
Mene, intend to convey, import, portend, purpose
Mercer, dealer in textiles, esp. silk and velvet
Mery(-e), agreeable, pleasant, happy
Mickle, much
Mo, more
Molde, earth
Momme, mumble
Mone, moon
Mote, might
Mourwen, morning
Moughte (*noun*), moth
Mow(-n), may
Mowlde, head
Moyster, moisture, sap
Muse, ponder, speculate
Myrre, myrrh
Myscheef, misfortune, distress, harm, evil
Mysse, fault, sin

N

Namely, especially
Ne, nor, no
Nece, niece
Nelde, needle
Nis, Nys, is not

Nolle, head
Non, noon
Nones, Noyns (often with 'for the'), time, occasion, spur of the moment, purpose; thus, very, exceedingly (Occ. a mere tag)
Noppy, strong, potent, foaming, heady (usu. of drink)
Nou, now
Nouther, neither
Nowrd, North
Nyse, fastidious, foolish
Nyw, new

O

O, one
On, Oon, one
On-avysed, without warning
Onpreyse, dispraise
Ons, Onys, once
Ony, any
Onys, one's
Or, ere, before
Orysont, horizon
Oten, made of (an) oat(s)
Othe, oath
Ottis, oats
Ouer, hour
Ougly, ugly
Outraye, vanquish, overcome, crush
Out-wrest, force, strain
Overronne, crushed, overwhelmed
Overthwarte, set-back, rebuff
Ower, oar

P

Panche, paunch, stomach
Pappes, breasts
Park(-e), enclosed hunting ground (see notes)
Parten, part, divide, share out
Pas(-se), surpass, excel

275

Pastaunce, sport, dalliance, 'fun'

Pe(a)se (*vb*), appease, pacify; (*noun*) pea

Peason, peas

Pend, shut up, enclosed

Pens, pence

Percase, perhaps

Perche, parch, dry up

Perde, by God, truly

Peres, equals, companions

Perfaict, perfect

Persaunt, piercing, keen, sharp

Perse, pierce

Peynted, feigned, deceiving

Peysed, weighed, balanced

Phrensie, frenzy

Pie, Py, magpie

Pike, Pyke, pick

Pikid, chosen, selected

Pinche (At), find fault with, blame

Plight (*vb*), plighted, pledged

(In) Plight, in condition, in 'trim'

Pok, bag, sack

Port, bearing

Powre, pour

Prane, prawn

Pranked, decked, adorned, 'dolled up'

Pray, prey

Prease, Prese, Presse, crowd, throng

Prest (*adj*), neat, trim, spry

Prime, 6 a.m., the first hour of the day

Procede, begin legal processes

Profe, experience

Pystle, Pystyl, epistle

Pyth, substance, matter

Q

Quat, what

Quen, when

Quite, Quyt, repaid, requited, revenged

Quod, quoth, said

Qwen, when

R

Raft, bereft, deprived

Rak(e)hell, thoughtless, heedless

Rathere, sooner, quicker, earlier

Reaulme, realm, kingdom

Recomfort, comfort, consolation, support

Rede (*vb*), study, deliberate, advise

Reed, red

Reft, deprived

Renne, run

Repyne, fret, complain

Resort (*vb*), return, go

Restie, rancid

Reven (*adj*), cracked

Reverte, turn away, change direction

Rewe, regret, pity

Reyne (*vb*), rain down, water

Rive, split, tear, rend

Rode (*noun*), cross, rood

Romish, Roman, Latin

Ron, Ronne, run

Ropy, glutinous, sticky

Rote (*vb*), rot

Roune, whisper (to speke roune')

Rout (*noun*), crowd; (*vb*) snore

Rowyngly, in a whisper

Rowte, snore

Rowth (*adj*), rough

Ruthe, pity, sorrow, grief

Ruthfull, grievous, pitiful

Ryall, royal, regal, grand

Ryd, decide, advise

Ryght(as), just as if

Rympled, wrinkled

Rynde, bark of a tree

276

Ryveld, wrinkled, wizened

S

Saey, say
Safe, apart from, except
Sare, sore
Sawus, sayings, promises
Scace, scarce, scarcely
Scale, ladder
Scanne, attempt
Schylde, preserve, protect
Sclender, Sklender, slim, slender
Seare, Sere, dry, dried
Seelden, seldom
Seely, Sely, simple, innocent, foolish, happy, good, holy
Seeth, Seth, cook by boiling
Sel, good luck
Selle, cell
Semys, seems
Senaws, sinews
Senckis, sinks
Sentence, discourse, opinion
Sewe, follow, pursue
Sheddeth scatters
Shene, bright, shining
Shent, disgraced, reproached, punished
Shere (*vb*), swerve, veer away
Shever, shiver, shake to pieces
Shoder, shudder
Shone (*noun*), shoes
Shoringnesse, unevenness
Shoyng, showing
Sike, such; sick
Sines, Sins, Syns, since
Skill, ability, powers of discrimination, expertise, knowledge
Skomme, scum
Slawyn, slain

Slepur, Slip(p)er, slippery, unstable
Slo(n), slay
Smal(l)e, slender, slim, small
Smoky, steaming, misty
So, as
Somdele, somewhat
Son, soon
Sonde, gift
Sone, soon
Soon, sun
Soot, sweet
Sort, set, company
Sory, dismal, distressed
Sotell, subtle
Sothe, truth
Sothfastnesse, truthfulness
Sound (*noun*), swoon, faint
Sowde, South
Spared, saved, reserved
Spere, sphere
Splayen, spread out, display
Spon, spoon
Spore, spur
Sprete, spirit
Spurnyd, tripped
Stale (*vb*), stole
Stede, place
Steere, stir
Stent (*noun*), end, stop, limit; (*vb*) ceased
Stern, merciless, cruel, harsh
Stithe, anvil
Stound(e), moment, esp. 'bad moment', state of amazement; blow, stroke
Strange, cold, unfriendly, indifferent
Straungeness(e), female indifference
Suer, sure, certain
Suete, sweet
Suld, should

Swarvyng, swerving
Swich, Swych, such
Swoune, swoon
Syb, related, akin
Sykke, sigh
Sykyrnesse, certainty, assurance, security, safety
Sypres, cypress
Syve, sieve

T

Tache, Tachche, quality, blemish (cf. 'a touch of his father about him')
Take, start growing successfully
Tan, taken
Tapites, tapestries, coverings
Tawarde, towards
Tene, sorrow, trouble, vexation
Ther(-e), where
Thilke, this
Tho, Thoo, then; those
Thorrough, through
Thowt, thought
Thrawle, captivity, bondage; slave
Thriftles, worthless, useless, wasteful
Throw, moment, brief space
Tickle, unstable, inconstant
To, two; too
Tong, tongue
Tord(e), turd, excrement
Tornyd, turned
Toye, trifle, whim
Trace, Tras, trace, track, trail, way of life
Train, tail of a bird
Transmewe, change, transform
Trayled, followed
Trayn(e), deceive
Trowe, believe, suppose
Trowght, truth

Tweyne, two, pair
Tyde, time, season, period
Tylesherd, shard, piece of tile
Tysing, enticing

U

Unmyt, unfitted
Unnethes, scarcely, hardly
Unpacyent, impatient
Unquyt, without penalty, unrequited, unrevenged
Unrest (*noun*), absence of rest, turmoil
Unsowndy, unsound, poor
Untruthe, falsehood, deceit

V

Vaine (*noun*), vein
Vavore, favour
Verray, indisputably true
Vesture, clothing, covering
Voiden, remove, depart, empty

W

Wan(-ne), gloomy, pallid, pale, feeble
Want, lack
Wanton, lively, rebellious, unrestrained, frisky, lecherous
Warke, work
Wawe, wave
Way, Wey, road, track
Wayne, wain, wagon
Wede, clothing
Wedow, widow
Welaway, alas, woe is me!
Wende, believed
Wene, doubt, surmise, conjecture
Westron, Western
Whylome, once
Whon, one
Wicket, small gate or door

278

Will(e), wish, desire (esp. sexual), pleasure

Wist, Wyst, knew, known

Withhalt, keep back, detain

Wit(t), Wyt(t), knowledge, wit, cleverness, intelligence, common sense

Wod, Wood, mad

Woll, Wull, wool

Wonder, wondrous, wonderfully

Wondys, wounds

Wonnyng(e), dwelling (place)

Worght, worth

Worould, world

Wortes, herbs, any kind of cabbage

Woxen, grown, become

Wrack(e), wreck, destruction, violence

Wreaker, Wreaking, avenger, avenging

Wrethed, twisted together

Wretyn, written

Wrythen, twisted, wrung

Wydnes, width

Wygge, waggle about

Wyght, creature, fellow, being

Wymple, woman's head-dress (see notes)

Wynch(s)e, wince, shy (of a horse)

Wywys, wives

Y

Yede, Yeding, went, going

Yerk, jerk, pull out quickly

Yerne, quickly, eagerly

Yeve, give

Yghe, eye

Ygoe, ago

Yit, yet, still

Ynow, enough

Yode, Yowde, went

Yol, Christmas

(Of) Yore, long ago

Yre, ire, anger

Yyng, young

INDEX OF FIRST LINES

(Burdens and refrains are printed in italics)